VIOLENCE AGAINST INDIGENOUS WOMEN

INDIGENOUS STUDIES SERIES

The Indigenous Studies Series builds on the successes of the past and is inspired by recent critical conversations about Indigenous epistemological frameworks. Recognizing the need to encourage burgeoning scholarship, the series welcomes manuscripts drawing upon Indigenous intellectual traditions and philosophies, particularly in discussions situated within the Humanities.

Series Editor:
Dr. Deanna Reder (Métis), Associate Professor, First Nations Studies and English, Simon Fraser University

Advisory Board:
Dr. Jo-ann Archibald (Sto:lo), Associate Dean, Indigenous Education, University of British Columbia
Dr. Kristina Bidwell (Labrador-Métis), Associate Professor, English, University of Saskatchewan
Dr. Daniel Heath Justice (Cherokee), Associate Professor, English, Canada Research Chair in Indigenous Literature and Expressive Culture, University of British Columbia
Dr. Eldon Yellowhorn (Piikani), Associate Professor, Archaeology, Director of First Nations Studies, Simon Fraser University

VIOLENCE AGAINST INDIGENOUS WOMEN

LITERATURE | ACTIVISM | RESISTANCE

ALLISON HARGREAVES

WILFRID LAURIER
UNIVERSITY PRESS

Inspiring Lives.

This book has been published with the help of a grant from the Canadian Federation for the Humanities and Social Sciences, through the Awards to Scholarly Publications Program, using funds provided by the Social Sciences and Humanities Research Council of Canada. Wilfrid Laurier University Press acknowledges the support of the Canada Council for the Arts for our publishing program. We acknowledge the financial support of the Government of Canada through the Canada Book Fund for our publishing activities. This work was supported by the Research Support Fund.

Library and Archives Canada Cataloguing in Publication

Hargreaves, Allison, 1981–, author
    Violence against indigenous women : literature, activism, resistance / Allison Hargreaves.

(Indigenous studies series)
Includes bibliographical references and index.
Issued in print and electronic formats.
ISBN 978-1-77112-239-9 (softcover).—ISBN 978-1-77112-250-4 (EPUB).
ISBN 978-1-77112-249-8 (PDF)

    1. Canadian literature—Indian authors—History and criticism. 2. Canadian literature—Women authors—History and criticism. 3. Canadian literature (English)—21st century—History and criticism. 4. Storytelling—Social aspects—Canada. 5. Violence in literature. 6. Indians in literature. 7. Indian women—Violence against—Canada—Case studies. 8. Indian women activists—Canada—Case studies. 9. Feminism—Canada—Case studies. I. Title. II. Series: Indigenous studies series

PS8089.5.I6H39 2017   C810.9'928708997071   C2017-901914-7
                                                      C2017-901915-5

Cover image: *Muse* (acrylic on canvas; 30 × 24 in.) by Dominique Normand. Cover design by Lara Minja. Interior design and typesetting by James Leahy.

© 2017 Wilfrid Laurier University Press
Waterloo, Ontario, Canada
www.wlupress.wlu.ca

Every reasonable effort has been made to acquire permission for copyright material used in this text, and to acknowledge all such indebtedness accurately. Any errors and omissions called to the publisher's attention will be corrected in future printings.

No part of this publication may be reproduced, stored in a retrieval system, or transmitted, in any form or by any means, without the prior written consent of the publisher or a licence from the Canadian Copyright Licensing Agency (Access Copyright). For an Access Copyright licence, visit http://www.accesscopyright.ca or call toll free to 1-800-893-5777.

CONTENTS

Preface   vii
Acknowledgements   xiii

INTRODUCTION
Violence against Indigenous Women: Representation and Resistance   1

CHAPTER ONE
Finding Dawn and the Missing Women Commission of Inquiry: Story-Based Methods in Anti-Violence Research and Remembrance   29

CHAPTER TWO
Narrative Appeals: The *Stolen Sisters* Report and Storytelling in Activist Discourse and Poetry   65

CHAPTER THREE
Compelling Disclosures: Storytelling in Feminist Anti-Violence Discourse and Indigenous Women's Memoir   101

CHAPTER FOUR
Recognition, Remembrance, and Redress: The Politics of Memorialization in the Cases of Helen Betty Osborne and Anna Mae Pictou-Aquash   133

CONCLUSION
Thinking beyond the National Inquiry: *A Red Girl's Reasoning*   165

Notes   187
Bibliography   243
Index   271

PREFACE

It seems that the most useful prefaces serve as a place of introduction—and not just to the subject matter, but also to the writer who situates herself in the work. In *Indigenous Methodologies*, Margaret Kovach (Nêhiýaw/Saulteaux) recalls Māori scholar Graham Smith's instructions to begin with a prologue. The idea, she says, is to narrate for readers the information required to "make sense of the story to follow."[1] As Kovach's own prologue explores, it can be difficult to narrate the origins of one's work. But one can hopefully say something about the relationships—to people, places, and stories—that have informed that work.

While I was revising this manuscript with the feedback of my reviewers, my ten-year-old stepdaughter asked me: when did I first "find out" that I had to write this book? The phrasing charmed me; I had the humorous image of myself receiving surprise notification in the mail. But this was a really good question, and its phrasing intuited something important about research and writing: that to whatever extent we choose our work, it also chooses us. This is not to efface our personal accountability as academics and teachers, but to say that many factors of history, social relations, and time converge and give shape to the choices we make. Though curious about the topic of the book, my stepdaughter was more interested in just that—in how and why it had become a daily labour for me. At first, I explained how the book began as work written for a doctoral degree while I was studying at Western University in London, Ontario, and that I had been reworking the project since moving to the Okanagan and taking up my job in Kelowna as a teacher at UBC. But this isn't really what she meant. It wasn't so much a timeline she was looking for, as a sense of those larger convergences: why me, and why this book? I realized that to answer this question was a much bigger task—bigger, certainly, than writing a book. For how do we talk to our families, to our students, and to our communities about ongoing colonial violence? And how do we promote both public and intimate engagements with this knowledge as a lived commitment to social transformation—one that goes beyond a mere "awareness of things not previously known"?[2] These are the questions that motivate me; this book is one possible response.

I came to this project through literature. As an adolescent reader seeking escape, I saw literature as a way to imagine my world otherwise. As a young adult, I saw it could also name problems with the way the world was. Drawn by the possibility of something that could both prescribe socio-political ills as well as imagine alternatives, I decided to study literature as an undergraduate at the University of Alberta. It wasn't until quite late in my degree that I took a course in Indigenous Literatures. Tellingly, this wasn't required credit for an English degree. And soon after my work in this course began, I started to see the problem with that: of all the texts I had studied, I hadn't yet read the stories of the peoples on whose land I was living. How could one graduate with a credible specialization in literature without engaging with Indigenous literary traditions? This initial questioning soon led to much deeper doubts about my life and learning to date. It was a gradual, sinking feeling of betrayal, which many of my own students—both Indigenous and non-Indigenous—also describe: why didn't I know? While reading the work of Syilx poet and novelist Jeannette Armstrong, I came across this explanation: the "dominating [culture] ... seeks to affirm itself."[3] This colonial reality can be transformed, she says, but very few of its beneficiaries "will desire or choose to hear these truths unless they are voiced clearly to people who have no way to know that there are good alternatives."[4]

So, I pursued further studies—moving from what I now knew as Cree territory in central Alberta to Anishinaabe, Haudenosaunee, Leni-Lunaape, and Attawandaron territory in southwest Ontario. I read authors like Maria Campbell, Beatrice Culleton, Lee Maracle, Marilyn Dumont, and Beth Brant, in whose words Canada's colonial history and present are "voiced clearly" and with persuasive force. I read them for the truths my upbringing and education had overlooked or denied. But such literature won't let us stay forever gathering "awareness of things not previously known"; part of its power is to call us to account. More than awareness, Rachel Flowers (Leey'qsun) suggests, the real "labor of settlers should be to imagine alternative ways to be in relation with Indigenous peoples."[5] Literature can help us to do this imaginative work—a labour no less important than solidarity organizing and direct action, for we need such imaginings to guide our movements toward social change. I saw this first-hand in my solidarity organizing with a coalition of Indigenous and non-Indigenous peoples while living in London, and I see it in my classroom today: both literature and activism are relational sites where personal forms of reckoning interact with lived social relations of accountability. In this framework, it is not enough to "know about" colonial violence, or to promote its greater public visibility. (Nor will one-off, symbolic forms of political recognition such as official apologies or public commissions of inquiry serve to permanently alter oppressive relations of power.) Rather, we have to imagine and enact our relationships differently, and with the goals of decolonization in mind.

I have tried to do this work in my teaching, and now also with this book—taking direction from Indigenous women's literature on how to understand and transform the different relationships we all have to colonialism in this country. In doing so, I speak from the perspective of a settler scholar and teacher. As Flowers defines it, "settler" is a relational term that "denaturalizes and politicizes the presence of non-Indigenous people on Indigenous lands."[6] In adopting this term, I signal both my status as a guest on traditional and unceded Syilx (Okanagan) territory, where I now live and work, as well as the politicized perspective from which I approach Indigenous-authored texts. I sometimes hesitate to use the language of allyship, although many have modelled its use in Indigenous literary scholarship with nuance and eloquence.[7] There can be something declarative or wholesale about the term "ally" when used to name a self-appointed identity rather than a relational practice. True allied scholarship, activism, or teaching demonstrates a resolute commitment to transforming colonial relationships, while at the same time recognizing this work as socially and politically contingent—as responsive to the shifting circumstances of strategy, necessity, location, and trust. When I use the word ally, this is what I mean.

The choices I have made in this book are informed by my experiences of teaching and learning as an allied settler scholar. My own classroom and community are made up of both Indigenous and non-Indigenous peoples who come together to learn and unlearn, and whose lived connections to the literature are necessarily diverse. The texts provide us with a place to gather and to think about these connections reflexively. Many of the texts discussed in this book are ones I have taught, both as aesthetic creations and as works of social analysis and intervention. In examining the issue of *gendered* colonial violence, specifically, I focus on texts that illuminate the structural facets of gendered dispossession—those designed by colonial policy and law—and on texts that identify and resist the harmful misrepresentations of Indigenous women that abound in mainstream media, education, and public memory. I choose these texts because they have something to offer all readers, but especially those critically approaching this issue for the first time: in these works, we see how women do not simply go missing or disappear, but rather are targeted for violence in ways that are *made possible* by the colonial state—a violence, statistically speaking, most often carried out by white men, who remain, as Sarah Hunt (Kwagiulth) says, "unmarked by the violence they perpetrate, not at fault for carrying out a form of violation that is as old as colonialism itself."[8] In these texts, we see also the limitations of many mainstream awareness and anti-violence campaigns—initiatives that too often look to settler governments and institutions for leadership and change. But it is possible to imagine what Armstrong calls "good alternatives," and to take direction from Indigenous women's literature in performing that task. Looking to the voices of contemporary Indigenous women writers, this book argues for the important role that literature and storytelling can play in responding to gendered colonial violence.

Indigenous communities have been organizing against violence since newcomers first arrived, but the cases of missing and murdered women have only recently garnered broad public attention. With the advent of provincial and national inquiries into missing and murdered Indigenous women and girls, a larger public conversation is now under way.

Indigenous women's literature is a critical site of knowledge making and critique that can influence the conversation and change the terms of debate. My hope is that *Violence against Indigenous Women* provides a foundation for reading this literature in the context of Indigenous feminist scholarship and activism and the ongoing intellectual history of Indigenous women's resistance.

ACKNOWLEDGEMENTS

This project spans a decade of my life, countless conversations and events, and many different beginnings. Much gratitude is owed to the many people who have enriched my thinking and my life along the way.

I want to thank Cheryl Suzack for teaching the course that first introduced me to Indigenous literary studies. That course put me on my current path, and I am forever indebted to her for this. Cheryl also offered me much-needed intellectual and professional mentorship throughout my Master's degree at the University of Alberta. For her careful attention at that pivotal moment, I am grateful. I am also very grateful to the members of my doctoral supervisory committee at Western University: Julia Emberley, Kim Solga, and Pauline Wakeham. Their steady engagement and support helped shape earlier versions of this book, while their example as mentors helped shape me as a teacher. To Pauline, whose support extended far beyond the bounds of that degree, and whose keen intellect and generous spirit have taught me so much: thank you. For their sustaining camaraderie, and for their work as scholars and teachers, many thanks are also due to Michelle Coupal, Ann Gagné, Erica Kelly, Brooke Pratt, Amber Riaz, Somaya Sabry, and Alia Somani. Thanks also to Tyler Chartrand, who read and engaged with early drafts of the project and who offered support in a hundred ways. The staff and volunteers at the Sexual Assault Centre London helped me think through many aspects of this project; I am especially grateful to Estella Rosa Irías Girón for her fierce compassion and insight. I am much indebted to the members of the London Coalition in Solidarity with Indigenous Peoples, and to Gloria Alvernaz Mulcahy and Darlene Ritchie especially, for their leadership, energy, and wisdom.

I am lucky to enjoy the rich engagement, encouragement, and challenge of many good friends and colleagues here in the Okanagan. My most heartfelt thanks to Melissa Jacques, David Jefferess, Ruthann Lee, and Lally Grauer—for your scholarship, your humour, and for the gift of many long walks, talks, and cups of tea. I owe so much to each of you; my thanks is never enough. For their continued collaboration and support, many thanks also to Jeannette Armstrong, Margo Tamez, and Greg Younging. To Kelly Fosbery, Jeannine Kuemmerle, Dan Odenbach, Adrienne Vedan, and everyone at APS: thank you for your tireless work on behalf of our students, and for everything you do to make the university a more livable place. And for their passion, engagement, and insight, I owe infinite thanks to my students—too many to name—whose activism and scholarship inspire me daily. For her own fierce work, and for many good conversations, a special thanks is owed to Nicola Campbell. For our hikes and grounding chats, I am grateful also to Michele Johnson.

It has been my great fortune to learn from so many communities. I have been much enriched and supported by early members of the Canadian Applied Literature Association (many of whom are now also active in the Indigenous Literary Studies Association). Much gratitude and respect go to Michelle Coupal, Amber Dean, Jo-Ann Episkenew, Tara Hyland-Russell, Deanna Reder, and Sue Spearey for their community, commitment, and encouragement. Jo-Ann: your work continues to bring fresh insight and to animate the transformative capacity of literature and story. This is a gift for which I remember you daily. To the AlterKnowledge community, for many good discussions, and to the Alternator Centre for Contemporary Art for hosting us, my sincere thanks. And for their collaboration, their teaching, and their generosity, my thanks to the Ki-Low-Na Friendship Society, and especially to Edna Terbasket and Ronni Roesler.

Thanks are due to Samantha Baldwin for her assistance in preparing the manuscript, and for chasing down many references in the process. For her beautiful artwork, which appears on the cover of this book, thanks to Dominique Normand. And for her extraordinary patience and expertise, many thanks go to my editor, Siobhan McMenemy. Big thanks, too, to everyone at Wilfrid Laurier University Press for their commitment to this book, and to Lisa Quinn for her crucial guidance in this project's earlier stages. Much gratitude to my reviewers, who engaged my work with real generosity and meticulous care.

To my family: Dad, Mom, Jennifer, Matthew, and Margaret, thank you for your humour, your unwavering support, and your love. For Mike, Kasey, and Ella: words can't express my gratitude. For your warmth, wit, patience, and presence, I owe you the world.

I also wish to acknowledge the funding and support of the Social Sciences and Humanities Research Council, the University of British Columbia's Individual Research Grant, and the Faculty of Creative and Critical Studies' Research Support Fund.

INTRODUCTION

Violence against Indigenous Women: Representation and Resistance

This book is concerned with the social issue of violence against Indigenous women in Canada, and the politics of literary, policy, and activist forms of resistance. I have three main contentions: first, that this violence is systemic in nature and colonial in origin; second, that representation matters to the material history of violence and to its resistance by Indigenous peoples and their allies; and third, that Indigenous women writers contribute vital insights into the analysis of gendered colonial violence while envisioning new, non-violent realities. Michi Saagiig Nishnaabeg scholar Leanne Simpson says: "As long as [there] has been colonialism on our lands, there has been resistance."[1] Contemporary literature plays an important role in analyzing colonialism and in enacting resistance. Understood within Indigenous storytelling epistemologies, literature is a powerful means of knowledge transmission and social critique, and a way to envision what Simpson terms "decolonized spaces and transformed realities that we have collectively yet to imagine."[2] While the disappearances of Indigenous women in Canada continue to be met with official forms of inaction or, just as problematically, with government-sponsored initiatives that arguably re-embed colonial relations of power, Indigenous literature imparts crucial lessons in anti-violence critique and social change. More than reshaping the terms of mainstream anti-violence debate, then, this literature also models Indigenous modes of research, remembrance, and reclamation.

Violence against Indigenous women is an ongoing crisis with roots deep in Canada's colonial history. The Canadian nation-state is premised upon historical and ongoing invasion, settlement, and expropriation of Indigenous lands—the result of which has been the dispossession of Indigenous peoples from ancestral land, language, and identity, and the planned elimination of Indigenous peoples "as a legal and social fact."[3] This dispossession is both gendered *and* colonial. As Grand Chief Edward John (Dakelh) stated in his October 2011 submission to the BC Missing Women Commission of Inquiry, women were "specifically targeted" in federal policies of forced removal and assimilation designed to undermine the political and familial structures of Indigenous communities.[4] These policies have contributed directly to the high rates at which Indigenous women are targeted for violence, and account for the statistics often rehearsed in media coverage of missing women cases: as of March 31, 2010, the Native Women's Association of Canada (NWAC) had documented 582 cases of missing and murdered Indigenous women,[5] while in 2013 the University of Ottawa doctoral researcher Maryanne Pearce indicated the number may be as high as 824.[6] A 2014 RCMP report suggests the actual number is higher still—reporting 1,181 cases between 1980 and 2012 alone.[7]

Statistics like these are perhaps more meaningful when taken in comparative terms: Indigenous women are targeted for gendered violence at much higher rates than non-Indigenous women in Canada. For instance, a government statistic finds that Indigenous women aged twenty-five to forty-four are five times more likely to die as the result of violence than all other women.[8] Similarly, the Standing Committee on the Status of Women reported to Parliament that Indigenous women and girls "are as likely to be killed by a stranger or an acquaintance as they are by an intimate partner."[9] This is very different from the situation of non-Indigenous women, whose homicide rates are far "more often attributed to intimate partner violence."[10] In short, comparative statistics help reveal the systemic and colonial origins of violence that merely appears interpersonal (violence committed by and against individuals). As independent counsellor for the BC Inquiry Robyn Gervais (Métis) points out, women have not vanished from Vancouver's Downtown Eastside by the hands of a serial killer alone—nor are the hundreds of missing and murdered women across Canada responsible for their vulnerability to violence because of "poor lifestyle choices," as is so often argued.¹¹ Rather, this violence occurs—can only occur—with the tacit collusion of the police and the justice system, and with the relative indifference of the Canadian public.

These shifting statistics tell only part of the story. They do, however, suggest a social issue in urgent need of action and redress. With the advent of the National Inquiry into Missing and Murdered Indigenous Women and Girls, the solution may seem nearer at hand. In this book, however, I question whether such forms of intervention can bring about the social and political transformation required to end violence. The National Inquiry's terms of reference provide for an investigation into the systemic causes of violence, and direct the commissioners to gather the experiences of family members and survivors, to make recommendations on ways to commemorate missing and murdered women, and to promote reconciliation by raising public awareness.[12] These are important forms of action, born of a decades-long struggle by anti-violence activists and the families of missing women to gain national recognition for the problem of violence. Yet, as Lubicon Cree scholar Robyn Bourgeois cautions, such strategies may not be as straightforwardly resistive as they appear: pursued within a context of ongoing "settler colonial domination," initiatives seeking improved knowledge, visibility, and awareness, "while appearing to offer a valid pathway of resistance, [may] *actually* serve to undermine these efforts by securing the colonial Canadian state's authority over indigenous peoples and territories."[13] Drawing from a body of critical scholarship which questions the potential of "recognition-based models of liberal pluralism" to transform the colonial relationship between Indigenous peoples and the state,[14] this book troubles the now commonplace activist tenet that increased visibility for the issue of missing and murdered women will lead necessarily to social change.

In mainstream initiatives to gather, publicize, and commemorate Indigenous women's stories of violence, the inclusion of Indigenous voices in dominant Canadian discourse is often believed to redress historical exclusions and to ensure a more just and equitable future for all. As Leey'qsun scholar Rachel Flowers observes, however, there is "always a risk of having our messages co-opted, difference erased, and the presumption that the colonized want or are willing to share our futures."[15]

Further to her critique of what Dian Million (Athabascan) calls the "adaptive inclusions" of liberal multiculturalism,[16] then, Flowers points to an incommensurability between Indigenous peoples' resistance, and the appropriative practices by which Indigenous stories of resistance are solicited and received in settler Canadian contexts. Rather than try to reconcile or transcend this incommensurability—which would entail a kind of colonial violence itself—I turn to Indigenous women's literature to help theorize decolonizing approaches to anti-violence resistance. Eve Tuck (Unangax) and K. Wayne Yang remind us that decolonization is not a metaphor. It is not just another way to advocate inclusion and equity, to "alleviate the impacts of colonization," to "reconcile settler guilt or complicity," or to "rescue settler futurity."[17] Instead, decolonization entails a profound transformation of colonial relations of power—a transformation "accountable to Indigenous sovereignty and futures," rather than to the ideal of Indigenous reconciliation with the Canadian state.[18] When read against material contexts of resistance in which Indigenous voices are co-opted to serve the interests of a "premature attempt at reconciliation,"[19] Indigenous women's literature unsettles the common-sense appeals to settler legitimacy, benevolence, and permanence that prevail in some dominant anti-violence initiatives. Tuck and Yang call this an "ethic of incommensurability"—this possibility to recognize "what is distinct, what is sovereign for project(s) of decolonization in relation to human and civil rights based social justice projects."[20] The literature I discuss herein performs this ethic of incommensurability by clarifying those aspects of either mainstream feminist organizing or state-sponsored initiatives that "cannot be aligned or allied" with Indigenous women's anti-violence resistance.[21] Kwagiulth legal geographer Sarah Hunt observes that Indigenous women's writing reveals "both the prevalence of violence ... and the strength of resistance to this violence."[22] Further to this, contemporary Indigenous women's literature comprises a significant (if often overlooked) archive of anti-violence theory and method.

A brief note on terminology may be helpful here—particularly with regard to terms like "Indigenous," and "Indigenous literature." As Anishinaabe literary scholar Cheryl Suzack notes, "one of the challenges of undertaking ... work in relation to aboriginal or indigenous peoples is the concern for appropriate terminology when discussing differently constituted cultural, political, and nation locations."[23] While often specifying the distinct national or community affiliations of individual authors I cite, I use the term "Indigenous" to refer collectively to the First Peoples of what is now called North America. "Aboriginal" primarily denotes the "customary and constitutional term in Canada for reference to Indigenous peoples"[24]—including First Nations, Métis, and Inuit peoples. In this way, "Aboriginal"—like "Indian"—is a "legal and social construction of the [Canadian] state."[25] By contrast, the term "Indigenous" signals a strategic departure from state-defined identity categories, and refers more inclusively to original peoples and their ancestors—many of whose nations and traditional territories are now "bisect[ed]" by the "artificial" borders and terms imposed by colonial nation-states.[26] I also use the term "Indigenous" because of its common application in international human rights discourse as employed by the United Nations and non-governmental organizations such as Amnesty International.

I understand "literature" to include written creative works as well as visual and oral texts. The texts explored throughout this book include documentary film, poetry, memoir, graphic fiction, drama, and narrative film. More broadly, I understand literature as both "artistic expression and political instrument"[27]—as an aesthetic project inseparable from the social and political contexts of its production and reception. This book presupposes a dynamic relation between literature and the world; in making these connections I draw from scholars in the field of Indigenous literary studies whose work explores literature's application to policy analysis and social debate. Daniel Heath Justice (Cherokee) describes Indigenous literature as an "expression of intellectual agency as well as aesthetic accomplishment" with a "role to play in the struggle for sovereignty, decolonization, and the reestablishment of Indigenous values."[28] As a critical project, analyzing literature thus entails what Muskogee Creek literary critic Craig Womack calls the "challenge of relating literature to the real world in hopes of seeing social change."[29] In engaging this challenge, I aim not to "subsume literature into politics," as Justice warns against, but instead to place "the text into constructive tension between its various contexts and its content."[30] Cree-Métis literary scholar Jo-Ann Episkenew calls this "socially responsible criticism"—and advocates examining "the *text* of works of Aboriginal literature [within] the *context* from which it is written."[31] By reading Indigenous women's texts within the context of ongoing colonial violence and resistance, my purpose is to inquire into the relationship between violence and representation, to explore literary contributions to anti-violence debate, and to foreground the work of Indigenous women writers in these conversations.

I began this project as a student of literary studies, reading texts whose interventions I understood in thematic terms to be resisting violence against Indigenous women in important ways. What I hadn't grasped in those early stages, however, were the methodological implications of that literary work; that is, that literature does more than describe violence—it can actually instruct its readers in decolonizing approaches to anti-violence resistance. Readers from Indigenous literary studies may recognize this challenge as disciplinary in origin, and as reflective of a particular moment in the development of the field. It's been eighteen years since the publication of Māori scholar Linda Tuhiwai Smith's *Decolonizing Methodologies: Research and Indigenous Peoples* (1999), and its impact is now deeply felt in the realm of Indigenous literary scholarship—a field primed for these interventions by its own contemporaneous turn to literary nationalist approaches that foreground Indigenous world views and nation-based intellectual traditions. The influences of these movements aside, however, students in the humanities still rarely receive formal training in Indigenous research methods or participatory, community-based approaches. Students of Indigenous literature today will likely develop a firm sense of the political stakes of representation, as well as a language in which to theorize story's capacity to "change the course of events in both the material and the spiritual worlds,"[32] but may not receive any overt instruction in the research frameworks by which to link this important discursive work to material sites of struggle in ways other than descriptive ones. While Indigenous methodologist Margaret Kovach (Nêhiýaw/Saulteaux) discusses what it meant in her own research to negotiate a "shortage of literature on Indigenous conceptual frameworks (specifically examples) linking tribal knowledges with congruent methodologies for human subject research,"[33] the humanities-trained scholar whose work often does not directly involve "human subjects" negotiates a different set of challenges.

Indigenous literature supplies in the realm of creative expression those conceptual frameworks Kovach calls for in her work on research methodologies. It offers practice-based as well as thematic contributions to anti-violence debate. It redresses the under-representation of Indigenous women's voices in the academy, in news media, and in mainstream feminist anti-violence movements themselves—not merely by fostering broader public recognition, but by articulating specifically "Indigenous solutions to the problems continued colonialism creates."[34] These approaches are now being theorized by a growing field of literary nationalist critics "alert for critical methods and voices that seem to arise out of the literature itself."[35] Reflecting on the characteristics of this movement, Anishinaabe critic Niigonwedom James Sinclair says: "Literary nationalism examines stories, poetry, songs, nonfiction works and autobiographies as processes deeply invested in the continuance of a People; it seeks to identify a political (and at times polemical) subjectivity at the centre of Native literary endeavors, while at the same time celebrating the interconnectedness of Native peoples with other cultures through treaties, nation-to-nation sovereignty struggles, models of cultural adaptation, and linguistic exchanges."[36] Notably, while the politically interventionist potential of Indigenous literature informed my thinking on this project from the beginning, my education in these matters took place first not in the literature classroom, but in the community halls and meeting rooms of anti-violence organizations.

It was in sexual assault crisis support work, and in solidarity organizing with an Indigenous/non-Indigenous coalition group, that I first understood the political stakes of representation where violence against women is concerned. Whether I was working with coalition members to organize our community's annual memorial march for missing and murdered Indigenous women, or partnering with feminist service providers to revise the "diversity" trainings offered to volunteers at a local crisis support line, I struggled to reconcile the projects and protocols of each setting—as well as my positioning as a non-Indigenous ally within them. In the coalition, we worked with the leadership of Indigenous women whose analysis of gendered violence was firmly tied to a lived analysis of settler colonialism. For these organizers, violence against

Indigenous women was unquestionably of colonial origin and took place strategically at the level of policy and legislation, as well as being something that men do to women. This was reflected in our organizing; as coalition members we took direction from Indigenous women, and pursued activities premised upon holding colonial structures accountable for violence in our communities. For instance, one of our major activities was to organize the city of London's memorial march for missing and murdered Indigenous women, held annually in solidarity with the February 14th Women's Memorial March in Vancouver. This march began with prayer and drumming on the steps of the courthouse, and then proceeded the length of our busiest downtown street to the steps of the city's police service headquarters. On these steps, leaders in anti-violence organizing gave speeches demanding that local authorities answer to the crisis of missing and murdered Indigenous women. The march thus expressed in both form (the route we took, the protocol we followed) and content (the speeches that were given, the call for accountability that was made) an act of Indigenous-led public memorial that critiqued the Canadian justice system. As one organizer said on the steps of the police headquarters, the justice system has not merely failed to protect the missing and murdered, but has actually been instrumental to this violence in the first place—displacing Indigenous women and children through policy and legislation designed expressly for this purpose. Rhetorically, then, the march began and ended on the steps of these institutions not to demand inclusion or protection for Indigenous peoples within those institutions' walls, but to assert the incommensurability of Indigenous and Euro-Canadian structures of justice and accountability, and to insist on the need for a different political relationship between Indigenous peoples and the colonial nation-state.

While the coalition worked firmly within a decolonial frame of reference that centred Indigenous women's voices and knowledges, the anti-violence work of our local mainstream feminist agencies took a more "additive" approach to organizing. Typically, this approach entails merely adding a "multicultural component" to pre-existing services developed largely with the "interests of white, middle class women in mind."[37] This approach is rooted historically in understandings of gendered violence as primarily a "tool of patriarchal control" to which such factors as race and class are of secondary significance.[38] Premised upon the tenets of an earlier mainstream feminist movement that had advocated for the "legal recognition of domestic and sexual violence,"[39] this dominant approach to anti-violence is often inattentive to Canada's legal institutions as contributing to the high rates at which Indigenous women are targeted for violence in the first place. As Mohawk legal scholar Patricia Monture explains, "Canadian laws are not an Aboriginal answer."[40] In Monture's analysis, Indigenous women's marginalization is furthered rather than alleviated by an inclusionary politics that would advocate better representation for Indigenous and racialized women while leaving state-sponsored systems of dispossession intact.

Through my solidarity work with the coalition, I understood Canadian institutions of law and governance as fundamentally embedded in colonial relations of power—relations that had been unjustly imposed, and could therefore be challenged or changed. In my feminist crisis support network, however, I was asked to assume the legitimacy and intransience of these institutions—merely seeking better representation and inclusion for marginalized women therein. In this way, a major tension emerged for me between mainstream feminist and decolonial solidarity organizing. This tension informed how I came to understand the activist implications of contemporary Indigenous women's literature, where the incommensurability of these projects came into sharper relief. As Hawaiian scholar Maile Arvin explains: "Feminism writ large is not a viable 'we' because it is whitestream and so often the vehicle to further colonial and imperial projects."[41] Indigenous women's literature, by contrast, often interrogates the colonial origins of gendered violence, tracing it to state policy and legislation. As Episkenew says, the "policies of the settler government have taken many forms"; however, their goal has often been the same—"to make Indigenous cultures disappear."[42]

Violence against Indigenous Women: Colonial Policy and the Mandate to "Disappear"

While it is beyond the scope of this book to explore each of these policies and the body of Indigenous-authored literature that exposes and resists them,[43] there are some government policies whose specifically gendered effects need mention here. Beverley Jacobs (Mohawk) and

Andrea Williams (Anishinaabe) point to the residential school system and the Indian Act in particular as having a "direct link to the disappearance and murder of hundreds of Aboriginal women in Canada."[44]

The Indian Act is a piece of legislation that structures all aspects of the relationship between Indigenous peoples and the federal government, and which defines "Indian status" under Canadian law. Legislative efforts to define status—who was and was not "Indian" under the law—pre-date Canada's formation as a federal state. With Confederation and the 1867 British North America Act the federal government claimed sole legislative jurisdiction in all matters related to "Indians, and Lands reserved for the Indians."[45] In 1876, the newly formed Canadian government consolidated pre-existing legislation into a single federal "Act Respecting Indians"; the 1876 Indian Act, with its many subsequent amendments, continues to define Indian status today. Paternalistically appropriating Indigenous peoples' "right to identify themselves," this legislation also established the reserve system, delineated the band government structure, and defined band membership and rights.[46] In this way, the Indian Act was the legislative expression of the colonial government's goal to efface Indigenous modes of governance, nationhood, and belonging—replacing these instead with a colonial structure administered by the Department of Indian Affairs and Northern Development (now Indigenous and Northern Affairs). Its intentions were thus assimilative from the outset. And although the Indian Act is sometimes interpreted as a "seeming affirmation of band rights to self-government and territories," it was always designed, as Joanne Barker (Lenape) points out, "with the explicit intent of assimilating Indians into Canadian society as hard-working, tax-paying, Christian citizens."[47] Perhaps no aspect of the act was more clearly assimilative than the gendered provisions by which generations of Indigenous women and their children were systematically disenfranchised from Indigenous identity and rights as encoded in the Indian Act.[48]

As Shari M. Huhndorf (Yup'ik) and Cheryl Suzack (Anishinaabe) explain, colonial legislation deliberately "reordered gender relations to subordinate women."[49] The Indian Act did so in many ways: by promoting and normalizing male-dominated forms of political organization, by privileging Euro-Western family structures, and by imposing restrictive identity categories that removed Indian status from women who married non-status or non-Indigenous men. This legislated sex discrimination not only imposed patriarchal modes of familial organization, inheritance, and descent, but also denied women community resources and political participation if they "married out."[50] With the 1876 Indian Act, the federal government consolidated the discriminatory provisions of earlier legislation and enshrined in law "Indian status" as defined by patrilineal descent: any woman who married a non-Indigenous man would lose her status, whereas an Indigenous man could confer status, through marriage, upon his non-Indigenous partner and her children. Indian status entitles one to vote in band elections, live in reserve housing, and access other band resources.[51] In defining women's status as entirely dependent on men, the 1876 Indian Act was integral to the colonial state's gradual displacement of tens of thousands of women from Indigenous identity and community over the following century.[52] It also disenfranchised women from participation in political governance while promoting the authority of men in this realm. The result, as Winona Stevenson (Cree) remarks, was a "major disruption of traditional kinship systems, matrilineal descent patterns, and matrilocal, post-marital residency patterns."[53] Although the Indian Act was amended in 1985 to remove its discriminatory membership provisions, the amendments themselves embed "continuing discrimination by differentiating between section 6(1), 6(2) and 6(3) categories of membership—framing a status hierarchy prejudicial to reinstated women and their children and thus perpetuating the sex discrimination of the pre-1985 Act."[54]

While the Indian Act subordinated women by displacing them from Indigenous identity, community, and rights via legislative means,[55] the residential school system accomplished a related assimilative agenda by means of forced removal and "re-education." Indigenous children were removed from their families and communities for over a century in order to attend these church-run, government-funded schools. From the time that residential schools were first operated according to this partnership in the early nineteenth century, until the last government-operated facility closed its doors in 1996, over 150,000 Indigenous children are estimated to have attended.[56] These schools had as their expressed purpose to "civilize and Christianize."[57] The government hoped that after a few generations of enforced dislocation, Indigenous peoples' own languages, knowledge systems, and governance structures would disappear. The genocidal intent of this system is memorably captured by the words of Confederation-era poet and superintendent of the Department of Indian Affairs (1913–32) Duncan Campbell Scott, who said: "The happiest future for the Indian race is absorption into the general population."[58]

It was under Scott's direction that amendments to the Indian Act in 1920 made attendance at a residential or day school compulsory under law for all status children between the ages of seven and fifteen.[59] Before this time attendance was strongly encouraged, with some parents reluctantly sending their children out of financial duress or in hopes that their children might attain the promised benefits of a formal, Euro-Western education. However, these benefits were rarely delivered. Schools were typically underfunded, overcrowded, and reliant in their daily operations on the physical labour of students whose work in such vocational capacities meant that less than half their time was spent in the classroom. After 1920, when attendance laws were increasingly enforced, parents who refused to send their children could be threatened with arrest. In many cases, Indian Agents (sometimes with the assistance of RCMP officers) would forcibly take children from their families in the fall.[60] While in the schools, children were often subject to psychological, physical, and sexual abuse, as well as known health hazards, malnutrition, and neglect. When they returned to their home communities as young adults, they did so often having lost not only their language and cultural knowledge, but also "life skills, parenting skills, self-respect, and, for many, respect for others."[61] Women and men were denied the opportunity to take up traditional roles and responsibilities; trans-generational family and community bonds were disrupted; and survivors of residential school suffered these traumas in addition to a host of related social ills that result from "inequality, injustice, and oppression within social and political norms and institutions."[62] In short, many former students returned home after years spent in the austerity, violence, and privation of residential schools with few skills and many traumatic memories.[63]

As the residential school era drew to a close, contiguous policies of child removal came into effect: cultural and linguistic dislocation promoted by the schools was subsequently carried out through the child welfare system, contributing to what is often termed the "Sixties Scoop."[64] As Cree/Assinniboine/Saulteaux social work professor Raven Sinclair explains: "The 'Sixties Scoop' describes a period in Aboriginal history in Canada in which thousands of Aboriginal children were removed from birth families and placed in non-Aboriginal environments."[65] While the period between the 1960s and mid-1980s saw a rapid statistical increase in the number of children apprehended and adopted,[66] it is important to note that this dramatic overrepresentation of Indigenous children in the child welfare system continues today. Cindy Blackstock (Gitksan) reminds us: "The number of First Nations children in care outside their own homes today [2008] is three times the number of children in residential schools at the height of their operation."[67]

Years of institutionalized violence and child removal have taken their calculated toll.[68] In communities wracked by generations of dislocation and loss, such social issues as poverty, addiction, and lateral violence have become increasingly normalized. In this environment, women are the targets of gendered violence in family settings and in their communities more broadly. Moreover, women face related challenges in settler-colonial Canada, including economic disadvantage, discriminatory treatment in the justice system, and a higher vulnerability to gendered violence perpetrated by non-Indigenous men. In this complex history of colonial disenfranchisement, gender has become a determinant of one's health and safety, of one's access to land and other community resources, and of one's official claim to Indigenous identity. In the following section, I discuss the corresponding role played by *representation* in perpetuating gendered violence, and also in affording possible pathways of resistance. Colonial policy and legislation are themselves a discursive form of violence, with direct material and physical effects. As Janice Acoose (Nehiowe/Métis/Anishinaabe) points out, such violence—whether in physical or legislative forms—is often also tied to racist and sexist stereotypes.[69]

Representing Gendered Colonial Violence: Recognition, Visibility, and Resistance

Violence against Indigenous women has emerged as an issue of urgent concern, now garnering national and international attention. Significant academic studies addressing Indigenous women's gendered experiences of colonialism have been published in both Canada and the US in the last decade,[70] and anti-violence activists have developed numerous public campaigns. Some of these campaigns have produced community-based research as well as large-scale awareness-raising initiatives—often national in scope—to promote greater public visibility for missing and murdered Indigenous women. The Native Women's Association of Canada's federally funded "Sisters in Spirit" campaign is one example of this at the national level: launched in 2005, this five-year research, education, and policy initiative featured significant public awareness and memorial activities which continue today in the form of the annual Sisters in Spirit vigils held in communities across Canada every October 4th. The work of the "Walk4Justice" group is a grassroots example of activism and awareness-raising which likewise drew national attention to the issue of gendered colonial violence. Robyn Bourgeois explains how Walk4Justice, co-founded in 2008 by Gladys Radek (Gitxsan/Wet'suwet'en) and Bernie Williams (Haida Gwaii), "undertook a number of provincial (British Columbia) and national walks to raise awareness and demand a national inquiry around the Highway of Tears and other cases of missing and murdered Indigenous women and girls from across Canada."[71]

The focus of many campaigns, then, has been to draw greater public visibility to violence against Indigenous women in Canada. In their analysis of media coverage in the cases of missing and murdered women, Yasmin Jiwani and Mary Lynn Young comment that "little attention has been paid" to missing and murdered women in mainstream news sources—and those representations that exist are often one-dimensional, pathologizing, and stereotypical.[72] Sharon McIvor and Teressa A. Nahanee likewise analyze Indigenous women's invisibility as victims of violence under the law,[73] while critics like Dara Culhane have explored the effective erasure of Indigenous women from dominant public discourse.⁷⁴ In short, many anti-violence scholars and activists have noted at once the "severity and pervasiveness" of violence against Indigenous women, as well as the apparent lack of "political will to address the crisis."⁷⁵ The persistence of the problem is thus articulated in relation to its lack of serious representation in both public and critical discourse. It would seem that in policy, politics, and law, as well as in mainstream reportage, gendered racial violence remains chronically under-represented and systemically overlooked—leading many critics to ask, as Susan Gingell does: "What will it take for ... people to develop a sense of outrage at this open season on indigenous women?"⁷⁶

In addition to the apparent invisibility of violence, a related site of resistance and critique has emerged to address the misrepresentation of Indigenous women. Critics point to a host of demeaning images and concepts that normalize women's invisibility as legitimate victims of violence and that code Indigenous bodies as inherently disposable and "rapable."⁷⁷ Explaining this phenomenon in her research on colonial violence, Cree-Métis scholar Emma LaRocque emphasizes the history of dehumanizing imagery and language to which Indigenous women have been subject: "A complex of white North American cultural myths, as expressed in literature and popular culture, has perpetuated racist/sexist stereotypes about Aboriginal women. A direct relationship between racist/sexist stereotypes and violence can be seen, for example, in the dehumanizing portrayal of Aboriginal women as 'squaws,' which renders all Aboriginal female persons vulnerable to physical, verbal and sexual violence."⁷⁸

As might be expected from a society that benefits materially from the continued dehumanization of Indigenous peoples, Canada's national imaginary fantasizes Indigenous women as either vanishing (as in the colonial trope of the noble but doomed "Indian princess"), or as disposable (as in the stereotype of the ignoble, promiscuous "squaw drudge").⁷⁹ At the same time, mainstream representations often disavow the actual disappearance or murder of Indigenous women as the material consequence of these racist misrepresentations. It is for this reason that LaRocque and others identify a "direct relationship" between dehumanizing stereotypes, ongoing violence against Indigenous women, and a general climate of public apathy.⁸⁰

In short, gendered colonial violence has often been theorized in causal relation to the indifference or distorted misinformation with which it is met. It is a problem characterized at once as epidemic in proportion and yet "invisible" to an indifferent dominant gaze. As such, many anti-violence projects pursue increased public visibility as synonymous with social justice for Indigenous women. This prevailing critical attitude holds that violence can be resisted by countering ignorance with awareness, and by promoting more informed, compassionate citizens. If Indigenous people "receive little mention in the collective myth of the Canadian nation-state,"[81] then accessible and sympathetic stories from Indigenous peoples' perspectives are hoped to redress this. However, while increased public awareness is important, it may not always lead directly to improved material conditions or to the political transformations required to end violence.

For instance, while public visibility is often assumed to be constitutive of political recognition for Indigenous peoples, such recognition is typically advocated in mere symbolic rather than substantive terms.[82] Citing Mohawk political scientist Taiaiake Alfred, Dene theorist Glen Coulthard explains how colonial recognition politics "[appear] to address ... colonial history through symbolic act of redress while in actuality 'further entrenching in law and practice the real bases of its control.'"[83] Dominant conceptions of advocacy, awareness, and change are often premised upon this liberal politics of recognition as well as a progressivist narrative of history—and can be traced, in their origins, to the modern emergence of the Enlightenment subject as rational, self-actualizing, and always improving. Of course, these narratives of subjecthood and history are themselves deeply implicated in the colonial project; the emergence of the modern subject coincides with its "Other" as produced through material and discursive practices designed to dehumanize Indigenous peoples in the bid to secure land and resources for the imperial centre and the settler colonial state. That the contemporary language of anti-violence activism and advocacy should so often make claims for Indigenous peoples' humanity, then—and for the inherent value in Indigenous women's emergence from marginalized obscurity into public visibility—preserves uncritically those dominant constructions of humanity and of progressive historical change upon which the colonial project is founded and maintained. Speaking to this problematic, Linda Tuhiwai Smith questions the presumed value of truth-telling and of "history in its modernist construction" for Indigenous peoples and the project of decolonization:

> We assume that when "the truth comes out" it will prove that what happened was wrong or illegal and that therefore the system (tribunals, the courts, the government) will set things right. We believe that history is all about justice, that understanding history will enlighten our decisions about the future. *Wrong.* History is also about power. In fact history is mostly about power.... In this sense history is not important for indigenous peoples because a thousand accounts of the "truth" will not alter the "fact" that indigenous peoples are still marginal and do not possess the power to transform history into justice.[84]

Smith vitally questions the instrumental uses to which some historical "truths" have been put. Often mobilized in ways that legitimize rather than decolonize colonial institutions (Smith's tribunals, courts, and governments), this modernist conception of history actually constructs Indigenous people as reliant for justice on the very structures that perpetuate colonial violence in the first place.[85] It moreover recuperates for settlers a position of benevolent innocence from which to approach the problem of violence. Yet, violence against Indigenous women is not an unhappy historical accident that now must be recognized and righted in order for the continued march of Western progress to unfold; rather, this violence is endemic to the existence of the modern colonial nation-state itself. The tenets of mainstream anti-violence under discussion in this book—namely, that broader visibility, public recognition, and state-sponsored action will end gendered colonial violence—too often presuppose the legitimacy of the colonial nation-state, privilege Euro-Western constructions of history and social change, and dismiss or appropriate out of context the voices of Indigenous feminist critics, activists, and writers whose work addresses the problems of violence and resistance. Drawing attention to the incommensurability between liberal, recognition-based politics of visibility and redress, and the decolonizing efforts of Indigenous women's anti-violence activism and literature, I attempt in this book to distinguish between these different ways in which Indigenous stories of violence are told and received in settler Canadian contexts.

Contrary to the claim that "nowhere [is] anyone prepared to tackle the root causes that give rise to these appalling acts" of gendered colonial violence,[86] in fact many such efforts do exist—and they now urgently require our critical attention. This is to say that how violence finds public expression is as much deserving of critical consideration as the fact of colonial violence itself. Of those instances in which public knowledge about violence is made, I ask: by what pedagogies is this victimry expressed? By what standards is violence constructed as *unjust* rather than "deserve[d]?"[87] My project is to account for those places where silence and marginalization are ostensibly opposed, where "societal inaction" is met with "action,"[88] and where Indigenous women's concerns emerge into public visibility. My goal is to highlight the insidious and unforeseen ways in which colonial violence is perpetuated in the present—not only by virtue of its "invisibility" to an indifferent public, but also by the very strategies devised toward its "visibility" and inclusion in anti-violence discourse itself. In this sense, I am as much concerned with the representational means by which violence and its survivors gain public expression as I am with any prescriptive approach to the problem of violence itself. This is because I question whether decolonized approaches to anti-violence can be reached within our current dominant frameworks, "which problematically attempt to reconcile settler guilt and complicity, and rescue settler futurity."[89] Instead of proposing prescriptive solutions, then, I look to Indigenous women's literature as a significant site of knowledge and resistance—one that, when read with and against dominant anti-violence initiatives, both demonstrates the incommensurability of sovereign Indigenous and settler colonial projects and sets forth instead a different set of possibilities.

Indigenous women's literature can help us to think critically about violence, representation, and resistance. Reading Indigenous literature in dialogue with the consciousness-raising efforts of community-based activism, or with the official texts of policy reform and government-sponsored redress, I canvas the insights of Indigenous women writers whose critiques of violence and representation can denaturalize or unsettle dominant, liberal strategies of anti-violence resistance. In this, I don't mean simply to privilege literary methods of social "conscientization"[90] over activist or policy-related efforts for change. Nor do I believe literature's value resides principally in its ability to inspire empathy among readers for whom the experience of colonial violence is normatively constructed as distant or unrelatable. Rather, I emphasize how literature can help us to think critically about actual anti-violence strategies, discourses, and debates—including the very notion of empathy itself. The *Oxford English Dictionary* defines empathy as "the quality or power of projecting one's personality into or mentally identifying oneself with an object of contemplation, and so fully understanding or appreciating it."[91] Literature's capacity for promoting imaginative empathy and social understanding has long been celebrated (and debated) in Euro-Western intellectual traditions,[92] but its application in the example of contemporary Indigenous literature is further complicated by settler reading practices which may seek (under the guise of identification) to collapse crucial power differences between settler and Indigenous subject positions in the name of reconciliation. Feminist performance theorist Elin Diamond calls this tendency the "mimetic pleasure of identification"—or, the pleasure of "becoming or inhabiting the other"—and cautions against the appropriative and authoritative moves that identification fosters.[93] Thus, while Jo-Ann Episkenew has made a persuasive case for the power of empathy, stating that "by reading Indigenous literature, settlers come to understand Indigenous people as fellow human beings,"[94] to this I would add Tuck and Yang's caveat that decolonized relations ultimately entail "abandoning the hope that settlers may one day be commensurable to Native peoples."[95] This applies as readily to the literary-critical realm as to the realm of social justice organizing.

Apart from its capacity to unsettle commonplace settler assumptions about violence and resistance, of course, Indigenous women's literature has its own role to play in sustaining Indigenous communities, readerships, and futures. Mishuana Goeman (Tonawanda Seneca) states in *Mark My Words*: "Just as the colonizer never left the Americas, neither did the Native people who continue to engage with land, nation, and community in their own tribally specific and gendered ways."[96] For Goeman, literature is uniquely positioned to carry out this work. She states:

The imaginative possibilities and creations offered in the play of a poem, imagery of a novel, or complex relationships set up in a short story provide avenues beyond a recovery of a violent history of erasure and provide imaginative modes to unsettle settler space. That is, the literary (as opposed to other forms of discourse, such as journalism, surveys, BIA/field reports, Indian agents' diaries, etc., in which Native women are continually a shadow presence) tenders an avenue for the "imaginative" creation of new possibilities, which must happen through imaginative modes precisely because the "real" of settler colonial society is built on the violent erasures of alternative modes of mapping and geographic understandings.[97]

This book explores the intellectual contributions of Indigenous literature to the project of anti-violence resistance, and puts the methodological insights of literary studies to work in grappling with both violence and the representational politics of resistance. I do this by reading Indigenous women's texts with and against anti-violence initiatives and awareness-raising campaigns themselves. The literature, itself implicitly concerned with questions of method and approach, can help us to theorize the gaps and limitations of contemporary anti-violence campaigns, and to articulate new possibilities and understandings.

Indigenous Women's Literature

This study is contemporary in its scope, and focuses primarily on the creative work of Indigenous women writers and thinkers in Canada, post-*Halfbreed* (1973). There is a long history of Indigenous women's literary production in Canada—dating back at least to the work of Tekahionwake (E. Pauline Johnson) and Hum-Ishu-Ma (Mourning Dove) in the late nineteenth and early twentieth centuries. Many critics, however, cite Métis writer Maria Campbell's groundbreaking autobiography *Halfbreed* as an important turning point in Indigenous literary production in Canada.[98] *Halfbreed* is notable not only for its complex reception history (exemplifying many debates that have characterized the field since its emergence in Canadian universities the 1980s and '90s),[99] but also for its contributions to Indigenous feminist analyses of identity legislation and other forms of gendered disenfranchisement.[100]

This disenfranchisement is embedded in colonial policy and law, as well as in popular representations of Indigeneity in Canadian culture and literature—and the project of much *Halfbreed* scholarship has been to understand the relationship between these discursive and material sites of marginalization. As Janice Acoose argues, Campbell's autobiography intervened in a dominant literary tradition that had constructed Indigenous women's lives from within the framework of "white-euro-canadian-christian patriarchy."[101] In analyzing this dominant literary tradition, Acoose examines historical and contemporary misrepresentations of Indigenous women as constructed to foster "cultural attitudes that justify violence."[102] Acoose traces these constructions from their inception in fourteenth-century "New World" ethnography to their manifestation in the twentieth-century Canadian literary canon, and argues for the important analytical work accomplished by Indigenous women writers like Campbell who not only expose this history of misrepresentation but also model Indigenous resurgence.

Although I do not discuss Campbell's *Halfbreed* (others have done this elsewhere), I am interested in a body of work made possible, in part, by its publication. I also build upon the work of critics like Acoose whose analyses of *Halfbreed* theorize gendered colonial violence as enacted in both material and discursive realms. Many of these critics also contribute an analysis of creative texts as having a material impact in the world. As Daniel Heath Justice explains, "the literary is never far from its context, especially among Native people, for whom words are generally regarded as having profound, world-altering power."[103] This claim for the "world-altering" implications of creative work informs the literary criticism of Acoose, Episkenew, Suzack, and others for whom the politically resistive capacity of *Halfbreed* resides in its affirmation, through story, of Indigenous models of kinship, governance, knowledge, and lifeways.

Working with a post-*Halfbreed* canon of Indigenous literature, I analyze primarily women-authored texts that reflect on gendered experiences of colonization and resistance. Although there are a number of contemporary male writers who deal in compelling ways with gendered colonial violence in their work, this book's project is to highlight the intellectual contributions of Indigenous women writers. For instance, acclaimed Cree playwright, essayist, and novelist Tomson Highway often foregrounds issues of violence against Indigenous women in his work. Much has been written about his invocation of the Helen Betty Osborne murder in particular. Highway attended high school with Osborne in The Pas, Manitoba, and recalls her murder's impact on him in an often-quoted 1994 interview with Joanne Tompkins and Lisa Male: "What I want my work to do is … prevent that kind of thing happening to another native woman."[104] The murder "changed me," he says, "and I will write this sort of stuff until the world stops treating women so poorly."[105] The recurring treatment of Osborne's murder has generated much debate—as have other instances of gendered violence in Highway's work.[106] Critics have questioned whether this work resists gendered colonial violence, or if it merely reproduces violence in representational form.[107] Although the debates over Highway's work are themselves beyond the scope of this book, they do highlight the considerable risks involved in staging creative interventions into the material problem of violence. Many of the women writers I investigate engage these risks directly by theorizing the politics of representation where the missing and murdered are concerned.

Throughout the book, I analyze several examples of public knowledge making and remembrance about missing and murdered women. Many of these examples are galvanized by actual instances of violence against Indigenous women in contemporary Canada and have played a role in shaping subsequent anti-violence activism and policy recommendations. For instance, the book begin and ends with chapters on prominent missing and murdered women's cases and literary responses to each: the missing and murdered women of Vancouver as culminating in the Missing Women Commission of Inquiry in 2010, and the murder of Helen Betty Osborne in 1971 as leading to the Aboriginal Justice Inquiry of Manitoba in 1988. Each chapter offers a case study in anti-violence that investigates the question of resistance by juxtaposing activist and policy documents with literary or other creative texts. By reading Indigenous-authored literature about violence in dialogue with these examples, I emphasize not only the thematic contributions of literature to anti-violence debate, but also the possibility that literature can imagine resistance differently. Despite the seeming proliferation of local and national campaigns now mobilized around this cause, some anti-violence initiatives have in fact narrowed rather than opened up a space for politicized, oppositional public engagement by foreclosing understandings of the root causes of gendered colonial violence. As Sarah Hunt remarks, "Why are we so hesitant to name white male violence as a root cause, yet so comfortable naming all the 'risk factors' associated with the lives of Indigenous girls who have died? Why are we not looking more closely at the 'risk factors' that lead to violence in the lives of the perpetrators?"[108] While politicians, journalists, and even some anti-violence advocates themselves often "blam[e] native people for the violence they face,"[109] literature takes aim at the structural facets of settler colonialism that empower perpetrators to act with impunity. In this way, literature offers a rich and often overlooked contribution to policy analysis and activist debate.

Each chapter begins with a different site of recent anti-violence activism (an awareness-raising campaign, a program in "diversity," or a state-sponsored initiative in legislative reform), and then explores the possibilities and limits of each site through related examples of Indigenous literary or creative production. This literary work not only performs the telling of gendered colonial trauma, but also occasions critical reflection about how resistive knowledge about violence gets made. Juxtaposing contemporary Indigenous literature with examples of anti-violence activism, I demonstrate literature's capacity to engage meaningfully with material contexts of struggle, and to emphasize how activist resistance is itself discursively constituted. The project of ending violence requires action-based strategies, but these strategies should not be taken for granted as necessarily resistive. We must always pay attention to questions of representation; literature can help us to perform this analytical task.

Chapter 1 interrogates the 2010 public commission of inquiry into the missing women investigation which led to the eventual arrest and conviction of serial killer Robert Pickton. Pursuant to the Public Inquiries Act, this commission's terms of reference provided for a fact-finding mission resulting in recommended changes for the conduct of police investigations into missing women and cases of suspected multiple homicides in British Columbia. With its narrow terms of reference and an equally limited temporal scope, however, the inquiry did not invite an analysis of colonial violence as ongoing and systemic. Moreover, the inquiry was not inclusive of the many grassroots organizations and other witnesses whose expertise would have contributed to this perspective. As it was, the inquiry's processes severely limited the kinds of recommendations it could make, as well as the public understanding it would produce. Métis filmmaker Christine Welsh's 2006 documentary *Finding Dawn* offers a useful counterpoint to the provincial inquiry. Modelling Indigenous methods of research and storytelling, the film documents accessible examples of how families and communities engage daily in the work of remembrance, protest, and change.

Chapter 2 takes as its point of departure a prominent multi-year anti-violence campaign in research, education, and policy change: the Native Women's Association of Canada's (NWAC) "Sisters in Spirit" campaign. Launched in 2004 as part of an effort to identify the "root causes and trends leading to racialized sexualized violence,"[110] this initiative was also concerned to "raise awareness" and to "build political will to address this crisis."[111] NWAC's qualitative research practices seek to document and disseminate "through life stories or storytelling, the experiences of missing and murdered Aboriginal women and girls" as narrated by their families.[112] While the "storytelling" pursued with the families is grounded in Indigenous methods and protocols, the women's stories themselves have been used more widely in public education campaigns and for the development of anti-violence recommendations in policy, justice, and policing reform. For instance, in the case of NWAC's partnership with Amnesty International, the life narratives of missing and murdered women are refracted through a human rights discourse of rights and redress. The 2004 Amnesty International report *Stolen Sisters: Discrimination and Violence against Indigenous Women in Canada* is an example of this. While this report does raise public awareness through its accessible format and wide circulation, it relies on women's biographical narratives to substantiate its recommendations— not all of which are unproblematic. Commemorative poetry, however, can help us to think critically about the report's recommendations, as well as its instrumental representation of missing women's lives. Like the *Stolen Sisters* report, Marilyn Dumont's (Cree-Métis) poem "Helen

Betty Osborne" explores remembrance as a way to raise awareness and to oppose violence, and makes reference to the stories of actual missing or murdered women in order to do this. Crucially, the poem also queries the ethical possibilities and limits of using stories toward particular pedagogical ends. In this way, Dumont critically intervenes into the way women's stories are circulated in activist discourse.

Chapter 3 further explores how women's stories of violence or discrimination have been solicited for their perceived pedagogical capacities, this time in the context of promoting multicultural "diversity" and "cross-cultural sensitivity" in mainstream feminist service agencies. Thinking through the history of anti-racist reform in feminist social service agencies in the 1990s, this chapter takes up the case study of one agency's well-publicized struggle to implement a more inclusive service mandate: Nellie's shelter in Toronto. Nellie's is one of Canada's oldest women's shelters, and the conflict there became a flashpoint for broader debates about institutional racism and white privilege taking place in various feminist organizations in the 1990s. These debates also took place in the publishing industry, where writers like Lenore Keeshig-Tobias (Anishinaabe) and Jeannette Armstrong (Syilx) critiqued the industry's continued marginalization of Indigenous authors. While feminist service agencies and publishers alike solicited Indigenous and racialized women's voices in order to educate white interlocutors, these initiatives nonetheless kept exclusionary structures and practices intact. This problematic likewise informs the reception of Dene (Chipewyan) writer-activist Morningstar Mercredi's 2006 memoir *Morningstar: A Warrior's Spirit*, which some reviewers have interpreted as providing readers an unmediated and authentic form of knowledge about gendered colonial violence. *A Warrior's Spirit* illustrates the tensions and contradictions surrounding the pursuit of anti-violence consciousness-raising when reception practices re-embed the very power asymmetries the work seeks to address.

Chapter 4 explores instances of public commemoration of missing and murdered Indigenous women in Canada. By public commemoration, I refer not only to public memorials and protest marches, but also to the processes of public inquiry, legislative reform, or formal government apology that are intended to honour the life and deeds of a particular person while expressing communal grief at that person's violent passing. Dominant forms of commemoration often uphold normative standards as to what constitutes a legitimately "grievable" victim of violence—prioritizing for public remembrance the lives and deaths of women who "resist to the utmost,"[113] or who are thought not to have been "doing something to deserve it, something to bring it on [themselves]."[114] While the increased public representation of such cases seems to promote rather than to foreclose social justice for Indigenous women, the opposite may actually be true when commemorative efforts normalize violence in Indigenous lives. I illustrate this by examining commemorative representations of Helen Betty Osborne (Cree) and Anna Mae Pictou-Aquash (Mi'kmaq) that posit these women's violent deaths as somehow inevitable, or as recoupable tragedies insofar as they fulfill an instructive, awareness-raising potential. In Osborne's case I discuss Cree writer David Robertson's commemorative graphic novel *The Life of Helen Betty Osborne* (2008). I read the novel in dialogue with the government of Manitoba's public apology to the Osborne family in July of 2000, as well as the Memorial Foundation Act established later that year. In the case of Anna Mae Pictou-Aquash, I analyze Algonquin playwright Yvette Nolan's 2006 commemorative play *Annie Mae's Movement* for how it both resists and subtly reproduces the popular tendency to make this activist's murder into a martyrdom. In each case, dominant forms of remembrance accord meaning to these women's deaths retrospectively, ironically recuperating violence as instructive when it conforms to certain narrative structures.

Dominant forms of anti-violence intervention have often overlooked the insights of Indigenous women and of writers and artists particularly. The juxtaposition of literary texts with activist sites of resistance allows not only for a critical account of gendered colonial violence to emerge, but also underscores Indigenous women's vital contributions to the process. This work is urgently required in our present moment, in which violence is not so much invisible to the public (as some critics have argued), but is actually misrepresented in ways that pathologize Indigenous women while normalizing systemic colonial violence in their lives. To weave into the discussion Indigenous-authored approaches to anti-violence and social change is to shift the public conversation. In looking to Indigenous women's literature for possible answers, rather than to state-sponsored policies or initiatives alone, I hope to demonstrate the important theoretical and practical contributions made by Indigenous literature in helping all readers to imagine beyond the possibilities, limits, and gaps of these initiatives.

CHAPTER ONE

Finding Dawn and the Missing Women Commission of Inquiry: Story-Based Methods in Anti-Violence Research and Remembrance

In the opening sequence of her 2006 National Film Board documentary *Finding Dawn*, Métis filmmaker Christine Welsh asks: "What is it about numbers? What do they tell us? Do they help us understand?" As the camera surveys a fragmented succession of rainy night-time streets, Welsh's voiceover states: "One woman goes missing. Then another. And another. For a long time, only those who know and love them pay attention. Until the numbers start to add up."[1] The camera then shifts our gaze, leaving the darkened streets of Vancouver behind in order to resituate us at the site of the excavated Pickton farm—a locale that remains significantly unnamed in the film itself. Our encounter with this site begins from above, by means of a broad aerial pan of the farm and its surroundings, and then shifts to the ground below, where forensic investigators search for "traces of missing women." It is here, in February of 2004, that a twenty-third woman is identified from DNA found at the farm. "But like all the others," Welsh emphasizes, "she is much more than a number. She has a name. Her name is Dawn Crey." This is how *Finding Dawn* begins.

An expedient point of departure that establishes the statistical gravity of a situation too frequently ignored—with, the film tells us, over sixty women missing from Vancouver's Downtown Eastside—this opening does more than expose an apparent empirical "truth about violence against [Indigenous] women" in Canada;[2] it also pries open, at the outset, a broader question about how public knowledge about this truth gets made. Addressed to a present moment characterized not only by an ongoing epidemic of gendered and racialized violence, but also by proliferating representational treatments of it,[3] *Finding Dawn* constitutes an intervention into both the social issue of violence itself and its expression in dominant public discourse. For instance, in naming Dawn, and in unnaming the Pickton farm, the opening to Welsh's film performs a conceptual break from the representational strategies that characterize much of the recent mainstream media coverage of the missing and murdered women cases—including the tendency to render disappeared women as anonymous figures whose lives and livelihoods are made to signal an apparent willing vulnerability to violence.[4] *Finding Dawn* overturns this and other mainstays of the missing women representational inventory, provisionally offering in its opening sequence the well-worn trope of a lone woman on a rain-slick, darkened city street only in order to replace it with the story of a woman who, like many of the missing women, "started out somewhere else."[5] Similarly, the aerial pan of the unnamed Pickton farm-site is offered not so much as a vision bearing the truth of "what really happened [there],"[6] but rather, as an image that deliberately undermines the fiction of definitive knowledge and closure underlying some representations of the police investigation into the missing women's case.[7] As Welsh puts it, finding Dawn's DNA perhaps generates more questions than it does answers; it cannot tell us who she was or why we lost her, nor can it account for Dawn's story as "part of a much bigger picture" of ongoing colonial social suffering. In efforts to attend to this "bigger picture," *Finding Dawn* tells the stories of several women whose lives (like Dawn's) are shown beyond the often individualized and pathologizing accounts of mental illness, poverty, sex work, and addiction associated with Vancouver's Downtown Eastside. Instead, Welsh explains these women's lives in terms of the intergenerational impacts of residential schooling and assimilative child welfare policy, the state-sponsored invasion and expropriation of Indigenous lands, and an ongoing history of gendered racism and sexual violence against Indigenous women. In telling these stories, the film takes care to position these women not as isolated, culpable, or victimized figures, but as each belonging to, and now senselessly missing from, a broader network of familial and community relations whose present work it is, in the words of Dawn's sister Lorraine, to "let it not be forgotten."[8]

In the context of the missing and murdered women, then, what might it mean to remember? More specifically, what might it mean to make official public knowledge about the missing and murdered, and where do such projects of memory making intersect with or diverge from the critical processes of remembrance here evoked by Lorraine Crey, and theorized by the film itself? In this chapter, I discuss *Finding Dawn*'s contributions to our thinking about these questions, and to Indigenous feminist theorizations of gendered colonial violence more broadly.

Since its 2006 Vancouver premiere at the Amnesty International Film Festival, where it won the Gold Audience Award, *Finding Dawn* has become an influential documentary resource on the issue of missing and murdered women.[9] Given the film's popularity as a teaching text and as an awareness-raising tool, I analyze how the film's representational strategies intervene into dominant forms of knowledge and memory about violence. I also discuss how the film models Indigenous research methodologies of storytelling that honour communal expressions of agency, activism, and resistance. Toward that end, I read *Finding Dawn* with and against another prominent instrument of knowledge making about the missing women cases: British Columbia's Missing Women Commission of Inquiry (2010–12). In doing so, I mean to think through the possibilities and limits of this provincial inquiry as a research body and as mode of public knowledge making about gendered colonial violence in Canada. In analyzing the inquiry, I draw from its official terms of reference and mandate, as well as from the transcripts of various key proceedings and from the final report released publicly in December 2012. I also draw from the oral submissions made by participants at the seven Northern Community Forums held in September 2011 in communities along the Highway of Tears in northern BC. These public consultation forums were appended to the inquiry's original mandate as part of a "study commission" designed to fulfill a broader policy advisory capacity than intended by the original evidentiary hearings held in Vancouver. I am interested in how Indigenous participants' oral submissions at the Northern Community Forums together articulated an analytical intervention into the problem of gendered colonial violence in BC and in Canada, as well as a methodological intervention into the limited mandate, powers, and processes of the inquiry itself.

In analyzing these oral submissions in dialogue with *Finding Dawn*, I foreground Indigenous women's voices in anti-violence policy debate. Moreover, I want to acknowledge women's contributions to each of these "fact-finding" projects—the inquiry and the documentary film—as representing a politically engaged Indigenous feminist research practice. This practice is modelled implicitly by *Finding Dawn,* in which Welsh wrests the stories of missing and murdered from their individualized expression in extractive modes of knowledge making (of which the Missing Women Commission of Inquiry is one example) in order to provide a more capacious, holistic, and agential analysis through story. In taking my methodological and analytical cues from Welsh's film, I hope to theorize not only the limitations of the inquiry, but also to suggest something of the significant but often overlooked analytical capacity of Indigenous-authored literature and film in modelling Indigenous research methodologies, in furthering Indigenous survivance, and in contributing vitally to matters of policy, policing, and law.

Violence against Indigenous Women in BC

As is the case across Canada and particularly in Western Canada, violence against Indigenous women is a matter of urgent material and political concern. In my own home province of British Columbia, the Native Women's Association of Canada (NWAC) has documented 160 cases of women and girls who have gone missing or been murdered since the 1960s. This means that Indigenous women go missing and are murdered at a higher rate in BC than in any other province or territory in Canada. BC also has the highest rate of unsolved murders of Indigenous women.[10] Amid tacit and official forms of indifference, often with scarce police resources and other supports being devoted to the cause, a number of BC cases have recently attracted sustained local and national media attention. These include the many cases of women who've gone missing or been murdered along the 800 km stretch of the northern Highway 16—known locally and in the media as the Highway of Tears—and the more publicized example of the Vancouver missing women whose disappearances would later be yet more widely known because of the Pickton case. Robert Pickton, a pig farmer from Port

Coquitlam, was charged with the murders of twenty-six women who went missing from Vancouver between the early 1990s and 2002, and was found guilty in December 2007 of the six charges with which the Crown initially proceeded. A disproportionate number of these women were Indigenous, as is the case with the some thirty women who have disappeared along the Highway of Tears since the late 1970s and whose cases remain largely unsolved.[11] The challenge of whether and how to link these disparate sites from which so many women have gone missing in BC—the urban lower mainland and Vancouver's Downtown Eastside (DTES), on one hand, and the northern Highway of Tears, on the other—is an ongoing matter of debate. As I discuss in a later section, the Missing Women Commission of Inquiry would belatedly attempt to address this challenge through its "study commission."

The work of linking the disparate BC cases suggests a number of questions vital to local and national discussions about anti-violence. In particular, these cases demonstrate the importance of addressing localized, interpersonal instances of violence as part of a broader pattern of *state-sponsored* violence. As many activists suggest, local responses must account for the socio-economic and geographical specificities of a given case, while nonetheless understanding the missing women problem as systemic in nature and colonial in origin—that is, as disproportionately affecting *Indigenous* women whose social and spatial "risk" factors are overdetermined by colonial state policies dating back to before Confederation.[12] In the example of BC's prominent cases, the specific conditions under which women have gone missing are, in each instance, distinct, and thus require different community-based responses.[13]

The DTES is an urban setting in which Indigenous women's vulnerability to predatory violence is informed by their overrepresentation in street-level sex work. The Highway of Tears, by contrast, is a remote stretch of highway along which women of various northern communities are compelled, by poverty and limited transportation options, to travel by hitchhiking. In each case, however, the circumstances under which women have gone missing are informed by a common history of displacement, marginalization, and gendered aggression that has targeted Indigenous women specifically. These circumstances, though expressed differently in the DTES than along the Highway of Tears, thus urgently require analyses that can envision both site-specific interventions—or "band-aids," as Vancouver-based Indigenous feminist activist Tina Beads puts it[14]—and broad-based, radical policy change. As Christine Welsh states in *Finding Dawn*, Canada is a country whose history is "steeped in violence against native people"; Indigenous women are at risk of violence "no matter where we live, our circumstances, or our lifestyles."

In this analysis, women go missing not despite the efforts of policing bodies and other institutions, but because of them. This is not to say that some police officers and advocates haven't expended enormous efforts in the missing women cases. On the contrary, many front-line workers have worked tirelessly to bring the missing home. What I want to emphasize, however, is how this present situation is irrevocably shaped by a colonial history that conditions the circumstances under which women arrive, live, and work under the daily threat of violence—whether in the DTES or along the Highway of Tears. This colonial history likewise structures the relationship between missing women and those who police and protect them. As a particularly evocative example, we might consider the "literal translation of the word for police" in the Carrier language, spoken by Dakelh communities along the Highway of Tears: *Nilhchuk-un*, or "those who take us away."[15] A reference to the RCMP's role in removing Indigenous children from their homes and enforcing their compulsory attendance at residential schools, this word captures a long history of state-sponsored displacement in which the police have been instrumental. As one RCMP-commissioned report puts it: "The police were not perceived as a source for help but rather as an authority figure who takes members of the community away from the reserve or makes arrests for wrong-doing"[16] Understood from this perspective, the police have been an oppressive force whose historical complicity with colonial policies of child removal and assimilation now finds contemporary expression in patterns of over-policing and under-protection that continue to put Indigenous women at risk.[17] This adversarial relationship between Indigenous communities and the police plays out in a number of ways,[18] from the more overt example of police brutality to the "slow violence" of institutional indifference and chronically under-resourced investigations into missing women cases.[19] Though the latter examples may not constitute outright or intentional forms of physical harm per se, they are nonetheless embedded within a complex of state-sponsored violence upon which Canada was founded—practices with which the police are historically complicit. Enabled by a broader set of legislative and policy initiatives, the everyday complicity and indifference on the part of the justice system and the Canadian public needs not be "conscious, intentional, or malicious" (though, in historical fact, it often has been); as Karen Warren has said, "it only needs to be pervasive to be effective."[20]

As this history makes clear, interpersonal expressions of violence against Indigenous women have at their root a legacy of state violence in the form of colonial displacement and assimilation meant to evict Indigenous peoples from the land. Women whose economic and social marginalization has been structured through centuries of oppressive legislation and policy thus arrive on the streets of Vancouver or on remote northern highways not as a matter of individual choice alone, but often by economic necessity or as a result of other related conditions. Similarly, the men who exploit these conditions, who seek such women out, and who lure women into situations of further vulnerability and isolation, do not act alone but with the full force of this history at their backs. As Sherene Razack remarks, such violence is informed by a long history of colonial policy and constitutes in the very moment of its expression the "making of the white, masculine self as dominant through practices of violence directed at a colonized woman."[21] The challenge of analyzing and of resisting these "practices of violence" as assertions of colonial domination thus requires an accounting for how gendered violence has been legislated as a tool of colonialism and racism. Indigenous feminist theory and practice offer such an analysis—one that can understand the missing and murdered women cases in Vancouver and along the Highway of Tears as the logical and anticipated outcome of legal directives intended to attack Indigenous women *as Indigenous women* in their home territories. This analysis is missing from the official terms and methods of the Missing Women Commission of Inquiry.

"Indigenous feminism" is often defined in terms of its constituent parts. Although there has been significant debate as to "what term—*Indigenous* or *feminism*—should take precedence" in projects concerned with gendered decolonization,[22] *Finding Dawn* implicitly advocates the inseparability of these terms. While the film never uses the language of Indigenous feminism to describe its project directly, it performs this analysis by accounting for the simultaneity with which gendered and racialized forms of violence have been mobilized against Indigenous women throughout Canada's colonial history and present. Hence Indigenous feminism's mutual commitments: it both "takes gender seriously as a social organizing process" that has systemically subordinated women to men,[23] and also "confronts the dominant myths and political, social and economic practices that dignify, deny or perpetuate colonialism" as the "enforced appropriation of Aboriginal nations' land and resources."[24] A key strategy in the colonial appropriation of land and resources has been the deliberate dismantling of Indigenous kinship relations through the targeting of women and children for forced dislocation and assimilation. This is seen clearly in the examples of the Indian Act and the residential schools system, and in the subsequent gendered violence these forced removals make possible. In analyzing these assaults on women and children as the calculated means by which colonial governments have undermined Indigenous peoples' sovereignty on their lands, *Finding Dawn* promotes gendered justice as integral to the struggle for self-determination. And, while colonial governments have sought to dispossess Indigenous peoples of their lands, languages, and nations in part by dismembering "strong kin relations in which women had significant authority,"[25] *Finding Dawn* purposefully *re-members* missing and murdered women and the territories and familial networks from which they have been removed. Significantly, this process of remembering is pursued through story as a methodology that can contextualize these removals historically, while also affirming missing women's relations to one another, to their communities, and to their ancestral lands in the present.

Part of *Finding Dawn*'s analytical contribution to feminist anti-violence, then, is to position the seemingly disparate stories of missing and murdered women in relation to one another, and to the families, communities, and territories from which they are missing. In doing so, the film foregrounds not only Indigenous women's vulnerability to violence across different material circumstances, but also the politically resistive ways women are actively remembered (and are remembering) within different familial and community-based networks. Interviewing the families of missing women, as well as activists, scholars, and survivors of violence in different territories across Western Canada, Welsh's qualitative research practice employs what Margaret Kovach has called "story as Indigenous methodology."[26] For Kovach, story functions as a way of advancing holistic, contextualized knowledge in terms of both content and method.[27] In this understanding, story both makes meaning and reflects upon the ways in which we come to know. As Neal McLeod (Cree) says of storytelling in *Cree Narrative Memory*, "there are elements of description and analysis: the storyteller describes events and experiences, but also analyzes this experience."[28] *Finding Dawn* draws together a series of oral histories—that is, "personal narratives of place, happenings, and experiences" of the missing and of those who work daily to remember[29]—in order to both describe and analyze the issue of missing and murdered women. Through story the film tells its audience empirical facts, but also theorizes different community-held knowledges about violence as constituted in part by the methods through which this information is sought, told, organized, and represented. In short, the film theorizes—through story as an Indigenous methodology—that what we can know about violence depends upon the form taken by our research and dissemination endeavours. This applies whether in the realm of activism, commemoration, scholarship, or teaching—all sites explored throughout Welsh's documentary.

As a very different kind of fact-finding mission, the Missing Women Commission of Inquiry shares *Finding Dawn*'s thematic commitment to the project of anti-violence and likewise draws from the qualitative knowledge of those who are on the front lines. As part of its policy-based mandate, the inquiry collected the testimony of families, grass-roots organizers, service providers, and representatives of policing bodies. Unlike *Finding Dawn*, however, the inquiry took an instrumental approach to the treatment of testimony. Necessarily bound by the constraints of the provincial Public Inquiries Act, by time limitations, and also by its own terms of reference, the inquiry arguably performed what Kovach would term "an extractive" research exercise in order to fulfill its mandate.[30] Rather than being guided by and responsive to the stories of its participants, and then shaped in its processes by the directives embedded therein, the inquiry was—in the words of its own final report—"captive of its Terms of Reference."[31] The inquiry was tasked with responding in a timely and efficient manner to a particular set of government-issued imperatives, and thus could not shape its processes reciprocally, in relation to its participants. As such, its methods and purposes were grounded not in the holistic approaches theorized by Kovach and performed implicitly in *Finding Dawn*, but in Euro-Western traditions of research and of public knowledge making that presume the legitimacy of colonial governments as well as their suitability to address social issues of colonial origin. In response to these limitations, fifteen different organizations boycotted the inquiry in April 2012.[32] Citing the inquiry's impractical timelines, its narrow terms of reference, its failure to provide publicly funded lawyers to community stakeholders, and its unwillingness to hear testimony from key witnesses, these organizations refused to participate in the Policy Forums or Study Commissions, stating: "The Commission has lost all credibility among Aboriginal, sex work, human rights and women's organizations that work with and are comprised of the very women most affected by the issues this Inquiry is charged with investigating."[33] Instead, the inquiry seemed to become part of the broader history of "researchers, scientists and development professionals entering [Indigenous] communities to study, to develop or to empower them."[34] For this reason, the inquiry's approach necessarily stands in contrast, both conceptually and in terms of its methodological execution, to the more holistic and decolonizing analysis undertaken by *Finding Dawn*.

This discussion is not intended fault the inquiry for what it could not have done, but to ask genuine questions about its limitations as an "investigative technique" and as a mode of "social influence" where issues of colonial violence are concerned.[35] This is to be attentive to the public inquiry's origins as a particular form of research and intervention. Prior to and following Confederation, public inquiries became an important mechanism by which the settler-colonial state established its "Indian" policy. The recommendations of early commissions of inquiry predictably called for and justified oppressive state intervention into Indigenous politics and lifeways. In contemporary Canada, the public inquiry remains a significant form of fact-finding and public knowledge making with respect to Indigenous peoples, with many commissions of inquiry (both provincial and federal) mandated to inspect and make policy recommendations regarding matters of social injustice as experienced by Indigenous peoples. The Royal Commission on Aboriginal Peoples is one of the most notable examples; this inquiry was formed by the federal government in 1991 following the failed Meech Lake Accord and the armed standoff at Oka between the Mohawks of Kanesatake, the Sûreté du Québec, and the Canadian military.[36] Despite its scope and significance, this commission nonetheless reproduced problematic recommendations. In *Red Skin, White Masks*, Glen Coulthard details how "many critics have convincingly argued that its vision still ultimately situated Indigenous lands and political authority in a subordinate position within the political and economic framework of Canadian sovereignty."[37] Ironically, the social injustices with which contemporary inquiries are tasked to contend are in many cases a direct result of the dispossession enforced by historical and ongoing colonial policy as the legacy of public inquiry. There is some irony involved in relying upon state-appointed bodies to fix (even at arm's length) the problems for which the state is responsible in the first place.[38] Appointed by the executive branch of government in exceptional cases where a matter of public concern has reached a level of crisis or contention such that it cannot be dealt with by ordinary governmental or judicial means, public inquiries have long served in Canada as a means of "*restoring confidence* in government processes" and institutions.[39] In this sense, public inquiry—as a research mechanism and as an instrument of social influence—serves as much to restore dominant public opinion in the police as it does to deal with the colonial violence inherent to law enforcement and the justice system in Canada.

The Missing Women Commission of Inquiry

The Missing Women Commission of Inquiry (MWCI) was established in response to the Robert Pickton case and the many questions it raised, and which remained unanswered following the 2007 trial. However, it is important to note that questions were being asked of policing bodies as well as local and provincial governments long before the trial—even long before Pickton's arrest in 2002. Women had been going missing from the DTES of Vancouver in increasing numbers every year since the early 1990s. By the time of Pickton's arrest in 2002, over sixty women were on the missing women's list.[40] The Vancouver Police Department had formerly downplayed or outright denied the possibility that a serial killer could be at work in the DTES—in part out of the mistaken and discriminatory belief that DTES sex workers are transient.[41] The arrest of a single suspect, Pickton, made visible to the broader public what had long been known by grieving families and communities: that these disappearances would have been investigated differently had they involved women of less marginalized socio-economic circumstances, and that Pickton had been able to act with impunity only with the tacit collusion of systemically under-resourced and biased policing. Ernie Crey makes this point clear in his interview for *Finding Dawn*. A vocal advocate for the families of the missing women, and himself the brother of missing woman Dawn Crey, he states: "If these women had been from a wealthier part of Vancouver ... some upscale, tonier neighbourhood in Vancouver, and involved largely white women ... the investigation would have been thorough-going, it would have been well-financed, and there would have been a lot of police officers.... We would very likely have had a suspect in jail far earlier than was the case."[42]

In the aftermath of this deferred and underfunded police investigation plagued by poor leadership, infighting, and multi-jurisdictional challenges,[43] the families of missing women, as well as community leaders and activists like Crey, called for a public inquiry into the investigation. This was seen as one way of making accountable social memory about the conditions under which the missing disappeared, with the hope of safeguarding against the repetition of such atrocities in the future.[44] Following the Supreme Court's decision to stay the remaining twenty of the twenty-six murder charges brought against Pickton, the provincial government of British Columbia finally announced in September 2010 a commission of inquiry into the missing women investigations.[45] Commenting on the purpose of the inquiry, Commissioner Wally Oppal stated in a March 3, 2011, Status Report, "The issue of missing and murdered women raises many pressing and important social, political, and economic issues, one important aspect [of which] is the conduct of police forces in investigating cases of missing women."[46] It is this—the matter of police investigation—that would shape the mandate of the inquiry itself.

Pursuant to the provincial Public Inquiries Act, this commission's original terms of reference provided for a fact-finding and policy-based mission resulting in recommended changes for the conduct of police investigations into missing women and cases of suspected multiple homicides in British Columbia. Notably, the terms understand "investigations" to mean specifically those "conducted between January 23, 1997 and February 5, 2002, by police forces in British Columbia respecting women reported missing from the Downtown Eastside of the city of Vancouver."[47] Considering the scope of the issue, with concurrent cases along the Highway of Tears and elsewhere in BC and Canada, early commentators found these terms problematically narrow in focus and scope. While families and community stakeholders welcomed an inquiry into the Pickton investigation, many saw these original terms of reference as limiting the extent to which it might meaningfully address violence against Indigenous women as a systemic problem across BC and Canada. For example, several of the women missing from the DTES in fact came from northwest communities.[48] Women's continued disappearances along the highway and elsewhere in BC clearly posed a challenge to the inquiry's narrow design. In short, the inquiry's planned focus on the DTES was a missed opportunity to link the specific circumstances of the Pickton investigations to broader colonial patterns of systemic displacement and violence. For this reason the inquiry came under intense public scrutiny even before its work was formally under way.

Soon after the announcement of the inquiry, for instance, then–National Chief of the Assembly of First Nations, Shawn Atleo, and chairman of the First Nations Health Council, Grand Chief Doug Kelly, publically criticized the mandate as far from "commensurate with the serious magnitude of the issues."[49] This analysis was echoed by a number of the front-line service agencies, advocacy groups, and political organizations that initially applied for and were granted standing in the commission. Despite this scrutiny, Commissioner Oppal insisted in the early hearings that the inquiry must unfortunately "confine [itself] to the terms that the government has given."[50] This insistence was challenged by the claims of participants themselves, who emphasized by contrast the national scope of the problem, the systemic nature of violence, and the impossibility of understanding the particular case of the Vancouver missing women without investigating gendered discrimination and racism as foundational to Aboriginal public policy in Canada. As Hugh Braker, on behalf of the Native Courtworker and Counselling Association, stated in his submission: "Our belief is that aboriginal people in Canada have been discounted or marginalized since the beginning of this country."[51] Similarly, Donald Worme, senior counsel to the Assembly of First Nations, emphasized that "there are First Nations people across this country … that are affected by what we say is systemic racism."[52] From the outset, then, the failings of the Pickton investigation itself were theorized by these participants not as the discrete product of circumstantial error, only now discernible by what the Vancouver Police Department has termed "the benefit of hindsight,"[53] but rather as the logical outcome of colonial dispossession. This analytical contribution by participants in the early stages of the inquiry's work emphasized the need for research approaches that could understand interpersonal violence as systemically constituted, and as shaped by what Christine Welsh documents in her film as an ongoing history of "dislocation, loss of land, [and] loss of culture."[54] In this analysis, the failed police investigation was itself understood as a form of violence—one that the inquiry was at risk of perpetuating rather than redressing.

Ironically, of the thirteen applicants who made the case for an expanded mandate at the pre-hearing conferences, and to whom Commissioner Oppal originally granted either limited or full standing at the inquiry, not one was granted provincial funding for their legal representation at the official evidentiary hearings. Although the inquiry would subsequently appoint two independent lawyers to take guidance from advocacy groups in representing public interests at the hearings,[55] the BC Attorney General's decision to deny these groups funding (against Oppal's recommendations) damaged public confidence in the inquiry's processes irreparably. In the words of First Nations Summit counsel Stacey Edzerza Fox, the province's decision highlighted an unsavoury gap between its publicly stated commitment to addressing violence against

Indigenous women, "and its actions on the ground."[56] This inconsistency, Fox stated at the pre-hearing conference, "raises questions about the province's sincerity in relation to the inquiry specifically, and to its commitments to take steps to address missing and murdered aboriginal women generally."[57] What's more, this example illustrates the extent to which governments can and do impact the activities and findings of public inquiries—despite their ostensibly arm's-length status. In effectively maintaining a financial barrier to participation, the provincial government not only further marginalized the voices of Indigenous peoples, women, sex workers, and other stakeholders, but also shaped the kinds of knowledge that could be produced as part of the inquiry's hearing commission. As later stated in the April 2012 Open Letter signed by fifteen organizations refusing to participate in the inquiry's Policy Forums, "this Inquiry is not a meaningful and inclusive process. Instead, it has served to repeat the same discrimination and exclusion that we had hoped it was going to uncover."[58]

While the official methods, scope, and mandate of the inquiry were heavily circumscribed by government decisions, community-based organizations continued to champion their grassroots knowledge as offering a separate and more radically constituted "terms of reference" for the inquiry. As Nicole Schabus, counsel for the Downtown Eastside Women's Centre, pointed out, "these organizations already do this work that the commission is also looking into;"[59] they hold expert knowledge about the missing and murdered, about the mistrust between policing agencies and Indigenous peoples in Canada, and about how meaningful policy change might be made. This knowledge was central to the inquiry's work and to its public legitimacy, and on these grounds Oppal successfully lobbied the government for expanded terms of reference in March 2011. Though originally designated as a "hearing commission" only, at Oppal's request the inquiry was subsequently appointed as a joint hearing and study commission. This allowed for broader public consultation and for the formal judicial processes associated with evidentiary hearings in Vancouver to be supplemented by the more "flexible and inclusive" processes of a study commission.[60] The difference between the two types of commissions can be further explained in this way: while hearing commissions "investigate and make findings of fact where there is a possibility of finding misconduct," study commissions by contrast "conduct research and consult with ... the public."[61] Moreover, participants do not require legal standing in order to take part in a study commission's processes. Under this structure, the evidentiary hearings would remain primarily concerned with examining the role of the Vancouver Police Department (VPD), the RCMP, and the Criminal Justice Branch in the missing women investigations of the lower mainland. However, the newly added study commission would conduct public consultations, hold policy forums, and carry out interviews with key community members and experts from across BC. Significantly, communities along the Highway of Tears became a major site of public consultation for the study commission. As the commission explained: "Community input is required to assist in developing policy recommendations that are practical, workable and effective within the specific cultural and community context in this region."[62] The commission sought this input through a series of Northern Community Forums—public sessions inviting written or oral submissions on the inquiry's mandate as it pertains to missing women cases along the Highway of Tears.

The Northern Community Forums

I wanted to witness how the study commission would be carried out in the context of northern BC, where significant grassroots efforts around the missing and murdered already existed, so I travelled to Terrace in September 2011 to attend two of the seven scheduled Northern Community Forums. Women and girls have been disappearing from the Highway 16 corridor since the 1970s, with the majority of these cases remaining unsolved. The exact number of missing women and girls is unknown, but the police task force assigned to the Highway of Tears was investigating eighteen murders and disappearances, seventeen of which involved Indigenous women.[63] While the 2006 Highway of Tears Symposium report estimates that more than thirty women are missing,[64] some communities put the estimated number of missing as high as forty-three.[65] These statistics give some sense of the overwhelming loss with which many families and communities are dealing. What remains untold by the numbers alone, however, is what this loss means as a lived sense of "fear, frustration and sorrow" permeating whole communities.[66] Moreover, this cumulative sorrow is not tied solely to the missing women cases; it is also a response to the patterns of displacement, isolation, and intergenerational poverty resulting from the residential schools system, the Indian Act, and other forms of systemic colonial dispossession. Communities along the Highway of Tears have developed analyses of and strategic responses to this dispossession, as detailed in the 2006 Report of the Highway of Tears Symposium. The inquiry looked to follow up on this kind of community-led work when it initiated the Northern Community Forums in 2011—but it would do so through its own mechanisms of research and consultation.

In total the inquiry held seven public forums in communities from Prince Rupert at the coast to Smithers, some 350 km inland. Approximately 290 people participated, and eighty submissions (both oral and written) were presented to the commissioner. In the two forums I attended, I witnessed twenty oral submissions. Many of these were from local advocates and family members, though representatives from provincial organizations also participated. As described in the final report, seven topics emerged from the northern consultations: "geography, colonialism, discrimination and racism, residential schools, poverty, violence, and unhealthy lifestyles."[67] As an observer, however, I noticed an eighth topic that received critical attention from participants: the inquiry itself. That is, while many participants were glad to see the issue of violence against Indigenous women garner more serious consideration at the provincial level, several remarked upon the inquiry's limited mandate, its exclusionary methods of public engagement, and its narrow scope. Some also questioned whether any positive action would come of another data-gathering exercise funded by the government—particularly when the Highway of Tears Symposium had already generated thirty-three action-based recommendations still in need of funding and implementation. In this way, participants in the northwest echoed the objections of other commentators from across the province: namely, that "the inquiry focused only on the criminal aspect of violence after it had already occurred instead of looking at how to prevent it in the first place."[68]

The need for action-based preventative measures shaped many contributors' comments on the inquiry and its limitations. As Nisga'a participant Millie Percival commented in her written submission to the commission's report on the Northwest Consultations: "When the Missing Women's Commission toured the province, Mr. Oppal was so compassionate within the limits of his job. He thanked us for the information we provided, but he never told us what he would do with it.... Will meaningful measures be taken to help us to reinstate the parenting and social skills so that we do not stand by paralyzed in pain watching our families succumb to this vicious cycle?[69] Rhetorically, Percival's call for "meaningful measures" here takes the form of a question. Her question comments on the structural nature of the problem of violence, as well as the need for the commission to hear and act on the knowledge of participants in a consultative, pragmatic way. In this way, Percival subtly calls the inquiry to account. By responding to the questions of the visiting commissioner with questions of their own, participants offered alternative "terms of reference" that broadened the inquiry's findings and refocused the attention on questions of prevention. Moreover, participants implicitly modelled a different research framework in which such knowledge could be sought and disseminated—moving beyond the obvious constraints of the inquiry's structure and mandate in order to propose alternatives.

For example, the inquiry ostensibly designed the forums as "an informal venue in which interested members of the community could provide their input to the Commissioner."[70] And yet, as one participant in Terrace noted, the design of the process was "not truly Aboriginal."[71] The forums I attended were held in community settings—one at the Kitsumkalum Hall, the other at the Terrace Nisga'a Society—and were opened and closed by local elders with words of welcome and prayer. The participation was diverse; as the report notes, submissions were made by family members and friends of the missing and murdered, as well as "community members who were involved in search efforts, Chiefs ... elected politicians ... [and] social service providers."[72] However, despite the stated goals of offering open-ended and informal venues for participants to share their knowledge with the commission, the actual structure of the forums subtly reasserted the restrictive and formal methods for which the original hearing commission was critiqued. As Karen Whonnock—a lawyer and member of Moricetown Band—remarked in her submission at Kitsumkalum, the "procedure ... is predominantly European-Canadian."[73] In the forums I attended, the questions of interest to the commission were predetermined. The seating was arranged in rows facing a table at the front of the room where the commissioner and his counsel sat. Funding and time constraints meant that the forums were held in rapid succession—sometimes two or three a day, in disparate community settings. This format did not require of the commissioner and his counsel—nor of the other visitors in attendance—that they participate reciprocally and with responsibility to community protocol for guests seeking a partnership in knowledge creation. Whonnock further suggested that "Aboriginal communities weren't invited to participate in a manner which reflects their Aboriginal culture and heritage."[74]

Participants at the Prince George pre-hearing conference (held the previous January) had repeatedly emphasized that in order to appreciate the challenges and strengths of the communities along the Highway of Tears, the commissioner "need[ed] to experience northern living," to spend time in northern communities, and to genuinely take part in community events and life.[75] Yet the inquiry's imperative—to be above all a timely, efficient endeavour—meant that the sharing of knowledge, understood by Indigenous theorists like Linda Tuhiwai Smith as properly a "long term commitment"[76] observant of community-specific protocol as well as the principles of respect and reciprocity, here became against its stated intentions a form of research that would collect and record Indigenous knowledge for the benefit of those outside the community. In this vein, some participants expressed considerable skepticism about how the commission would act on the information collected at the forums, and whether this process would actually come to benefit the communities along the Highway of Tears: "The government continually conducts studies and surveys, but nothing is ever done."[77] In drawing attention to this in their submissions, participants implicitly noted, as Margaret Kovach does, that "earning trust is critical and may take time, upsetting the efficiency variable of research timelines."[78] This tension, between the timelines of the inquiry and the more "truly Aboriginal" processes advocated by some participants, thus contoured the consultation process of the Northern Forums and also stood as a site that was then theorized by participants themselves.

The seven questions to which participants were invited to speak were fairly narrowly construed in terms of the mandate itself, and thus asked participants to consider what kinds of barriers women faced in dealing with the police, how women's vulnerability to violence in northern BC could better be taken into account by the police, and how current police investigations of missing and murdered women could be conducted with greater sensitivity to these contexts.[79] This question-and-answer format as implied by the invitation to participation was ostensibly meant only to identify possible key issues for discussion and was "not intended to limit presentations."[80] However, the very structure and protocol followed in the forums themselves reified the more formal processes the study commission was supposed to eschew. As some theorists of Indigenous methodologies argue, an "informal relaxed gathering with open-ended questions proceeding in a conversational manner" would be better suited to Indigenous research processes.[81] The key problem I observed in my attendance at the Northern Community Forums, then, was that these forums risked constituting participants as objects of research rather than co-creators of knowledge. There is a long history of extractive research conducted by non-Indigenous researchers in Indigenous communities—research practices intended to produce knowledge about Indigenous peoples and experiences, rather than knowledge produced from within and for the benefit of those peoples and communities. The history of public inquiry in Canada is part of this history. In this case, the risk of this instrumental and extractive practice was clear: given the inquiry's terms of reference, which included a stated interest in the conduct of police investigations, the commission was collecting knowledge in order to improve the policing practices of *Nilhchuk-un*, or "those who take us away."

Tellingly, when the commissioner asked participants about the practical barriers they encountered when reporting a missing person to the police, participants often chose to relate stories of historical mistrust and violence in the relations between policing bodies and Indigenous peoples. When asked about transportation initiatives to reduce instances of high-risk hitchhiking, some people spoke of the broader context of the north—in terms not only of geography, but also the history of residential schools, of systemic discrimination, of poverty, of racism. In these ways the submissions strategically responded to and reframed the specific research questions being asked, subtly embedding in the process a more radical critique of colonialism than would be possible by merely responding straightforwardly to the commission's terms. By not responding to the commission on its own terms, then, and by offering instead a different kind of knowledge by means of heterogeneous narrative practices (ranging from overt political appeal to personal storytelling), presenters implemented what Margaret Kovach has called "story as method." This sought from the commissioner as interlocutor (and others in attendance) a mode of listening that was not passive but instead relational. Kovach explains: "By listening intently to one another [researcher and participant], story as method elevates the research from an extractive exercise serving the fragmentation of knowledge to a holistic endeavour that situates research firmly within the nest of relationship."[82] In this formulation, narratives as requested in the context of extractive knowledge making can be reconstituted by the fact of the listener having been made "part of the event too."[83] Given the ways in which participants' submissions issued an analytical challenge to the limited terms of the inquiry, but also implied a different set of research questions and methods, they seemed then to instruct listeners toward a different listening practice and thus embedded a teaching about listening and about research itself.

Against the commission's "extractive method" of research and consultation, the contributions of participants stood as a subtle method for asserting holistic and relational knowledge that—more than producing alternative information about the missing and murdered—actually embedded Indigenous ways of knowing and reconstituted Euro-Western narratives of intervention and social change. Participants did not issue a challenge to the commission on its own terms, in the vein of what Linda Tuhiwai Smith calls "writing back" or "talking back."[84] Rather, their testimony enacted Indigenous knowledge about and strategies for social analysis and change. While the commission framed its task as one of identifying and "overcoming the continuing impact of colonialism,"[85] participants spoke of what would be necessary to transforming these relations of power—and not as historical conditions, but also as present, lived realities. As Leanne Simpson intimates, Western theories of social injustice and social change are skilled at inquiring into and diagnosing immediate social ills. By contrast, she emphasizes Indigenous resurgence as a longer-term visioning process—intrinsic to many Indigenous intellectual traditions of social change—of imagining more just realities. Simpson thus argues that social transformation is a creative process of continual enactment, rather than a finite process spurred only by inquiry and critique. Storytelling, she says, is one physical, temporal, spiritual, and cognitive site that affords a means not only of critiquing colonization, but also of envisioning balance and modelling non-hierarchical social relations.[86]

Through their stories, many participants in the Northern Community Forums foresaw what meaningful social change might look like, outside of the commission's temporally and geographically bound mandate and agenda. In this way, participants theorized through their submissions the possibility of "negotiat[ing] with settler governments and the legal system"[87] without succumbing to the government's terms of reference—proposing instead "Indigenous solutions to the problems continued colonialism creates."[88] The results of these efforts are not without their limitations, of course; the findings of the Study Commission, including the Northern Community Forums, are marginal to the inquiry's official final report and are instead collected in a series of supplementary publications. Nevertheless, the participants' contributions offer a meaningful counter-discourse where such limitations can be exposed and better understood. *Finding Dawn* likewise offers a separate "terms of reference" for the research and representation of gendered colonial violence—modelling a responsive and relational approach to memory and knowledge making about the missing women cases in BC and across Western Canada. These interventions couldn't be more urgent or timely. Given the shortcomings of the BC provincial inquiry, and the fact that the national inquiry is now under way, it is imperative that we take methodological and analytical cues from the communities most affected by this violence. *Finding Dawn* models "pathways of action that are beyond the boundaries of a colonial mentality" by which the provincial inquiry was necessarily bound.[89]

Finding Dawn: Re-Search and Remembrance

In many ways, *Finding Dawn* is about what Anishinaabe scholar Kathleen Absolon would call "re-search"—that is, "journeys of learning, being and doing" that centre the seeking and gathering of knowledge from an Indigenous perspective.[90] The film follows family-led searches for three missing women: Dawn Crey, Ramona Wilson, and Daleen Bosse. In following these searches, *Finding Dawn* takes viewers on a journey of sorts—one that begins in Vancouver's DTES, from which Crey disappeared, travels north to the Highway of Tears, where Wilson was last seen, and then heads east across the prairies to Saskatoon, where Bosse went missing. Then, in the film's final sections, filmmaker Christine Welsh completes the search in all four directions—first journeying south from Saskatoon to Regina, where she interviews Indigenous literary scholar Janice Acoose, and then finally travelling west to the coast, where she interviews anti-violence activist Fay Blaney. In these concluding sections, Acoose and Blaney are each interviewed about their own journeys of "learning, being and doing" by which they transformed personal histories of violence in order to become educators and leaders in their communities. In this way the film positions these women not as objects of research to be better known and understood, nor as victims of colonial violence in need of assistance or intervention, but as "agent[s] of change" who impart teachings in anti-violence analysis and protocol.[91] The film brings us into Acoose's First Nations University classroom, where students discuss the work of Cree-Métis poet Marilyn Dumont, and into a boardroom, where Blaney leads a community action group in developing anti-violence response protocol. These examples bring balance to Welsh's re-search process by documenting not only the search for missing women, but also the diverse forms of anti-violence work undertaken by Indigenous women across Canada. *Finding Dawn* thus models several pathways of hope, resilience, and transformation. As Welsh states at the end of the film: "I set out on this journey to find Dawn, but I also found Fay. I found Janice. I found the people who strive and search and hope." While Crey, Wilson, and Bosse are the women whose individual stories lend an initial organizing principle to the film, each story is held in the broader nest of relations created by Welsh's own journey of re-search—to seek and assert hopeful interventions into the issue of gendered colonial violence and its remembrance.

Methodologically, then, this documentary film reflects upon responsible research practices. It explores how our chosen modes of inquiry impact our findings and affect the terms on which we might then imagine or pursue social transformation. When Welsh asks at the opening of the film, "What is it about numbers? What do they tell us? Do they help us understand?" she is asking questions not only about the prevalence of violence—that "relentless adding up of numbers"[92]—but also about the means by which we make public knowledge about it. She signals with these framing questions a tension between the quantifying rhetoric of fact-finding missions, and a kind of knowledge that cannot be known, counted, or studied in a Euro-Western, empirical sense. After all, the empirical facts of Dawn Crey's case can tell us some things—that she went missing in November 2000; that her name was added to the missing women's list in February 2001; that her DNA was found on the Pickton farm in 2004—but there are so many things that these facts cannot tell us. In contrast to the quantitative rhetoric of statistical reports and the extractive logic of some government-sponsored research practices, Welsh interrogates the analytical potential of story as a method of inquiry into violence, and into how we come to know.

In *Kaandossiwin: How We Come to Know*, Kathleen Absolon explains a "wholeistic framework for Indigenous methodologies" as observed through her work with a series of graduate students who centre Indigenous world views and knowledge to their research in the academy.[93] She does so through the metaphor of the petal flower—a diagram she first develops after it arrives to her in a dream. The petal flower framework is a holistic way to show the relationship between different but interdependent aspects of Indigenous research:[94] the roots (foundational principles), the flower centre (the self as located in the research), the leaves (process and journey), the stem (methodological supports), the petals (different ways of searching), and the environment (the broader research context).[95] Through this framework Absolon emphasizes the important connections between the researcher's knowledge-seeking paradigm, purpose, and findings.

This all begins at the roots—the foundation from which a research project is developed. Shaped by world view, the roots provide the invisible but ever-present grounding of a research project as "manifested in actions, behaviours, ethics and methods."[96] Though unseen and existing below the surface, the roots necessarily inform each of the choices made by the researcher throughout the research process. In the case of *Finding Dawn*, one of the foundational paradigms for its research is an Indigenous feminist approach to the issue of missing and murdered women. This approach puts apparently interpersonal forms of violence in the context of systemic, state-sponsored violence, while connecting but never collapsing the different women's stories that it tells. It thus highlights the interdependence of gendered and colonial forms of systemic dislocation and violence, and affirms women's agency in remembering, analyzing, and transforming this violence from an Indigenous perspective. In her account of Indigenous methodologies, Absolon begins with "the roots" in order to describe research as a "search for congruency with the re-researcher's own worldview."[97] With this in mind, I will begin by seeking incongruities between the film's popularly received project of remembrance, and the project of critical Indigenous remembrance at the film's roots.

At its roots, *Finding Dawn* remembers missing women in interviews with family members whose storied reflections highlight the connections between honouring memory and asserting sovereign Indigenous presence and resilience. This process involves, on the surface, putting "a human face to what has happened" to so many Indigenous women in this country.[98] As such, the film's project is often popularly received as a "humanizing" one wherein the formerly faceless or nameless women who populate dominant public discourse are reframed by the documentary's effort to put "faces to the names."[99] In putting "a human face to the mounting number of victims,"[100] it is argued, the film "forge[s] awareness of the violence" while reminding viewers "that these women existed in the lives of all who loved them."[101] Indigenous women have been denied dignity and humanity throughout Canadian colonial history—the argument goes—and the film restores women's fundamental humanity by "tak[ing] viewers into the lives of these women and young girls."[102] Through the details of these women's lives and deaths, viewers are introduced to this issue of "national disgrace,"[103] and are thus presumably transformed, by the act of watching the film itself, into more caring and socially responsible citizens.

This line of argument has enormous intellectual and affective appeal, which I've seen at work in popular and academic reception as well as in teaching settings where I've shown the film. As one reviewer notes of *Finding Dawn*'s pedagogical potential, "I can't imagine a single student who would be unmoved by the eloquent testimonials of strong parents and caring siblings as they struggle to cope with the devastation of lost daughters and sisters."[104] While I wouldn't discount the complex pedagogical value of affect, nor the evocative role of family testimonials in the film, I do want to complicate the root ends to which this affect is presumed to work, and for whom. Are the film's depictions of struggle and loss here presumed to affirm Indigenous women's inherent dignity, or are they imagined to affirm non-Indigenous viewers for their "discovery" of this dignity? The problem I observe is this: if we understand the film as primarily an exercise in uncovering how Indigenous women have been dehumanized by "widespread attitudes in our society,"[105] then its pedagogical value rests in how it positions viewers to verify Indigenous women's true humanity, and in doing so to validate (as *fait accompli*) their roles as allies in the project of anti-racism. The discovery and verification of Indigenous women's humanity become the primary work the film is assumed to facilitate, which not only assumes a uniform non-Indigenous viewer for whom this humanity was formerly in question, but also flattens out the complex forms of storytelling and response that are modelled (for both Indigenous and non-Indigenous viewers) by the film itself. As Andrea Smith points out, an argument which presumes that "the problem facing Native peoples is that they have been 'dehumanized'" invites as its solution only the attainment of more knowledge and better understanding.[106] This overlooks the ways in which "the human"—as a universal, self-determining subject—is an ideological project historically constituted through the oppression of others.[107] Moreover, this formulation locates political agency and the potential for social transformation not with Indigenous women but with the non-Indigenous viewer, who becomes, again, the arbiter of humanity—and whose own humanity (mobility, agency, and capacity to change or to affect others) is what's always been at stake. Indigenous women's humanity and worth are positioned by this logic as objects of discovery to be uncovered by the universal seeking subject who, through the seemingly personalized connection with the missing and murdered made possible by the film, moves from ignorance or indifference toward awareness. In this enlightenment model of social change, it is the non-Indigenous viewer's "humanity" that is ultimately affirmed, whose knowledge is centred, and whose transformation is presumably sought and attained.

Finding Dawn can be understood outside of this extractive and "discovery-driven" paradigm, however. Looking at the film through an Indigenous methods framework, we can see how its root project is not merely one of raising awareness, of "humanizing" victims of violence, or of adding valuable memorial reflections to an existing body of statistical data.[108] Rather, the film seeks to model and enact possible research and storytelling practices within an Indigenous framework of knowledge making. These practices locate knowledge and authority with Indigenous peoples themselves, and demonstrate through Indigenous-led examples a range of activist responses to the issue of gendered colonial violence. In this way the film focuses on acts of "resilience and strength"[109] not only as awareness-raising endeavours meant to humanize Indigenous peoples in the face of colonial victimization, but more importantly as ways of modelling responsive action from an Indigenous perspective. This is not to deny the reality or effect of dehumanizing misrepresentations, nor to discount the value or possibility of raising awareness among non-Indigenous viewers. Rather, the film embeds critical Indigenous strategies through which to imagine research, remembrance, and social transformation differently. As Linda Tuhiwai Smith notes, "Non-indigenous research has been intent on documenting the demise and cultural assimilation of indigenous peoples. Instead it is possible to celebrate survival, or what Gerald Vizenor has called 'survivance.'"[110] It is this assertion of Indigenous survivance that is at the root of the film's work.

Vizenor's notion of survivance articulates "an active sense of presence over absence, deracination, and oblivion."[111] As the "continuance of stories, not a mere reaction,"¹¹² survivance is about ongoing acts of resistance that work by asserting the continued persistence of Indigenous peoples and knowledges. *Finding Dawn* documents several examples of persistence exercised by family members in remembrance of loved ones, and then models for viewers how one might read for presence rather than seeking only stories of dehumanization, disappearance, and demise. In the BC context, the stories of Dawn Crey and Ramona Wilson are meant to reframe common public perceptions of the prominent missing women cases of Vancouver and the Highway of Tears respectively, while foregrounding the survivance work of family members and activists in each site. While the BC Missing Women Commission of Inquiry was critiqued for its inattention to the significant grassroots work undertaken by women organizers, the film demonstrates pathways of anti-violence action and remembrance from the perspective of family members and local activists. *Finding Dawn* begins this work with the case of Dawn Crey.

Following the film's opening sequence, Dawn's story begins for us on the streets from which she disappeared. From the vantage point of a moving vehicle, Welsh's camera offers a series of fleeting tracking shots of the DTES streets. This is a familiar set of images for any viewer with a passing knowledge of Vancouver's inner city and its representation in local and national media; as anthropologist Dara Culhane points out, these streets have been a "favorite focus" of media photographers and researchers whose cameras regularly capture spectacles of social suffering for the "virtual voyeur."[113] This is among Canada's poorest neighborhoods, where Indigenous peoples and women are overrepresented, and where declared public health crises related to intravenous drug-use, street-level sex work, and HIV/AIDS are often met with a pathologizing rhetoric of intervention and "treatment." Culhane and others have critiqued this rhetoric for ignoring the structural facets of gendered and colonial disenfranchisement that impact how people arrive and live in the DTES.[114] Mainstream media, Culhane says, trade in "exotic and spectacular representation of drugs, sex, violence, and crime."[115] This is the backdrop against which women are often shown "hurry[ing] back and forth ... in and out of cars, alleyways, and parking lots,"[116] a popular image of subsistence-level sex work as constructed and consumed by the touristic gaze.

Of course, these images are not objective visual documents of "street-level" life. Rather, it is through such images that settler Canadians come to know themselves in the colonial geographies of our present. These representations naturalize the spatial dynamics of gendered colonialism; they are visual expressions of the "spatial containment" and "violent expulsion" that characterize the policy and policing practices often mobilized against Indigenous peoples in contemporary urban space.[117] A history of colonial displacement brought Dawn Crey and others to these inner-city streets, and a history of colonial violence is responsible for their predatory removal. Yet it remains a most persistent colonial fantasy that Indigenous women have an ill-fated agency in this—that they are in part authors of their own demise. The Vancouver Police Department's *Missing Women Investigation Review*, for example, states that "Downtown Eastside sex trade workers were *willingly* visiting the Pickton property in Coquitlam and some were being murdered there."[118] In this logic, women's disappearances and murders become both predictable and provoked on one hand (because these women are shown living so-called "high-risk" lifestyles, and to have gone "willingly" from the street corner to the site of their death), and sensationally anomalous on the other (because the daily social conditions of oppression that made their removal and subsequent murder possible are individualized, as is the figure of Pickton himself). According to the Vancouver-based Aboriginal Women's Action Network, this is just one example of "the victim blaming that pervades ... stories on the 'Missing Women'" in the news media and in official institutional responses.[119] By opening her segment on Dawn Crey in the way she does, Welsh draws attention to (and critiques) this victim-blaming rhetoric. The opening set of tracking shots by which she introduces the DTES streets thus perform a kind of citational gesture, offering familiar documentary images of decontextualized and presumed despair against which her comparatively relational and story-based form of knowledge making will unfold: "For the women who vanished from this community," Welsh says, "life here was a daily struggle and they did what they had to do to survive. Each of them had a story. And like Dawn, most of them started out somewhere else."[120]

This story neither begins nor ends on the streets of Vancouver. With a very different set of tracking shots, this time from a coastal mountain highway, Welsh purposefully replaces the streets from which Dawn disappeared with the traditional territory of the nation from which she came: the Stó:lô Nation. In a voiceover accompanying the visual footage of her eastward highway travel, Welsh explains: "I'm going to Chilliwack to meet Dawn's brother, Ernie Crey—a longtime activist for Aboriginal rights in BC." Tracking shots of the highway traffic put immediate distance between Welsh and the streets of the DTES, while subsequent wide shots convey a living landscape of the Stó:lô Nation, whose traditional territory "starts at the mouth of the Fraser river and extends deep into the canyons of the coastal mountains."[121] It is through this frame that Welsh positions Dawn in relation to both her tribal ancestry and her immediate family—thus subtly modelling for viewers one of the central tenets of Indigenous research methodologies: the importance of location and of situating the self.[122] As Kathleen Absolon and Cam Willet put it, "location is about relationships to land, language [and the] spiritual, cosmological, political, economical, environmental, and social elements in one's life."[123] More specifically, it is a way of explaining these relationships in order to create grounded and accountable knowledge. For theorists of Indigenous methodologies, then, situating yourself means more than saying who you are and where you come from;[124] it is also a means of "clarifying [your] perspective on the world" in land-based, community-specific, and historically grounded ways.[125] As Craig Womack says, "stories take place,"[126] and the geography of Dawn Crey's original homescape matters for the story Welsh seeks to tell. By this homescape, Welsh signals a broader ancestral network from which Dawn is missing. This network is shown in geographical and well as temporal dimensions to include but extend beyond the DTES (a community unto itself, formed and lived in traditional Coast Salish territory) and into the Stó:lô Nation's past and future. Against the comparatively decontextualized representations by which the public has become aware of Vancouver's missing women, then, Welsh produces a situated and relational account of Dawn Crey. This treatment serves both as a pointed means of reshaping dominant public perceptions and as a subtle way to model Indigenous methodological interventions into anti-violence research and public knowledge making.

Dawn's brother, Ernie Crey, observes this protocol in his own interview with Welsh when he positions himself and his sister within a tribal history that pre-dates the arrival of colonial interferences. "We are the Stó:lô people," he says by way of introduction, "the people of the river. We're a fishing community, a community that has lived here ... probably for as long as 9,000 years. Certainly since the last ice-age. This is the place we call home. And we grew up here."[127] By observing this principle of self-location, Ernie sets forth a particular epistemological lens through which viewers might interpret Dawn's personal history. Significantly, this is not a biographical portrait meant simply to remember Dawn more fully as "human" for an imagined viewer's benefit of understanding. Rather, Dawn is here re-membered into a specifically Stó:lô genealogy to which Ernie has lived responsibilities when telling his sister's story. As Stó:lô scholar Jo-ann Archibald says of storywork—or, the use of stories and storytelling for educational purposes—speakers must "identify their kinship and speak from their experiences."[128] Ernie's interview thus instructs viewers in Indigenous research and teaching methodologies while providing an important narrative of Stó:lô survivance, told as the continual occupation of traditional territories in the Fraser Canyon as captured visually by Welsh and explained in Ernie's oral account. This re-visioning of Dawn within her nation's past and future provides the communal context necessary to a more holistic understanding of her life and loss than could ever be conveyed by an account of life in the DTES alone. In this way, Welsh replaces what is too often a rhetoric of victimhood with one that honours presence, agency, and resistance from a Stó:lô perspective.

Significantly, while emphasizing survivance over victimhood, Welsh nonetheless offers a trenchant analysis of colonial policy and its effects. As Absolon and Willet suggest, "we need to know how we got into the mess we're in,"[129] and accounting directly for the genocidal impacts of colonial policy is part of this process. This does not entail a focus on stories of demise at the expense of promoting survivance. Rather, Welsh illuminates the past and present impacts of colonization in ways that can "make sense" of the current reality of missing women. For Welsh, this means locating Dawn's personal history in relation to the "much bigger picture" of European colonial settlement.[130] Colonial processes are shown to have had both historical and ongoing effects for multiple generations of Stó:lô people, including the Crey family. As Welsh explains, four generations of settlement displaced the Stó:lô from "their land, their livelihood and even their children, who were taken away first to residential schools, and then to foster homes." Dawn and her siblings were themselves taken from their mother and placed in foster homes throughout the Fraser Valley, and the telling of this fact makes Dawn's story resonate within a broader history of forced dislocation. While much public knowledge making about the missing women cases diagnoses this dislocation in a descriptive sense, *Finding Dawn* additionally performs a kind of healing remembrance through the method of locating the self. As Absolon states, locating oneself and others "connects us to family, community and nation. In that sense ... the research process cultivates a healing movement of being reconnected and remembered from the dismemberment and disconnections created by colonial policy and actions such as the *Indian Act* and residential schools."[131]

One of the challenges involved in this kind of survivance storywork is the necessary balance it must seek between an empowering account of "presence over absence, deracination, and oblivion" on one hand,[132] and an unflinching account of the real, lived effects of colonial violence on the other. Settler colonialism continues to mandate deracination and oblivion, after all, and many documentary and truth-telling projects now seek to challenge this mandate and to show its devastating effects. This emphasis can, however, construct for public consumption stories of victimhood that feed easily into the long-standing national myth that Indigenous peoples need intervention or rescue. These are images primarily of despair and "deficit,"[133] images of a "problem-ridden, broken existence serving to confirm stereotypes offered as explanations for the marginalization of native populations within Canadian society."[134] *Finding Dawn* suggests instead that it is possible to document and critique colonial violence while also acknowledging the agency, knowledge, and leadership of Indigenous peoples in directing this critique and in envisioning practices of dignity and freedom. Working from within an Indigenous intellectual paradigm, Welsh performs not just "an evisceration of colonial thinking" or a description of colonialism's effects, then, but what Leanne Simpson would call a "visioning process where we create new and just realities in which our ways of being can flourish."[135] For Welsh, this visioning process includes storytelling the lives of missing women within a larger web of relations. In doing so, Welsh short-circuits the colonial fantasy of Indigenous victimhood and instead shows how women are re-membered to their families, communities, and territories.

The film performs this critical remembrance through its documentation of annual memorial walks for the missing and murdered. From the Annual Women's Memorial March taking place in the DTES every February 14, to the Take Back the Highway demonstrations coordinated in communities along Highway 16 every year, memorial walks are shown in each of *Finding Dawn*'s case studies to enact an embodied assertion of collective action that turns our focus "away from the regimes of disappearance to resistance, survival, and possibility."[136] Walking serves not merely to mark a passing, or to document discrete instances of disappearance and "demise"—it is a strategic political expression of survivance and a form of knowledge making that connects communities. Drawing from Indigenous traditions of social movement, *Finding Dawn* frames walking as a kind of "community procession"—to use Leanne Simpson's phrase—as a kind of mobilization that takes place over time and space, and which involves "persistence, patience and slow, painful movement."[137] This is shown in relation both to annual memorial walks themselves and also to community-coordinated searches for the missing that take place in Northern BC and on the prairies.[138] Of one communal search effort, for example, Terrace-based radio host Lynne Terbasket comments: "The effort put into that was tremendous. I've never seen anything like it. It was an amazing effort. It was not successful, but we tried."[139] Terbasket's words serve as an important reminder in the film that "large-scale mobilizations" leading to "discernible immediate change" are not the only ways in which to understand resistance and "result."[140] Her comments further suggest, as Leanne Simpson does, that matters of "intent, commitment and vision" are at the heart of many community-led activist initiatives—the impacts of which may be incalculable and unknown at the time of their enactment but which constitute significant forms of resistance nonetheless.[141] Like the communal search effort that may yield nothing of clear evidentiary significance, the memorial walk is valued in *Finding Dawn* as a strategic, collectivized manifestation of vision and intent: family members are joined by friends and allies in claiming their inalienable connection to territory, in caretaking the memory of loved ones they've lost, and in setting forth a new vision for the future. The memorial walk is thus a way to "nurture life, motion, presence and emergence."[142]

Matilda Wilson's (Gitxsan) annual walk in honour of her daughter Ramona's memory is one of several examples offered in *Finding Dawn*, and might be the clearest instance in which the film articulates walking as a form of knowledge making about survivance. Here, walking becomes a kind of story that is told about the missing in northern BC, and also a communal ceremony through which the responsibilities of the living are exercised and sustained. Ramona Wilson went missing from the Highway of Tears near Smithers in June 1994 while hitchhiking to a nearby town where she had plans to join up with friends. The annual memorial walk traces the last known steps Ramona took along Highway 16, and in following these steps together, family and community members are able to "feel closer to her."[143] Ramona's older sister Brenda explains: "It's a healing process for us. And to have the support from other people makes it even better—gives us strength to go on and try to find answers of what happened to my sister."[144] Walking is here theorized as a *way to know*—a method or technique by which to search for answers and to gather strength from others in carrying this search forward. Close-up footage of walkers on the highway captures the footfalls of participants as they move forward along the route together, while audio content from home interviews with Brenda and Matilda Wilson accompanies this visual detail. Welsh's interviews serve to tell Ramona's story from her family's perspective and to explain the purpose and vision of the annual walk. In this way the film gives us an interpretive frame through which to understand the memorial walk as a form of critical Indigenous remembrance.

In her list of "twenty-five Indigenous projects," for example, Linda Tuhiwai Smith defines "remembering" as a research process that works by "connecting bodies with place and experience."[145] At its roots, the memorial walk enacts just this sort of connection, re-membering women to their territories and in relation to one another. Rather than an act of commemorative awareness raising premised upon the accumulating disappearances of Indigenous women, then, the walk is presented as a way for families and communities to assert an embodied Indigenous presence on the land. Footage of Ramona's mother Matilda approaching the roadside memorial at the walk's end is accompanied by this voiceover, in which Matilda pointedly explains the continued presence the walk is meant to demonstrate:

> We are showing people that we are not afraid. We will never be afraid. That we are here. We will always be here. If it's not me, it will be my children. And if it's not my children, it will be my grandchildren. And if it's not my grandchildren, it will be my great-grandchildren. I am fighting. I'm fighting for the loved ones. I'm fighting for the unsolved murders. I'm fighting for everything that I have. I never back down. I will always be here. This face will always be here.[146]

Through the rhetorical use of repetition and the evocative choice of the auxiliary verb "will"—expressing future-oriented notions of choice, determination, and persistence—Matilda Wilson's oral commentary annotates Welsh's visual footage of the walk with a powerful statement on intergenerational sovereignty and survivance. Reorienting our understanding of remembrance to include a forward-looking process of envisioning new futures, Matilda argues for the annual memorial walk as claiming Indigenous peoples' inexorable connection to the land over time: what "we are showing people," she says, is that "we will always be here."[147] Like Leanne Simpson's account of *Biskaabiiyang*—the Nishnaabeg concept of "looking back" in order to move forward[148]—Matilda's statement articulates remembrance as an active process of reclamation and vision that affirms Indigenous presence. The annual walk is the lived, embodied expression of that vision; it asserts a multi-generational resiliency which Ramona's murder deeply wounds but cannot break. Thus, while many dominant, mainstream interpretations of the missing women problem take "the disappearance of Indians as inevitable,"[149] the only inevitability expressed in this section of *Finding Dawn* is that of a continued Indigenous presence: as Matilda says, "This face will always be here."[150]

Leanne Simpson emphasizes that "as long as [there] has been colonialism on our lands, there has been resistance."[151] Colonialism has attempted the "obliteration of memory" as a "deliberate strategy of oppression."[152] It has done so through land theft, by way of legislated dispossession through the Indian Act, and in sequential policies of child removal (residential schools, contemporary child welfare policies) designed to fracture the multi-generational transmission of knowledge. *Finding Dawn* affirms critical Indigenous practices of remembrance that resist the calculated obliteration of memory these policies were designed to produce. In so doing, it asserts Indigenous-led research processes by which colonial histories are named and ongoing resistances are acknowledged—demonstrating the multi-generational connections that exist (despite colonial attempts to sever them) between Indigenous knowledges and their living, fluid expressions in the present. Matilda Wilson's memorial walk performs this connection as an embodied practice that not only makes visible the past story of Ramona's disappearance, but also constitutes an act of protest that will be carried forward for generations to come. Similarly, Ernie Crey's interview re-members Dawn to the Stó:lô Nation's history and future. Through these processes of re-search and remembrance, Welsh, like Absolon, emphasizes the "methodological concepts of reconnection, remembering, learning, recovering and reclaiming."[153] Through these concepts, Welsh rethinks with others what it means to remember the missing, and what it means to make public knowledge about this remembering—that it is not about making definitive, quantitative knowledge with questionable "reliability in Indigenous contexts."[154] Rather, it is about making a different kind of knowledge, about communally held practices of remembrance and resistance. As she says in closing, "We may never know what happened to Dawn, or to so many other women we've lost. But I do know that right across this country, there are people who will not give up hope. We will continue to honour the dead, and learn to take better care of the living. We will search for the missing, and call them home."[155]

CHAPTER TWO

Narrative Appeals: The *Stolen Sisters* Report and Storytelling in Activist Discourse and Poetry

While the BC Missing Women Commission of Inquiry has concluded its work, a national commission of inquiry has just begun. Announced by the federal government in December 2015, the National Inquiry into Missing and Murdered Indigenous Women and Girls has now completed its pre-inquiry design phase, consisting of cross-Canada meetings with families and front-line workers, an online survey, and mailed submissions. With this level of community input, the national commission is arguably well positioned to learn the lessons of the BC example; yet, as the government reviews the recommendations of key stakeholders and prepares the inquiry's terms of reference, it still remains to be seen whether a more consultative, inclusive, and action-based national inquiry will result. In the previous chapter, I discussed the limitations of the BC inquiry's narrow mandate and scope, and looked to Indigenous women's documentary storytelling for cues as to what a broader mandate and approach to ending violence could entail. Taking direction from the example of *Finding Dawn*, I emphasized the importance of Indigenous women's leadership, of community-accountable approaches, and of Indigenous feminist analyses of violence in particular. In this chapter, I continue to locate within Indigenous-authored texts the leadership and insights now needed for an informed national conversation about violence against Indigenous women. This knowledge can be found on the front lines of advocacy work and policy critique, but also in the examples of Indigenous-led remembrance and resistance found in women's writing.

This chapter first considers the research and advocacy role of the Native Women's Association of Canada (NWAC) in building momentum for an Indigenous feminist anti-violence movement in Canada, and in laying the groundwork for the national inquiry. Specifically, I discuss one of NWAC's key anti-violence initiatives, the Sisters in Spirit campaign, and the well-known 2004 report that preceded it: Amnesty International's *Stolen Sisters: A Human Rights Response to Discrimination and Violence against Indigenous Women in Canada*. Both the Sisters in Spirit campaign and the *Stolen Sisters* report make significant pedagogical use of the "life stories" of missing and murdered women to raise awareness, and to guide their policy recommendations. For instance, the second half of the *Stolen Sisters* report consists of nine biographical case studies, each devoted to storytelling the details of a different woman's life experiences leading to her disappearance or murder. Similarly, NWAC's campaign has collected the stories of missing and murdered women as told by their families, and has made them available in its public reports to families and communities. However, while NWAC frames its qualitative use of storytelling with Indigenous precepts of relational knowledge making in mind, Amnesty International employs a human rights framework. Engaging the commemorative poetry of Marilyn Dumont (Cree-Métis), I discuss the possibilities and limits of storytelling the lives of missing or murdered women within these very different paradigms. Storytelling can be a powerful qualitative tool for gathering and disseminating information about gendered colonial violence. It can also be a way to devise meaningful recommendations for social change. However, there are some ethical risks entailed in using the life narratives of missing and murdered women toward particular awareness-raising goals or in policy critique. In this chapter, I look to Dumont's poetry for further direction as to the application of this "story telling methodology" in anti-violence research and awareness raising.[1] Specifically, I discuss the stakes of telling story as a strategy of remembrance and as a catalyst toward action, asking: what is at risk in presuming a transparent relation between the telling of missing and murdered women's stories, and the hopeful outcome of social change? Moreover, I explore how literary forms of protest and remembrance afford us new ways of thinking through the representational strategies of activist rights campaigns.

The NWAC and the Sisters in Spirit Research

The Native Women's Association of Canada has a long history of anti-violence work conducted with an Indigenous feminist approach. Established in 1974, NWAC is one of five national Aboriginal organizations recognized by the government of Canada, and the only to represent women's concerns specifically.[2] Founded with the goal of promoting Indigenous women's well-being in all aspects of life, NWAC is active in several core policy areas, including: education, employment and labour, environment, health, human rights, and violence prevention with a focus on missing and murdered Indigenous women and girls.[3] Working across these policy areas in an intersectional way, NWAC has documented the violation of Indigenous human rights as a historical and continuing outcome of colonization—one which has had a specific effect on Indigenous women.[4] Intervening in the gendered legacies of colonization, NWAC characterizes its recent work in terms of a "national momentum built around taking action countering violence against Aboriginal women and girls."[5] As part of this national momentum, March 2004 saw the launch of the association's Sisters in Spirit campaign.

Designed to identify and address the root causes of sexualized and racialized violence, the Sisters in Spirit campaign was a five-year research, education, and policy initiative funded by Status of Women Canada.[6] In its early phases, the campaign conducted quantitative research and gathered statistical data about the number of missing women and the complex variables impacting women's vulnerability to violence. An outcome of this research was the creation of a national database documenting 582 cases of missing and murdered women as of March 31, 2010. The research revealed that "Aboriginal women are the most at risk group in Canada for issues related to violence."[7] Key statistical findings further showed that the majority of cases occurred in urban areas of the western provinces of Canada, that most of the missing and murdered women were under thirty-one years of age, and that many were mothers.[8] Where possible, the research also investigated the demographics of accused offenders and found that the majority were men—many of them under thirty years old. NWAC also found that both

Indigenous and non-Indigenous men were the perpetrators of violence against Indigenous women, and that most offenders (when their personal history was known) had themselves previously experienced "violence, neglect, or abuse."[9]

While collecting this quantitative demographic data, NWAC relied heavily on media, police, and national statistical reporting. For this reason, the association believes that the Sisters in Spirit database may account for only a fraction of the actual cases. As NWAC points out, "cases presented in the public domain" reflect only those that are reported to and acknowledged by the police and media.[10] National data collected by Statistics Canada is also likely to underestimate the number of cases; the General Social Survey, for instance, does not take into account barriers to participation impacting Indigenous women in remote communities, or barriers to disclosing violence more generally.[11] In addition to the problem of "under-counting," however, NWAC saw other limitations to their quantitative research: statistical data cannot reflect complex life experiences, nor the rich contextual knowledge of families and communities.[12] In order to address these gaps in the research, to centre the knowledge of Indigenous communities, and to honour women "lost to violence," the Sisters in Spirit campaign also pursued qualitative, interview-based research with the families.[13]

Conducted according to community-based participatory action methods, the project took a collaborative, relational approach to its research with families. NWAC positioned participating families not as research subjects, but as experts and co-creators of knowledge whose vision for change was integral to the research process.[14] As the association elaborates in a policy research paper about its methodology, this approach was meant to supplement the more "Western" methods employed by their quantitative data collection by seeking the stories of missing and murdered women as told directly by their families.[15] NWAC researcher Jennifer King explains: "Using the life cycle as a guide, families are invited to share the life story of their daughter, sister, mother, or grandmother. These stories also explore families' experiences in relation to the justice system, the media, victim services, and other institutional and community supports."[16] This story-based method offered the families a more inclusive and participant-driven process than most existing institutional means of reporting and recording violent crime. And because there were no specific criteria for participation, any family aware of NWAC's project might choose to share their story.[17] The interviews themselves were conducted according to a semi-structured, conversational format—giving the families control over the direction of the dialogue, as well as the option to decline certain questions or to revise a story's content at any point. In this way, the participating families were positioned as collaborators in NWAC's project to uncover the "root causes, trends, and experiences surrounding missing and murdered."[18]

In underlining the knowledge of families and communities, and in seeking this knowledge through conversational, story-based means, NWAC's qualitative research drew purposefully from Indigenous "ways of knowing."[19] In particular, the association cites the work of Nêhiýaw/ Saulteaux scholar Margaret Kovach on the topic of relationship-based research,[20] linking this to the "cultural and ethical values of caring, sharing, trust, and strength," which guided the researchers' interactions with the families.[21] The association also worked explicitly with Leey'qsun scholar Robina Anne Thomas's notion of storytelling as a traditional form of oral documentation and as a distinctly Indigenous mode of resistance to colonial violence.[22] As Thomas explains, a storytelling methodology "enables us to keep the teachings of our Ancestors, culture, and tradition alive throughout the entire research process."[23] When applied in the context of the Sisters in Spirit research, storytelling also offers a way to "give voice to a story that has not been fully told": the life narratives of missing and murdered women, and the experiences of their families.[24] These are stories of resistance, Thomas says, because they document and validate the experiences of Indigenous peoples living with colonization.[25] For those who have sustained unthinkable loss as a direct result of colonial violence, storytelling "respects and honours [them] while simultaneously documenting their reality" in a way that can lead to change.[26] The process of collecting, recording, and publicly disseminating the stories of missing and murdered women was thus about more than "simply finding out" about violence in an empirical sense; it was about promoting education, respect, and, ultimately, policy change.[27]

The Sisters in Spirit campaign followed a "research-for-change" process—meaning that the stories of missing and murdered women were sought and received with the purpose of addressing gendered colonial violence through policy change and education.[28] The storytelling methodology was central to this goal because it allowed researchers to identify from within the stories themselves a series of "preventative measures and effective solutions" that could inform concrete recommendations made to governments, media, police, courts, and service providers.[29] The process takes direction and leadership from those most affected by violence, honours their knowledge, and promotes its application to policy change. Sisters in Spirit has made recommendations for policy development in the areas of poverty reduction, homelessness reduction, and improved access to justice.[30] The campaign also encouraged the use of stories in education and awareness-raising activities. For instance, NWAC's online "Community Resource Guide" provides a series of toolkits for advocates, service workers, and educators. In this guide, NWAC encourages supporters to organize vigils in their own communities, and to use the life stories of missing and murdered women as a way to "educate [a]ttendees."[31] The Resource Guide offers similar support to teachers introducing the issue in their classrooms, welcoming them to "share and discuss the life stories" available online as part of the Sisters in Spirit program, while also pointing to other resources that can help teachers and students to approach the life stories respectfully.[32]

For all of its benefits, however, the storytelling methodology does entail some risk. For instance, NWAC researchers noted the challenges of making publicly accessible a story first shared in a "culturally appropriate and respectful" setting.[33] While a participant's initial act of storytelling occurs ideally in the context of trust carefully built and sustained through the research relationship, one of the broader audiences for that story is a public with whom trust and accountability have not been forged. Even though participants maintain control over the stories they have consented to share—that is, "what appears in the story and how it is presented"[34]—the task of interpretation ultimately rests elsewhere. This can be problematic because of the way that negative stereotypes continue to impact public and police perceptions. Confronting these misconceptions with the personal life narrative of a loved one is thus a powerful act of resistance as well as a responsibility of enormous ethical weight for both the families and the researchers to whom the stories have been entrusted. What of the responsibilities, then, of the stories' recipients—of the listeners or readers? Speaking of the task of "hearing others' stories," Kovach discusses interpretation as an act of "co-creation": "story is not only a means for hearing another's narrative, it also invites reflexivity" about the knowledge shared and one's own relationship to it.[35] In this model of storytelling, the listener is not a passive recipient of information to which he or she may then choose to respond. Rather, the listener is an active participant in the co-creation of knowledge, beholden to certain responsibilities by virtue of the reciprocity embedded in the act of storytelling itself. This accords storytelling powerful potential as a means of social change, but one potential difficulty is this: while NWAC researchers have carefully theorized their own research process in terms of Indigenous principles of reciprocity and respect, it is not always clear how these principles can be observed by "listeners" outside the immediate research relationship.[36] Of her work with the stories of residential school survivors, for example, Thomas says: "For me, there is always the fear of documenting our stories. Will the voices be heard?"[37]

Indigenous women's literature likewise has posed this question, and—in the case of Dumont's commemorative poetry—has offered some insights as to how a researcher or storyteller might navigate such difficult terrain. As NWAC researcher Jennifer King asks, "Should life experiences be reported," and, if so, "which experiences? What about personal and traumatic experiences like violence, addiction, or poverty?"[38] Dumont reflects on this problem from the perspective of a poet engaged in memorial practices, and her work has implications for how life narratives might be represented in media and awareness-raising campaigns. In particular, her poetry engages the question of responsible representation and of what constitutes a reciprocal "hearing" on the part of listeners or readers. It also implicitly critiques the instrumental use of life narratives. While some advocacy initiatives deploy life narratives strategically toward the goal of educating their readers and recommending a particular vision of change, Dumont's poetry models a critical vigilance about the way such stories are told and received. Before looking to Dumont's poetry for its insights, however, I turn first to a related project in anti-violence awareness-raising where storytelling is pursued: the Amnesty International *Stolen Sisters* report.

Amnesty International and the *Stolen Sisters* Report

Established in 1961, Amnesty International has perhaps the longest history of any non-governmental organization in the human rights advocacy movement. It is also the largest and most wide-reaching: with offices in eighty countries, Amnesty International has 4.5 million members worldwide.[39] Working with internationally recognized human rights standards as enshrined in the 1948 Universal Declaration of Human Rights and in subsequent international covenants, the organization researches, publicizes, and demands action on human rights violations across the globe. Amnesty International is especially known for its research and advocacy on issues like torture, detention, and enforced disappearances. The organization has also worked to defend the rights of Indigenous peoples, migrants and refugees, and women. In Canada, Amnesty International was active in pushing for the country's adoption of the UN Declaration on the Rights of Indigenous Peoples and has been particularly vocal on the issue of missing and murdered Indigenous women, calling it a national human rights crisis.

Amnesty International's "No More Stolen Sisters" campaign focuses explicitly on the issue of violence against Indigenous women in Canada and has argued persistently for a comprehensive national response to the crisis. The campaign made its first official call to action in October 2004 when it released *Stolen Sisters: A Human Rights Response to Discrimination and Violence against Indigenous Women in Canada*. Notably, the report's publication coincided with an important strategic moment in NWAC's own anti-violence campaign, appearing just two months after Sisters in Spirit submitted its first budget proposal to the federal government.[40] In fact, this timing was the product of planned inter-organizational co-operation. In the early stages of the Sisters in Spirit campaign, NWAC had called on human rights organizations to take action on violence against Indigenous women in Canada. Amnesty International responded to the call, working closely with lead researcher and consultant Beverley Jacobs (Mohawk) to produce the *Stolen Sisters* report. Jacobs, a lawyer by training, went on to serve as NWAC's president during key years for which the Sisters in Spirit campaign received federal funding (2005–2009). During this time, then, both NWAC and

Amnesty International ran concurrent anti-violence campaigns focused on reframing violence as a rights issue, rather than a criminal problem. The *Stolen Sisters* report was the first major report of either campaign to bring this message to the public through the life stories of missing and murdered women themselves. However, while NWAC framed its use of storytelling in terms of "traditional Aboriginal protocols, processes and understandings,"[41] Amnesty International's report storytells the lives of missing and murdered women within an international human rights paradigm. Both organizations use storytelling as a means to lobby the government for change, and both recommend reform-based solutions in policy, education, and policing. To a greater extent than NWAC, however, Amnesty International assumes the legitimacy of the colonial nation-state to protect Indigenous women's rights and deploys Indigenous women's stories unproblematically toward that end.

As Kay Schaffer and Sidonie Smith emphasize in their introduction to *Human Rights and Narrated Lives*, "life narratives have become one of the most potent vehicles for advancing human rights claims."[42] Human rights discourse is a prominent recognized mode of "addressing human suffering," injury, and harm,[43] and the use of life narratives within rights campaigns has become a key method for the telling and witnessing of rights violations. Life stories can "narrate alternative or counter-histories coming from the margins,"[44] and can also document specific rights violations in need of recognition and redress. For this reason, life stories are often solicited and circulated for their affective and evidentiary power within different human rights venues, including: "fact-finding in the field; handbooks and websites; nationally based human rights commissions; human rights commission reports; collections of testimonies; stories in the media; and other scattered venues through which narratives circulate."[45] In these venues, life stories render complex experiential knowledges of rights abuses intelligible within otherwise empiricist frames. Philosopher Shari Stone-Mediatore, speaking from her former experience as an intern for Amnesty International, outlines the persuasive value of storytelling in the context of human rights data: "I found that even seemingly self-evident, clear-cut data depend on stories for the persuasive force. For instance, while Amnesty International takes pains to quantify and objectively report human rights abuses, they often present Congressional testimony in the form of stories, stories that invite listeners into a world in which data has moral and emotional impact and in which a set of options other than those defined by military, strategy-focused paradigms can be envisioned."[46] Nor do the rhetorical advantages of storytelling extend only to listeners; as Mediatore affirms, storytelling provides a qualitative mode of expression for those experiences of dispossession and marginalization for which objective statistical data so often prove "inadequate."[47] Storytelling is thus a way not only to persuade listeners, but also to give voice to "the experiences of people struggling against oppression."[48]

And yet, as Schaffer and Smith remind us, there are tensions between this resistive potential of storytelling and the evidentiary purpose to which it is often put. The life narratives collected and retold by human rights advocates are meant to provide "credible and reliable data" on which verifiable claims about marginalization or victimry can be made, whether in the juridical context or in awareness-raising campaigns.[49] In this sense, there can be a strategic or instrumental purpose to this storytelling. This is quite different from storytelling as theorized by Indigenous researchers like Margaret Kovach, who emphasize storytelling as a "dynamic relationship between teller and listener" wherein knowledge is a holistic bundle for which the listener takes responsibility in analysis and understanding.[50] Facts and data cannot merely be abstracted from this process to meet other "empirical academic needs."[51] Cree scholar Winona Stevenson elaborates: "It is often the case in mainstream scholarship," by contrast, "that once a story is shared and recorded, 'facts' are extracted and the remaining 'superfluous' data set aside."[52] In the case of human rights discourse, Schaffer and Smith argue, "personal testimony, understood and judged unproblematically as evidentiary, turns the speaker into a victim and moulds his or her story into a case history, a piece of positivist evidence, with attendant gains and losses."[53] The primary gain is the articulation of an individual's story within the broader discursive context of rights, and of rights violations, "for the purposes of building a case and motivating action."[54] The loss, however, is that these stories are often made to conform to a certain narrative mould—a story of demonstrable victimry codified and contained within a "standardized, often chronological format."[55] This standardization may hold rhetorical advantages to the making of persuasive human rights claims, but it also flattens out each story's nuances and arguably constrains the kinds of recommendations that can result. In essence, the juridical frame subordinates communally held and communicated knowledges to the need for justiciable claims and concrete recommendations. Moreover, it presumes the legitimacy of the Canadian nation-state in carrying out these recommendations and in protecting the rights of Indigenous women. These are problems I hope to demonstrate with close attention to the *Stolen Sisters* report itself.

The *Stolen Sisters* report is a thirty-seven-page document that can be split into three main sections: first, a backgrounder that frames violence against Indigenous women in terms of international human rights discourse, and which identifies a number of interrelated systemic factors (both historical and ongoing) that put Indigenous women at risk of "racist, sexist attacks by private individuals;"[56] second, a series of nine narrative case studies that illustrate "common themes" and "root causes" of violence through storytelling the lives of missing and murdered women;[57] and third, a concluding section of recommendations for action and change.

The first section opens with an explanation of the human rights framework, premised upon the "inherent dignity and worth of every human being."[58] The section then clarifies Canada's responsibilities to uphold international human rights standards and to prevent with "due diligence" any violations of its citizens' human rights—whether by private individuals or by public officials themselves.[59] While the cases explored throughout the report "do not involve allegations of violence by police or other public officials,"[60] they do nonetheless evidence the state's direct failure to protect Indigenous women's fundamental right to be "safe and free from violence."[61] For instance, Amnesty International emphasizes the state's role in creating policy and legislation that render Indigenous women vulnerable to violence. Alongside the continual erosion of Indigenous peoples' traditional land base, the Indian Act and the residential schools system are cited as examples of state-sponsored initiatives with immediate consequences for Indigenous women's access to safety and security.[62] The report explains these initiatives as historic forms of government-mandated dispossession leading to situations of economic and social precarity in which violence is committed with impunity. In this way, the report characterizes both interpersonal attacks and systemic, state-sponsored forms of oppression as interlocking human rights issues: "When a woman is targeted for violence because of her gender or because of her Indigenous identity, her fundamental rights have been abused. And when she is not offered an adequate level of protection by state authorities because of her gender or because of her Indigenous identity, those rights have been violated."[63]

Having established in statistical fact the high rates of violence against Indigenous women, and having located responsibility for remedying this violence with the state, the report then moves in its second section to demonstrating the "human terms" of this problem.[64] This is accomplished largely through the use of the narrative case study form. The centrepiece of the *Stolen Sisters* document, nine narrative case studies make up the entire second section of the report. In these case studies, the individual stories of missing or murdered Indigenous women are told with the permission of their families.[65] Adapted from interviews conducted with the families and with the organizations or advocates who work with them, the stories are written in a third-person expository narrative mode. The purpose of these stories is to provide qualitative evidence of racist and sexist violence in Indigenous women's lives, and to call on all levels of government to take action. The stories thus alternate between relating select biographical details of a woman's life—the details of her home community, her family, her childhood and adolescence, and the known circumstances of her disappearance or death—and providing an expository interpretation of these biographical details for what they reveal about systemic discrimination and violence as human rights abuses. The report's lead case study is of Helen Betty Osborne. Osborne's case is often cited in the literature on missing and murdered Indigenous women, and was even the subject of a provincial justice inquiry in 1988. Her 1971 murder is also the earliest of the nine cases explored in the *Stolen Sisters* report (otherwise spanning 1991 to 2003). Its place both at the head of the report and as the first narrative case study is thus owed not only to its location in historical chronology but also to its archetypal power. Of its selected case studies, the report states: "In every instance, it is Amnesty International's view that Canadian authorities should have done more to ensure the safety of these women and girls."[66] Perhaps no case is so clear in this regard as Osborne's.

The narrative begins by establishing Osborne's birthplace in the Cree community of Norway House, north of Lake Winnipeg, and then relates a brief account of the assimilationist policy that forced her to pursue her education elsewhere at age seventeen—first at the Guy Hill Residential School, and then in the town of The Pas, Manitoba: "The federal government, pursuing a policy of cultural assimilation—and having decided that Indigenous communities offered no future for young people—wanted Indigenous children to get their education in predominantly non-Indigenous towns and cities."[67] This is an example of how the case study weaves biographical detail with pointed policy critique, referring to successive policies of assimilation which followed on the heels of the federal government's residential school system. Having already established in the previous section how residential schools aimed to erode Indigenous peoples' "sense of identity,"[68] the report then demonstrates how "the disruption of Indigenous families and communities is not a thing of the past."[69] The story of Osborne's displacement from her community in 1969, even as "the residential school system was being transformed and eventually phased out,"[70] speaks powerfully to this fact.

Osborne had dreamed of "becoming a teacher and helping her people,"[71] but was compelled to pursue her education outside her home community of Norway House. Drawing primarily from the *Report of the Aboriginal Justice Inquiry of Manitoba*, the *Stolen Sisters* case study goes on to describe Osborne's high school community of The Pas as "sharply divided between Indigenous and non-Indigenous residents," with each "group" maintaining its own side in movie theatres, bars, and school lunchrooms alike.[72] In The Pas, these racial tensions also manifested in gendered terms; the report comments on "a pattern of sexual harassment of Indigenous women and girls" into which both the police and the Department of Indian Affairs routinely "fail[ed] to intervene."[73] In efforts to underline the severity of the situation, and the extent of the authorities' indifference, Amnesty International quotes directly from the *Report of the Aboriginal Justice Inquiry*: "We know that cruising for sex was a common practice in The Pas in 1971. We know too that young Aboriginal women, often underage, were the usual objects of the practice. And we know that the RCMP did not feel that the practice necessitated any particular vigilance on its part."[74] Amnesty International thus wonders whether Osborne's life "might have been saved if police had taken action on a pattern of threats to Indigenous women's safety."[75]

After having described a setting rife with the "racism and sexism"[76] of both community members and the local authorities, the *Stolen Sisters* report then recounts the abduction and murder of nineteen-year-old Osborne. While walking home from a dance in the early morning hours of Saturday, November 13, 1971, Osborne was "accosted by four non-Indigenous men," who "forced her into their car," sexually assaulted her, and then took her "to a cabin owned by one of the men where she was beaten and stabbed to death ... possibly with a screwdriver."[77] A detailed interpretive account of the circumstances surrounding Osborne's murder and its subsequent investigation follows. The final passages of the case study enumerate the documented failures on the part of the Department of Indian Affairs, the RCMP, and the justice system to intervene, investigate, and arbitrate in the interests of Osborne and other Indigenous women. For instance, the report details how racism "marred the initial RCMP investigation" into Osborne's death, with police failing to "act on a tip naming the four non-Indigenous men responsible."[78] The case was left to lapse for over ten years before an officer pursued new information, soon gathering enough evidence for charges to be laid in October 1986.[79] In December 1987, sixteen years after Osborne's murder, one of the four men responsible was sentenced to life imprisonment.[80] The report, in agreement with the *Report of the Aboriginal Justice Inquiry*, concludes that "the most important factor obstructing justice in this case was the failure of members of the non-Indigenous community to bring forward evidence" toward assisting the original investigation.[81] This failure, like that of the RCMP to thoroughly investigate the murder, was found to be "at least partly motivated by racism."[82] In this way, the report establishes assimilationist policy as well as racist and sexist attitudes as the major contributing factors to Osborne's murder and its subsequent mishandling by the police: "Betty Osborne would be alive today had she not been an Aboriginal woman."[83]

The expository narrative mode employed throughout the Osborne case study alternates between biographical storytelling and policy critique. Key causal factors contributing to violence are strategically illuminated throughout the story—from the "history of government policies that have torn apart Indigenous families and … pushed a disproportionate number of Indigenous women into dangerous situations," to the failure of police to "provide Indigenous women with an adequate standard of protection."[84] In the Osborne case study and elsewhere in the *Stolen Sisters* report, women's stories provide the qualitative data from which Amnesty International draws its primary thesis: "that Canadian authorities should have done more to ensure the safety of these women and girls."[85] In keeping with its human rights framework of redress, the report concludes by citing Canadian officials' "clear and inescapable obligation to ensure the safety of Indigenous women."[86] The report thus establishes from within the biographies of missing and murdered women the root causes of violence, as well as the "Conclusions and Recommendations" about what should be done.

The report's final section calls on Canadian officials to implement measures "consistent with international human rights standards."[87] A set of recommendations in policy, policing, and education reform that constitute a "platform for action,"[88] these proposed measures look to rectify oppressive social relations through the very structures responsible for colonial violence in the first place. For instance, the report's indictment of racist police and RCMP investigations results in its recommendation that police training programs incorporate issues of "cultural sensitivity and violence against women."[89] Similarly, the report finds that learned colonial sensibilities have normalized gendered colonial violence in Canada; it therefore recommends expanded public education programs as a means of remedial action.[90] Other key recommendations include the following: All levels of government must "publicly condemn the high rates of violence against Indigenous women"; "undertake a review of outstanding recommendations from Canadian commissions, inquiries and inquests"; "support research into the extent and causes of violence against Indigenous women"; "ensure the provision of culturally appropriate services such as shelters and counseling for Indigenous women and girls"; and address, through improved funding and social programs, the "social and economic factors that lead to Indigenous women's extreme vulnerability to violence."[91]

Here, the report brushes up against some of the discursive limits of the rights framework of redress—the "enabling and constraining" circumstances,[92] as Sidonie Smith puts it, of the "juridical model of the human rights regime."[93] In telling the stories of missing and murdered women, the report witnesses individual acts of violence within a broader network of oppressive relations and articulates human rights claims as legitimate and potentially justiciable within an international framework of accountability. And yet the report's reliance on liberal, state-centred measures of reform throws into relief some of its limitations. In order to be a workable document, there are of course pragmatic limits to the kinds of recommendations the report can make. And certainly, if implemented, many of the proposed measures would have positive outcomes. However, many thinkers and activists question whether remedial initiatives have any meaningful or lasting effects in the daily lives of Indigenous women in Canada. As Indigenous feminist activist Tina Beads remarks in an interview with Rauna Kuokkanen, "while anti-racism training or cultural sensitivity training would be useful, I don't think it addresses the problem."[94] This is because the problem is somewhat deeper than a mere lack of awareness, tools, funding, or support: the problem is that Canada is *premised* upon the dispossession of Indigenous peoples. This is not likely to be solved by the Canadian government or its institutions, however much the international human rights framework relies on governments and state officials to protect and uphold their citizens' rights.[95] For these reasons, I see two interrelated problems with the *Stolen Sisters* report: the report pursues a paternalistic formulation of rights that relies on the benevolence of the Canadian government to protect Indigenous peoples; and it deploys the stories of missing and murdered women in ways that naturalize these formulations and derives recommendations accordingly.

While the report charts several government policies and initiatives that have contributed directly to circumstances of discrimination, inequality, and dispossession,[96] in keeping with international human rights discourse it nonetheless relies on governments to recognize and protect Indigenous peoples' rights.[97] Human rights are seen as the responsibility of the nation-state to safeguard, yet this paradigm is arguably at odds with Indigenous contexts of struggle against state authority.

As Elizabeth Povinelli suggests in her critique of multicultural recognition, "In this liberal imagination, state apparatuses, as well as its laws, principles of governance, and national attitudes need merely be *adjusted* to accommodate others."[98] This is in fact what political theorist Duncan Ivison advocates in his conception of a "postcolonial" liberalism that would provide "space within liberal democracies and liberal thought in which Aboriginal perspectives ... can not only be heard, but given equal opportunity to shape (and reshape) the forms of power and government acting on them."[99] At issue, then, is a debate about whether Indigenous rights can be articulated *within* the "legal and political discourses of the state"—and in other non-Indigenous institutions where Indigenous rights are framed[100]—or whether these frameworks are fundamentally assimilative and thus incompatible with Indigenous self-determination. For those in the latter camp, efforts to produce change from "within" are stymied by colonial power relations invested in their own perpetuation. For this reason, thinkers like Glen Coulthard have issued a call "to selectively 'turn away' from engaging the discourses and structures of settler-colonial power."[101] Leanne Simpson, citing Anishinaabe activist-scholar Winona LaDuke, puts it yet more succinctly: "Ultimately, we're not talking about getting a bigger piece of the pie—as Winona LaDuke says—we're talking about a different pie."[102]

In the case of the *Stolen Sisters* report, and the issue of gendered colonial violence more broadly, the need for practical and immediate solutions would seem sometimes to necessitate working "within" existing programs and institutions. Of course, imperatives for progressive social change are often couched in this persuasive pragmatic discourse: "Begin with the doable"; "set aside the intractable problems facing national and international life ... and concentrate instead on the levels and types of disagreements that can be resolved."[103] However, is it not the case that the "doable" is politically, materially, and ideologically constituted? The contemporary Canadian context in which the "doable" is shaped is one in which "colonial domination continues to be structurally committed to maintain—through force, fraud, and more recently, so-called 'negotiations'—ongoing state access to the land and resources that [provide] the foundation of colonial state-formation, settlement, and capitalist development."[104] When seen in this light, the ideal of "decreased harm through increased mutual understanding" is insufficient to the task of ending violence when pursued within the very institutions that have advanced colonial policies and practices in the first place.[105] Athabascan theorist Dian Million reminds us: "rape, murder, and sexualisation of Indigenous women has been constitutive to the founding of western nation-states" like Canada.[106] In such a reality, more vigilante policing or better education will not necessarily create conditions of safety for Indigenous women. While the *Stolen Sisters* report does bring the issue of gendered colonial violence into sharper focus for Canadian publics and authorities, and does so with the persuasive "discursive weight" of Amnesty International behind it,[107] the report is nonetheless constrained by its human rights framework to produce liberal measures of change.

Wendy Brown reminds us that human rights activism, like any form of activism, is a specific "moral-political project" that carries with it a "particular image of justice."[108] In the *Stolen Sisters* report, "justice" is largely interpreted to mean "prosecution and punishment" within the mainstream criminal justice system, as well as public acknowledgement and healing for survivors of violence.[109] The report clearly documents the failures of the justice system to protect Indigenous women, and even mentions that "the Canadian court system was imposed on Indigenous peoples without their consent and continues to be looked on with suspicion and mistrust"; yet the report also assumes in its proposed solutions that the trust of Indigenous people in this system can and should be established.[110] Million, echoing Sarah Deer, further clarifies the problem with this approach: "Making the disappeared visible as an object of colonial law is not the same as changing a society where rape is constitutive to deeper relations. 'Reform' hasn't stopped anything."[111] So, while the use of women's stories garners greater visibility for the issue of gendered colonial violence, it may also surreptitiously legitimize dominant structures of law and government as the place where acknowledgement and action must be sought.

By storytelling the lives of missing and murdered women, the report establishes and interprets the truth of rights violations through select biographic detail. The report thus presents life narrative as an unmediated forum through which to advance recommendations for change. The risk is that women's stories get mobilized and consumed in the service of an authenticating purpose: they become the representational strategy through which particular measures for addressing human rights violations are naturalized. The assumed "givenness" of a woman's remembered life and its apparent capacity to speak authentically to violence and discrimination performs an unproblematized link between Indigenous women's stories and particular calls to action. As Roger Simon warns, this can have the effect of "inoculat[ing] specific remembrance practices against critique as to what pedagogies they enact and what interests they serve."[112] The report's recommendations derive a kind of moral authority from their connection to Indigenous women's experiences of violence; meanwhile, incompatibilities between Indigenous practices of resistance and human rights activism problematically slip from view.

Both Amnesty International and their collaborator in the *Stolen Sisters* report, NWAC, deploy biographical storytelling as a means to raise awareness and generate recommendations for change. And for both organizations, these recommendations are aimed strategically at dominant political structures (change from "within"). However, NWAC's Sisters in Spirit campaign has been more publicly reflexive about the possibilities and limits of its approach—and about relying on the colonial state to initiate change. While Amnesty International employs a human rights storytelling approach that presents standardized narratives of victimry from which justiciable claims can arise, NWAC's parallel campaign has solicited and reproduced the stories of missing women with Indigenous methods of remembrance and of storytelling in mind. This includes a focus on reciprocal responsibilities for tellers and listeners, as well as a greater emphasis than in Amnesty International's case on survivance over victimry. As King reflects, NWAC researchers have a "responsibility to consider how the stories we publish represent the woman or girl involved and how the story might affect those close to her."[113] NWAC's emphasis on the strengths and needs of families and of communities is reflected in their stated hope that, more than conveying to readers the impacts of colonial violence, the women's stories will serve as a powerful reminder that "Aboriginal women and girls are strong, beautiful, proud and loved."[114]

Very different traditions of storytelling have shaped these overlapping campaigns' representations of material violence (and what needs to be done to counter it). I now turn to the possibilities presented by Indigenous women's literature—looking to the specific example of commemorative anti-violence poetry that, like the NWAC and Amnesty International campaigns, deploys biographical narrative as a means of intervention and critique. In reading this poetry within the broader context of life narratives in activist rights campaigns, I want to consider literature as more than a parallel site of protest whose work is primarily imaginative. That is, I read this poetry as itself engaged in activist praxis and debate. In the section that follows, I explore how poet Marilyn Dumont fosters new, critical ways of thinking through the stakes of mobilizing life narratives in activist sites of resistance.

Commemorative Anti-Violence Poetry: Marilyn Dumont's "Helen Betty Osborne"

As Michelle La Flamme notes in her review essay on Marilyn Dumont's 1996 collection *A Really Good Brown Girl*, this is "a collection of poems which deals with memory, the land, the body, family, and colonial conditions in Canada for Native people."[115] The Gerald Lampert Memorial Award–winning collection was re-released as a Brick Books "Classic" in 2015, and its themes remain highly relevant to contemporary anti-violence critique and activism. In her recent interview with Dumont, Métis-Icelandic poet and *Room* magazine editor Jónína Kirton reflects upon poetry as a "powerful and subversive tool of activism."[116] Dumont's response draws clear connections between poetry, activism, and analysis: "Writing has saved my emotional, spiritual, and intellectual life in a country where I wasn't supposed to exist, let alone thrive," she says. "It allows me to sort out the mess of structural inequity, bureaucratic obfuscation, colonial racism, and sexism."[117] A number of the poems in *Really Good* address colonial racism and sexism directly, foregrounding how material forms of violence interlock with discursive ones, and demonstrating the centrality of representation and remembrance to anti-violence critique. Engaging prescient questions around what constitutes a responsible representation of colonial violence, the poem "Helen Betty Osborne" in particular explores the possibilities and limits of storytelling where an individual's life narrative is concerned. As such, the poem offers possible solutions to that key question, raised over a decade later by NWAC researchers for the Sisters in Spirit campaign: how and when should life experiences be reported?[118]

As discussed, Osborne's case has been reported in a number of contexts—from the 1991 *Report of the Aboriginal Justice Inquiry of Manitoba* investigating her death, to the *Stolen Sisters* report, where her story appears both as a framing device and as a subsequent independent case study. Dumont's thirty-three-line poem does something quite different. There are generic distinctions, of course—things that the associative and elliptic qualities of poetry can accomplish, and which can't be done in the more positivist realm of justice inquiries or human rights reportage. But there are broader implications to Dumont's choices, formal and otherwise, which lend crucial insight to the issue of representation in the Osborne case. In the *Stolen Sisters* report, Osborne's story is deployed for its explanatory capacity as well as its affective dimensions; the report means to both raise awareness and incite a specific "ethical response" from its readers.[119] In Dumont's poem, the explanatory and affective power of Osborne's story figures as a point of departure for a broader reflection on gendered colonial violence and on the storytelling approach to anti-violence resistance. Combining commemoration with critical reflection, Dumont's work reflects on the use of life narratives in activist campaigns—and also offers implicit "recommendations" of its own. Notably, the poem avoids any paternalistic formulation of Indigenous women's rights and, despite its memorial qualities, eschews a sentimental or spectacularized approach to securing the engagement of its readers. Dumont instead suggests an Indigenous approach to storytelling a missing or murdered woman's life narrative—one arguably premised, in this case, on Cree precepts of "historicity and wâhkôtowin (kinship)."[120]

"Helen Betty Osborne" is a free-verse poem, meaning that it does not make use of a regular rhythmic pattern or rhyme scheme; rather, its verse approximates natural speech. As Dumont notes of her later work in *The Pemmican Eaters* (2015), many of her poems are written in free verse, yet she has also occasionally "experimented with writing in traditional form(s)."[121] In "Helen Betty Osborne," Dumont adapts the elegy—a lyrical lament for an individual's passing, and a poetic reflection on loss and grief—into a free-verse epistle addressed directly to Osborne herself. Osborne figures as both the subject of memorial contemplation and the intended recipient of the letter-poem: "Betty," it begins, "if I set out to write this poem about you / it might turn out instead / to be about me / or any one of / my female relatives."[122] In naming Osborne as the recipient, and by evoking others to whom the poem might also speak, Dumont locates Osborne within a broader web of relations with which the poem's speaker also identifies. Despite Osborne's irrevocable absence as the poem's main addressee, Dumont asserts the *presence* of living relations to whom Osborne is actively "re-membered."[123] In this way, the poem pursues "an active sense of presence over absence,"[124] and foregrounds a relational framework in which to tell and interpret Osborne's story.

This evocation of relations, of wâhkôtowin, happens at the level of surface themes or content as well as being a process performed toward linking past and future generations. Speaking to the Cree poetic process as one of connection through storytelling, Neal McLeod elaborates: "Because of this connection to other generations, there emerges an ethical dimension to Cree poetic discourse, namely, the moral responsibility to remember."[125] While McLeod is specifically referring to the ethical imperative among contemporary Cree storytellers and poets to ground their work in Cree narrative memory—to connect the strands of ancestral narrative to contemporary poetic practice—this concept can also help us to understand the relational dimensions of remembrance in Dumont's poem. Dumont refashions the elegy to instruct a holistic and communal process of memory that is as much about asserting continuity as it is about marking a disappearance. For instance, the opening lines about "any one of / my female relatives" indicate at once the greater statistical vulnerability of Indigenous women to violence, as well as the significance of "re-membering" one's living relations in anti-violence work. Janice Acoose explains re-membering as the "re-creation and re-attachment of important relations;"[126] in Dumont's poem, the opening lines "re-attach" the knowledge of families and communities, of her relations, at the outset. The elegy then becomes a possible lens through which "to *see* our Ancestors" despite the distortions and erasures of colonial history.[127] It marks for remembrance Osborne's passing, while turning our attention as readers to the broader history of violence—and resistance—of which Osborne's story is a part.

In its second stanza, the elegy further reframes remembrance as an opportunity for reclamation and "re-attachment," moving from the more intimate example of "my female relatives" to a much wider circle of relations:

> it might turn out to be
> about Anna Mae Aquash, Donald Marshall or Richard Cardinal,
> it might even turn out to be
> about our grandmothers,
> beasts of burden in the fur trade
> skinning, scraping, pounding, packing,
> left behind for 'British Standards of Womanhood,'
> left for white-melting-skinned women,
> not bits-of-brown women
> left here in this wilderness, this colony.[128]

Here, there are two sets of relations whose connections to Osborne are invoked: "our grandmothers, / beasts of burden in the fur trade," and the three named figures of Aquash, Marshall, and Cardinal. Each is a story in its own right, yet together they tell a broader critical narrative about Canada's history as a settler colonial state. Leey'qsun scholar Rachel Flowers explains: "The story of the settler colony is founded on disappearing peoples, from terra nullius to missing and murdered Indigenous women. Colonialism operates as a form of structured dispossession and the current relationship between Indigenous peoples and the state is part of that continuum. Ongoing extractionist politics continue to inform our place-based arts of resistance and critiques in our struggles not only *for* land but also informed *by* the land."[129] Dumont's poem explores this foundational premise of "disappearing peoples" as endemic to the settler state's continued existence, recalling hundreds of years of structured dispossession in the space of a single stanza. She names the women whose labour in Canada's first major extractionist economy, the fur trade, is so often misrepresented or erased. She further commemorates three contemporary figures whose names are synonymous with systemic injustice in Canada. In doing so, Dumont re-forges in poetic form the connections which colonial history has severed or effaced.

In naming Aquash, Marshall, and Cardinal, for instance, the poem links our remembrance of these individuals to the struggle to *name* systemic colonial violence in cases of injustice. In her analysis of recent public dialogue about missing and murdered women, Sarah Hunt observes the media's failure to name white male violence as a root cause.[130] Reporters and politicians continually emphasize "risk factors" in the lives of victims rather than focusing on perpetrators, she argues, which leads them to blame Indigenous people for the violence they face. Meanwhile, Hunt states, "they are unable to see that the Canadian justice system has been set up to serve a society built on Indigenous erasure, including brushing aside these seemingly endless murders." Though separated by time and place, the cases of Aquash, Marshall, and Cardinal are unquestionably a part of this trend. Aquash (Mi'kmaq) was an activist in the American Indian Movement whose 1976 murder went unsolved for nearly thirty years despite her family's repeated calls for justice.[131] Marshall (Mi'kmaq) was wrongly convicted of murder and served eleven years of a life sentence before being acquitted in 1983. Cardinal (Métis) was a youth in Alberta's foster care system whose 1984 suicide was caused directly by the abuse and neglect he experienced as a ward of the state. Each case evidences what the Amnesty International report would call the "painful human cost of government failure,"[132] yet in highlighting these particular examples the poem's analysis is clear: the justice and child welfare systems are not failing Indigenous peoples so much as they are fulfilling their intended purpose to replace—by active and violent imposition—pre-existing Indigenous legal and familial structures with Euro-Western ones. As Sherene Razack remarks of the Donald Marshall case and the subsequent provincial justice inquiry, Marshall was wrongly convicted not because of poor judgment on the part of individual law officials, but because the justice system is "organized to the cultural advantage of the dominant group"[133] Similarly, in the Osborne case, her murderers evaded justice for years. This is owed not merely to oversights on the part of investigating officers, but to the systemic disadvantage of Indigenous peoples in a justice system reluctant to name white male violence.

Implicit in the choice of Aqaush, Marshall, and Cardinal is a critique of the imposition of foreign legal and child protection structures with the patronizing presumption of their superiority. Also implicit here is a skepticism about whether these structures can or should be reformed for the greater inclusion of Indigenous people. A frequent argument in favour of reform is that cases like these indicate "malfunction"[134] but not racism per se—since racism in this understanding can "only consist of overt, intentional acts."[135] As such, better policy and training are touted as solutions. Cloaking as "individual incompetence" (the regrettable mistakes of a few) the work of systems designed for the very elimination of Indigenous peoples and institutions,[136] this argument emerges in the public commentary on both the Marshall and the Cardinal cases, as well as in the cases of missing and murdered women. It amounts, as Razack puts it, to a "widespread denial of racism in the justice system."[137] That Osborne's individual assailants attacked her with racist intent is undeniable; as Métis critic Emma LaRocque notes in her written submission to the Manitoba Aboriginal Justice Inquiry, "these youths grew up with twisted notions of 'Indian girls' as 'squaws'"—a "grotesque dehumanization has rendered all Native women and girls vulnerable to gross physical, psychological and sexual violence."[138] What the poem makes clear, however, is that dehumanizing stereotypes inform institutional practices as well as interpersonal ones. Naming Aqaush, Marshall, and Cardinal allows Dumont to analyze the relationship between Osborne's murderers, the "townsfolk" who colluded through their silence, and the justice system that failed to convict all but one of the men involved (sixteen years later).[139]

Like LaRocque's submission to the justice inquiry, Dumont's poem emphasizes the relationship between representational and physical forms of violence. It exposes the lived ramifications of dehumanizing "ideas about Indians"[140]—including the popular belief, clearly informing the Osborne case, that "native girls were easy."[141] Janice Acoose terms this the "easy squaw" stereotype,[142] and she traces its origins to the written texts of New World ethnographers and to the records of "explorers, fur traders, and christian missionaries" who came afterward.[143] Acoose's research reveals how this stereotype supported "cultural attitudes that justify imperialistic expansion."[144] She cites as one example the records of the Hudson's Bay Company (HBC), which she says contemporary historians too often take as "historically accurate" in their glaring misrepresentations of Indigenous women as immoral, lustful, and expendable.[145] As historian Sylvia Van Kirk points out, "The fur trade forms the basis of recorded history in Western Canada;"[146] that these archives contain such depraved images of Indigenous femininity thus explains, in part, the persistence of the "squaw" stereotype in contemporary Canadian culture. Acoose notes: "Such documents encourage the stereotypic representation of Indigenous women, fostering dangerous cultural attitudes that condone violence and murder."[147] In her poem, Dumont similarly attributes contemporary instances of violence to this legacy of degrading misrepresentations. These misrepresentations inform personal practices as well as social and economic ones, the poem argues—and it offers the infamous words of prominent HBC administrator Sir George Simpson as one example.

George Simpson was a governor-in-chief of Rupert's Land, serving HBC as deputy governor (1839–52) and governor (1852–56) at the height of the company's power. Van Kirk calls him "the most important personage in the nineteenth-century fur trade."[148] Simpson is best remembered as a shrewd and disciplined manager, as well a "classic practitioner" of a most "exploitative attitude toward native women."[149] Van Kirk explains how Simpson "formed a series of liaisons with young mixed-blood women whom he treated in a most callous manner."[150] Ktunaxa critic Shirley Green elaborates on this practice:

> Many [HBC employees] took Aboriginal women as wives, sometimes with the legal ceremony of marriage but often, in the phrase used in those days, as "country wives." The well-to-do men, or those who ranked higher in the organization ... would often later return to the British Isles to seek a wife from among those of their own social and economic class. Sometimes the country wife and her children would be passed along to another Bay employee. This was a common practice as women and children were viewed as chattels.... Sometimes the woman and her children were simply abandoned and left to fend for themselves, often far from their families.[151]

The practice—both of taking a wife and of deserting her—was widespread, as Green and others suggest, but Simpson was notably calculated in his approach. For instance, he openly counselled traders to use women in forging economic ties with "the savages," saying that "connubial alliances are the best security we can have of the goodwill of the Natives."[152] So often did this result in women being later deserted that the Council of the Northern Department of Rupert's Land actually passed an order in 1824 "requiring all officers and servants to make adequate provision for their Indian women."[153] Shirley Green's own great-aunt was one of the women whom Simpson callously discarded when he had tired of his latest "'bit o' brown,' 'his article' and 'his commodity' (*his words*)."[154] Though but one among many such incidents in Simpson's life, it represents for Green an inherited history of contempt and erasure hardly improved by the fact that Simpson made arrangements to pass his "commodity" on to another HBC employee. As a descendant of women in the fur trade, Green attests: "The impact of these colonizing corporations on the Indigenous peoples throughout the world was profound and the legacy of their policies continues to affect the descendants of these peoples."[155]

Official colonial history has largely erased Indigenous women (and their labour) from view, recording instead the deeds of men and the products of empire. Dumont's poem seeks to "re-member" her grandmothers in the fur trade—"skinning, scraping, pounding, packing"[156]—and to *name* as white male violence the exploitation perpetrated against them. Significantly, Dumont doesn't name Simpson directly; rather, he is identified by his own degrading words when the poem's speaker recalls the women "left for white-melting-skinned women, / not bits-of-brown women / left here in this wilderness."[157] Letting Simpson's demeaning language speak for itself in the structural context of colonial exploitation, the elegy condemns his treatment of Indigenous women without singling him out as an exceptional case. Too often in public discourse about gendered colonial violence, the acts of perpetrators are individualized and sensationalized, supporting the common presumption that white male violence is exceptional rather than business as usual in the settler colonial state. This was certainly evident in the Pickton case, as discussed in chapter 1, and in the earlier examples of the John Crawford or Gilbert Paul Jordan serial murders.[158] When compared outright to the acts of such men, Simpson's ugly turn of phrase may seem innocuous indeed. But Dumont's purpose is more subtle than that: by compressing the time and space between Simpson's exploits and the Osborne murder (a juxtaposition poetry is uniquely able to make), Dumont analyses both cases as being "about hunting season instead, / about 'open season' on native women."[159] As a student of mine once pointed out, the phrase "open season" implies rules of engagement—a sanctioned structure in which ordinary laws or restrictions are conditionally suspended. Incongruous examples though they may seem, Osborne's murderers share with Simpson the same rules of engagement: an understanding of Indigenous women as "(gendered) racial Other(s) whose degradation confirmed their own identities as white—that is, as men entitled to the land and the full benefits of citizenship."[160] In this context, Indigenous women are virtually inviolable under the law. The poem's comment on "hunting season" thus refers not only to the high rates of violence against Indigenous women, but also to this violence as committed with relative legal impunity throughout history.

Like the *Stolen Sisters* report, then, Dumont uses Osborne's case as a narrative point of departure to evidence the complex "reality of violence and discrimination against Indigenous women."[161] Yet, unlike the human rights organization, Dumont's poem presumes neither the unqualified resistive potential of raising awareness nor the unproblematic use of biographical storytelling in that project. Rather, the poem reimagines the commemorative properties of elegy in order to theorize a broader set of tensions inherent to the ideal of storytelling for "social change."[162] The elegy isn't ultimately *about* Osborne, despite being addressed *to* her; in this way, the poem troubles the assumed illustrative power of a single life narrative for the purposes of promoting social change and reflects instead upon the potential risks entailed in remembering the missing and murdered.

Often seen as giving political expression to the experiences of marginalized or oppressed subjects, storytelling has emerged as a prominent methodology not only in human rights discourse, but also in the fields of critical and anti-racist education, as well as in the awareness-raising campaigns of activist social movements themselves. As Sherene Razack explains, personal storytelling in these settings often refers to the process of giving voice, through narrative means, to an "experience of the world that is not admitted into dominant knowledge paradigms."[163] In this sense, storytelling would seem to produce what Sarita Srivastava and Margot Francis term "oppositional knowledge;"[164] in the activist contexts of popular education or awareness campaigns, marginalized subjects are granted a space from which to speak the "truth" of their experiences, while listeners are presumed to gain edifying knowledge of oppression as experienced by another. Through this process, an alternative discourse is thought to emerge—one that locates, from within stories themselves, both the root of a social problem, and the impetus for social change. However, there are considerable limits involved in uncritically assuming a necessary correlation between the telling of story and the hopeful outcome of social change. For one thing, this understanding supposes that, by mere virtue of hearing another's story of oppression, we have participated in an oppositional act. This formulation becomes yet more problematic in cases where the subject positions of either the teller or the listener are left untheorized or are otherwise divorced from the power relations that may structure each party's differential place in the storytelling act. For instance, in many settings where storytelling is used as a method for raising awareness around issues of gendered and racial oppression, women of colour are positioned as "authentic" objects of knowledge—their stories solicited and consumed for the educational (or perhaps even entertainment) benefit of white interlocutors.[165] When this happens, the storytelling method occludes rather than invites a critically reflexive interrogation of oppression—allowing listeners to retreat into an unimplicated position where the gratifying experience of consuming an "other's" narrative is substituted for a more sustained interrogation of one's own possible "complicity in the oppression of others."[166] In short, while storytelling has become a privileged methodology for the expression of oppression across different activist sites, it is often the case that oppressive power relations are reinforced rather than dismantled when listeners passively consume the personal narratives of others.

Rather than putting story forth as a transparent means of promoting awareness and social change, the poem complicates how public knowledge about violence is produced. For instance, Dumont strategically denies readers access to the details of Osborne's story. Specifically, the poem withholds all narrative details of Osborne's murder itself. While the *Stolen Sisters* report seems obliged by generic convention to offer a comparatively exhaustive account of Osborne's life and death—including details from the autopsy report in which the extent of Osborne's brutalization is recorded[167]— the poem, for its part, refuses to reproduce what Mohawk poet Beth Brant calls "the last secrets of her life."[168] In fact, no overt reference to Osborne's murder is made at all. She is named fully only in the poem's title. And the only specific image we have of Osborne is of a photograph: "it might turn out to be / about your face   young and hopeful / staring back at me   hollow now / from a black and white page."[169] This is to say that the poem reproduces in words the *image* of a photograph: a likeness twice removed. A school photograph comes to mind at the mention of her face, "young and hopeful / staring back at me"—perhaps the same one now commonly used on the posters at commemorative marches and in other visual materials of memorial. Upon closer inspection, however, this passage is about something else, too: the act of looking at a photograph. It is about the moment in which the speaker's gaze seems to meet Osborne's, "staring back at me … from a black and white page." It is a mediated encounter between the speaker and the subject of memorial reflection—one containing both the obstinate fact of Osborne's absence as well as the challenge of representing that absence ethically.

Roland Barthes says of photography that its referent "is not the same as the referent of other systems of representation" because—unlike painting or writing—the photograph always refers to "the *necessarily* real thing which has been placed before the lens, without which there would be no photograph."[170] In Dumont's poem, of course, there is no photograph—only the discursive representation of one. And through this image Dumont problematizes the presumed transparency of the memorial photograph, and of the commemorative life narrative, to confer authentic knowledge of its subject. Contrary to Barthes's notion of the photograph's "evidential power"—in which "our vision of it is *certain*"[171]—Dumont's representation undermines any fantasy of sovereign certitude. And not because she is dealing thematically with Osborne's death, and thus with the photo's (and the poem's) irrevocably absent referent, but because the fantasy of positivist truth and of authentic "ethnographic knowledge" is itself a violence.[172] In her discussion of ethnography, photography, and the camera as "political weapon,"[173] for instance,

Chippewa media studies scholar Gail Guthrie Valaskakis explores the violence entailed in photographs that "reveal neither the context and conditions of their production nor the complexities of the experiences they seem to fix and transmit over time."[174] While the poem in no way presents the photo of Osborne as ethnographic, it does deploy photography's association with "ultimate reality, authenticity, and authority" in order to question the ideal of transparent evidentiary truth in the public representation of Osborne's case.[175] This is not to say that Osborne or the violence perpetrated against her is somehow unreal. It is precisely because this violence is "*necessarily* real"—to use Barthes's phrase—that the question of representation matters so much.

As the poem's only direct depiction of Osborne, the image of the photograph draws attention to itself *as* representation—mediated not only by the speaker, who constructs for readers both the photograph and the act of looking, but also by the broader commemorative project of the poem itself: to remember Osborne within a relational framework that names an ongoing history of colonial violence while questioning the necessity (or even possibility) of evidential detail as a guarantor of ethical public response. By denying readers any narrative details of the case itself, and by instead placing fragments of Osborne's story in evocative relation to others, the poem argues that greater public visibility will not necessarily combat the "indifference" of Canadian citizens and public officials.[176] Rather, the poem's challenge to public indifference is enacted through an invitation to analytical historicity that requires of all readers their participation in the interpretative task. In other words, the poem requires for its interpretation the sustained critical engagement of its readers. Dumont frames a structural, systemic analysis of Osborne's murder, but suggests that readers must themselves do the work of naming gendered colonial violence and of imagining resistance—of engaging with such figures as Aquash, Marshall, Cardinal, and Simpson, and considering their relationships to one another and to the broader history of violence under discussion. Like the participatory qualitative process described by Sister in Spirit researchers, Dumont's poem invites readers to co-create Osborne's story. In this sense, the story is less an evidentiary artifact in Dumont's hands than a means of "implicating the audience" in the very processes of representation and resistance.[177]

It is often the case that anti-violence activists and scholars regret the inadequacy of statistics or charts to convey the actual experience of social suffering; as humanitarian physician Paul Farmer puts it, perhaps "the 'texture' of dire affliction is better felt in the gritty details of biography."[178] However, we don't often enough question our investment in these "gritty details," or the impetus to narrate the "human terms" of rights violations.[179] Dumont's poem queries this investment through a form of strategic silence—that is, through a selective refusal to narrate or otherwise clearly depict Osborne's murder—while still nonetheless exposing the murder as part of a history of colonial violence. In this way the poem offers practical solutions to the conundrum described by NWAC researcher Jennifer King with respect to the Sisters in Spirit campaign: namely, under what circumstances should "personal and traumatic experiences like violence, addiction, or poverty" be reported?[180] King states:

> Certainly, we do not advocate "hiding" these experiences, as hiding such issues acts only to silence (and in many cases shame) those who experience them. But is it the place or role of the media to report on such experiences without the consent or control of the woman involved or those who loved her? At the same time, does failing to report in a substantive way conceal the experiences of Aboriginal women and girls in Canada? Put another way: Is it better to report on Aboriginal women's experiences without providing the historical context of colonization than to not report at all? And if we ignore their experiences, how can we expect to create change? These are hard questions, without easy answers.[181]

While Dumont's poem in no way advocates "hiding" the traumatic experience of violence, it deliberately avoids reproducing both the biographical detail and the prescriptive recommendations so central to a document like Amnesty International's *Stolen Sisters* report. In so doing, the elegy complicates the implicit binary (between reporting and not reporting) upon which King's dilemma is based. Instead, the poem's vision of anti-violence advocates naming and historicizing white male violence, exposing ongoing systemic racism in the justice system, and centring questions of responsible representation in public debates about violence and resistance. Part of its advocacy for responsible representation is to model ways of naming violence without reproducing it discursively in ways that could be violating to an individual's memory.

Dumont is not alone in wrestling with these particular questions in poetic form, and by way of conclusion I note that not all Indigenous-authored commemorative poetry about Osborne shares Dumont's approach. For example, Mohawk poet Beth Brant's prose poem "Telling" engages a comparatively graphic rendering of the "last secrets of [Osborne's] life": "I have a dream about Betty Osborne. / The last secrets of her life. / Stabbed fifty-six times with a screw driver to keep the secrets of whitemen. / Betty, your crime was being a woman, an Indian. Your punishment, mutilation and death. / The town kept the secret of who killed you … / Who do I protect with the secrets given me? / My pen is a knife."[182] While Dumont's poem critically interrogates the resistive viability of "telling," Brant's performs a solicitous and even confessional rehearsal of detail as a proposed tool of resistance. As Brant puts it, perhaps the writer "has to tell. It is the weapon I know how to use."[183] Telling here becomes the necessary vehicle for expunging the "secrets" and "speechlessness" accompanying colonial silencing and denial.[184] The Pas "kept the secret of who killed [Osborne]";[185] Brant's job, as a writer, is "to tell."[186] With this, Brant evokes a binary wherein the keeping of "secrets" is aligned with the perpetuation of gendered colonial violence, and the telling of "secrets" with anti-colonial resistance.

The tension between speech and silence is one of the chief structural tropes of Brant's poem, with each of its stanzas alternately engaging the notion of colonially imposed silence—"*they* told us to be speechless"[187]—and the resistive "need to tell."[188] Speechlessness is explored through the poem's interlaid narratives about interpersonal violence such as domestic abuse: "[h]e told me not to tell."[189] These interpersonal instances are then compared with systemic forms of silencing that take place on a broader scale, including the colonial suppression of Indigenous languages and knowledges: "They stole our speech and raped our minds."[190] The figure of Helen Betty Osborne resides at the centre of this tension; her murder (and the silence around it) represents both an individual and systemically perpetrated violence against which the resistive act of "telling" is pitted. As in Dumont's poem, "telling" is not without its risks. Brant asks if "some stories [are] meant to be hidden" or unspoken, and if telling might not be a form of "betray[al]."[191] And yet, even when this poem queries the impetus to counter silence with speech it does not go so far as to question the foundational liberal conceit upon which "telling" is so often premised in activist discourse: that "silence and speech are opposites" and "that when an enforced silence is broken, what emerges is truth borne by the vessel of authenticity and experience."[192] For Brant, the writer ultimately "has to tell."[193] In this way, the poem's performative tension between speech and silence nevertheless leaves this binary and its assumptions intact.

This tension between speech and silence underwrites much anti-violence discourse surrounding missing and murdered Indigenous women in Canada, where the shattering of an imposed silence with the "truth" is positioned as a necessarily resistive act. In troubling this binary, I don't mean to suggest that "telling" serves no progressive ends, or that speaking the truth of violence or abuse is an inherently misguided practice. Brant's poem, for instance, argues compellingly for the exposure of exploitative relationships in which the abuser's power depends on the preservation of a victim's silence. However, the exposure of the "truth" can't always be so easily separated out from regulatory or disciplinary power. As Wendy Brown puts it, it is possible that this "ostensible tool of emancipation carries its own techniques of subjugation—that it converges with unemancipatory tendencies in contemporary culture, establishes regulatory norms, [and] coincides with the disciplinary power of ubiquitous confessional practices."[194] The storytelling method of raising awareness has been unproblematically celebrated as granting emancipatory political expression or "voice" to experiences not normally admitted into "dominant knowledge paradigms;"[195] in this chapter I have tried to show how the narrative appeals of some anti-violence campaigns, and the dominant paradigms they would seek to oppose, may uneasily converge. Foucault's comments on confession are helpful here:

> The obligation to confess is now relayed through so many different points, is so deeply ingrained in us, that we no longer perceive it as the effect of a power that constrains us; on the contrary, it seems to us that the truth, lodged in our most secret nature, "demands" only to surface; that if it fails

to do so, this is because a constraint holds it in place, the violence of power weighs it down, and it can finally be articulated only at the price of a kind of liberation. Confession frees, but power reduces one to silence; truth does not belong to the order of power, but shares an original affinity with freedom.[196]

It is this which is ultimately at issue in Amnesty International's *Stolen Sisters* report: the assumption that the act of telling women's stories is a breaking of imposed silence, that the means (and ends) of this telling aren't as important as the act of telling itself (these means and ends being self-evident, and in the interests of liberation), and that truth—belonging irrevocably to the order of freedom—seamlessly translates the authenticity and pathos of Indigenous women's experiences of violence into necessarily resistive recommendations for change. The silence of systematized exclusion and marginalization is apparently shattered by the emancipatory tool of storytelling; meanwhile, all that "remains is for Canadian officials to acknowledge the seriousness of the problem and to commit themselves to immediate action."[197] Notably, many of these actions entail a mere "adjustment" to existing programs and institutions.[198] This does not ultimately transform the colonial relationship between Indigenous women and the state, but rather works to reconcile women's experiences of state violence with "all levels of government."[199] It is a framework that assumes the legitimacy and permanence of the colonial state, and that mobilizes Indigenous women's stories as a way to authenticate reform-based solutions. By contrast, Dumont's poem troubles the naturalized conception of experiential knowledge and "voice" when refracted through a liberal framework of redress. Instead of turning to the state for recognition, the elegy turns to the speaker's "female relatives,"[200] to Aquash, Marshall, and Cardinal, and to "our grandmothers."[201] As Rachel Flowers explains: "It is crucial to center Indigenous women's voices while we build stronger relationships with one another, [and] healing from violence means rebuilding our strength rather than reinforcing state power."[202] In foregrounding relationships between Indigenous women as a foundational premise of her poem, and in subsequently refusing to reproduce prescriptive recommendations or closure for readers, Dumont's poem intervenes in some of the most troubling representational strategies of contemporary mainstream anti-violence resistance.

Dumont's refrain, "Betty, *if* I set out to write this poem about you,"[203] prompts readers' reflection on what might be lost or gained in storytelling as a means of remembrance and resistance. The causal subordinating conjunction "if" introduces, across multiple stanzas, a refrain consistently rejoined by lines that speak to the impossibility of establishing, within a single narrative, a stable interpretation of what that life can tell us: "Betty, if I set out to write this poem about you / it might turn out instead / to be about me / or any one of / my female relatives;"[204] "Betty, if I start to write a poem about you / it might turn out to be / about hunting season instead, / about 'open season' on native women."[205] Significantly, the poem's elliptic refrain defers the act of writing or telling Betty Osborne's story indefinitely, instead "confronting the impulse to claim to know or have authority over a struggle."[206] And, contrary to the teleological impulse of the Amnesty International report that compels its narratives toward the closure offered by recommended measures for state intervention, Dumont's poem arguably defies closure entirely, ending with the open-ended refrain: "Betty, if I write this poem."[207]

CHAPTER THREE

Compelling Disclosures: Storytelling in Feminist Anti-Violence Discourse and Indigenous Women's Memoir

On Wednesday, June 11, 2008, Beverley Jacobs (Mohawk) of the Native Women's Association of Canada stood before the House of Commons to deliver a statement—a statement, she said, about "respect [for] aboriginal women in this country."[1] In a performative moment of "collective reconciliation"[2] overdetermined by a host of irreconcilabilities (not least of all, the state's pursuit of a "post-colonial" resolution in a present shaped by both historical and ongoing colonialism), Jacobs answered the government of Canada's official apology to former students of residential schools not with a conciliatory expression of rapprochement, but with a request. Specifically, she said: "We have given thanks to you for your apology.... But in return, the Native Women's Association wants respect."[3] With this, Jacobs effectively reconstituted the apology's ostensible narrative of closure, and shifted the disproportionate burden of responsibility back to the apologizer. In redistributing the logic of uneven exchange implied by this public act of contrition—we say we're sorry, and you grant "forgiveness"[4]—Jacobs seems almost to say: in return for your apology, we ask for your respect.

This moment has a number of implications for how we might read statements of and responses to public apology in what Jennifer Henderson and Pauline Wakeham have termed Canada's contemporary "culture of redress."[5] We might ask, as Elizabeth Povinelli does, how moments like this demonstrate the extent to which "national pageants of shameful repentance and ... new recognition of subaltern worth remain inflected by the conditional,"[6] something Jacobs here underscores (and undercuts) by subtly tempering her "acceptance" of the apology with a conditional statement of her own. Canada's national display of repentance stages reconciliation as the self-evident outcome of an apology at once conditioned upon and guaranteed by the state's unqualified redemption for "past" wrongs. What interests me in this performance, then, is how the inclusion of Indigenous peoples (and their testimony), rather than serving the interests of dialogic exchange in the pursuit of social justice, is insidiously structured in service to the hegemonic interests of the state. Public apology offers evidence of the nation's supposed largesse— its willingness to make amends[7]—while the testimony of Indigenous respondents is used to solidify a script of gracious benevolence (on one hand) and grateful absolution (on the other). In this formulation, even statements outwardly critical of colonial power can be recast to serve a broader narrative of "post-colonial" reconciliation. For instance, then–National Chief Phil Fontaine of the Assembly of First Nations stood in the House of Commons and declared: "Brave survivors, through the telling of their painful stories, have stripped white supremacy of its authority and legitimacy. The irresistibility of speaking truth to power is real."[8] But what if we understood the telling of painful stories as sometimes bolstering, rather than straightforwardly dismantling, white supremacy? What if, by Fontaine's "speaking truth to power," we understood not only the resistive sense of "speaking back to power" with the "truth," but also the Foucauldian sense of speaking truth as an *effect* of power?[9]

It is with this problematic that I am concerned: how narrative disclosures of colonial violence, solicited in a context of professed mutual understanding and reconciliation, may function as amenable to (rather than always resistant of) colonial strategies of power. And what interests me in particular is the matter to which Beverley Jacobs specifically draws our attention—namely, the matter of gendered colonial violence as narrativized in the moment of cultural recognition. In the case of Canada's official apology, the House recognized and called upon Indigenous respondents whose oral testimony could be appropriated, in J. Kēhaulani Kauanui's (Kanaka Maoli) and Andrea Smith's terms, as "narratives of 'healing' to promote national (read federal) reconciliation."[10] In this chapter, I want to meditate on this *mise en discours* as part of a broader liberal ideology that embeds scripts of painful disclosure and conciliatory redress as a strategy for the dissimulation of colonial power. Toward this end, I begin by pursuing this narrative imperative out from the halls of Parliament and into another site of cultural recognition: the mainstream feminist anti-violence service industry. In doing so, I want to open up a reading of liberal ideology as disseminated not just in the rhetoric of state-mandated multiculturalism, or in the official expression of national apology and redress, but also in the seemingly unlikely quarters of anti-oppression movements themselves.

For this discussion I build upon the previous chapter, in which I sought to complicate the use of storytelling in recent activist anti-violence campaigns in Canada. Storytelling is popularly understood as a way to resist systemic silence and indifference toward violence against women. Awareness-raising projects, educative initiatives, and policy critique alike have relied on narrative accounts of violence in order to both evoke public empathy and promote social change. In chapter 2, I investigated the example of Amnesty International's action-oriented document *Stolen Sisters: Discrimination and Violence against Indigenous Women in Canada*. This document recommends significant policy, policing, and education reforms toward addressing gendered and racial violence in Canada; I problematized the prospect of locating, from within women's stories, the impetus to reform institutions that have historical and ongoing links to colonial state violence. Indigenous women's stories of gendered and racial violence get deployed as inscrutable narratives of "subaltern worth"[11]—narratives that are then solicited and consumed in ways that naturalize liberal measures of reform and inadvertently bolster colonial state power. In this chapter, I further interrogate this problematic, in part by analyzing the use of storytelling as a tool of recognition in the so-called "diversity" and "anti-oppression" initiatives of feminist anti-violence service agencies. However, while chapter 2 investigated the biographical narrativization of women's experiences of violence—that is, the telling of the stories of absent subjects, of women who are missing or murdered and therefore cannot "speak" for themselves—this chapter investigates instances where women are compelled to tell their own stories in particular kinds of activist forums. In each case, I am concerned with how acts of "telling" and of "hearing" experiences of violence are contoured by complex and sometimes uneven power relations that make possible some utterances, while circumscribing others.

This discussion involves different, and at times incommensurate, storytelling practices. For this reason, this chapter investigates the question of storytelling in two parts. I begin with a discussion of mainstream feminist anti-violence activism, where autobiographical storytelling has long been an important site for the production of experiential knowledge about gendered colonial violence. As a form of awareness raising and critique, personal storytelling played a vital role in mainstream feminist organizations in the 1990s, at a time when many agencies were transitioning from a one-size-fits-all service regime to "an integrated, anti-racist, feminist service delivery system."[12] Specifically, storytelling became one of the dominant discursive scripts through which racialized women's experiences of oppression were solicited for the perceived educative benefit of their white interlocutors. While this practice was ostensibly pursued with the goal of promoting improved knowledge and understanding within the anti-violence movement, it often ignored and even reinforced "power inequities based in race."[13] I discuss the problems with this practice in the context of feminist anti-violence work before moving into an exploration of how storytelling has been deployed in Indigenous women's writing in ways that sometimes uneasily conform to, and yet other times resist liberal imperatives promoting reconciled relations with Canada's genocidal past and present. Specifically, I analyze the example of Dene writer-activist Morningstar Mercredi's 2006 memoir *Morningstar: A Warrior's Spirit*. While this memoir chronicles the gendered and intergenerational impact of residential school trauma, and charts the autobiographical subject's "journey" toward healing, the text nevertheless refuses to reproduce closure as a self-evident outcome, and instead ends with reference to the Pickton case by way of drawing broader attention to the ongoing colonial violences of the present.

In juxtaposing these different sites of storytelling and reception, I mean to complicate the transformative potential often accorded storytelling in anti-violence organizing and in the popular reception of Indigenous-authored memoir. In particular, I want to problematize storytelling solicited and received for the ostensible purposes of white edification, and to listen closely for a different purpose to which such storytelling might occur—one focused instead on modelling feminist anti-colonial critique. In short, I am interested in how narratives of violence are produced and consumed across a multiplicity of sites that, when read in dialogue, point to a dissonance or incommensurability between different kinds of "telling"—a dissonance that belies the liberal *mise en discours* that would "capture" and recast the telling of trauma toward a manufactured moment of conciliatory closure.[14] I look to Indigenous women's writing for its capacity to unsettle this comforting narrative of closure and absolution while providing non-Indigenous readers with the opportunity to "decentre [themselves] and to learn and act from a place of responsibility rather than guilt."[15] While I began with Jacobs's statement (and its refusal to reciprocate the government's apology with forgiveness) as a way of pointing up the colonial asymmetries of power embedded in the moment of conciliatory redress, I now turn my attention to a place where the ambiguous impetus of "speaking truth to power" has been problematically ingrained (and, at times, resisted) in feminist initiatives that strive to address racialized gendered violence.

Feminist Anti-Violence and the Anti-Oppression Model

Many women have been, and continue to be, marginalized by mainstream feminist theory and practice. To the extent that mainstream feminism historically articulated a homogeneous vision of gendered relations in which patriarchal domination and women's victimhood are presumed universal, this formulation has effaced both the historical specificity of different women's experiences, as well the particular "effects of contemporary imperialism" and class-based oppression.[16] For this reason, mainstream feminist approaches to anti-violence work have been dubiously received by many Indigenous scholars and activists. In her survey of Indigenous women's critiques of dominant feminist paradigms, for example, Métis scholar Verna St. Denis explains how many women have "rejected feminism as irrelevant"[17] because "gender inequality is neither the only nor the most important form of oppression they face."[18] In this view, violence against Indigenous women is understood as *colonial* in origin, rather than stemming from male supremacy first and foremost; as such, "colonization, racism and economic disparity are more pressing concerns."[19]

Self-identified Indigenous feminist critics, though embracing rather than eschewing the contested term of "feminism," similarly emphasize "how both racism and sexism fuse when brought to bear on Aboriginal women."[20] More than an additive and hierarchized approach in which categories of exclusion are appended to a privileged foundational analysis of gendered oppression, Indigenous feminist theory highlights gendered and racial oppression as systemically interlocking within the broader context of colonial domination. Likewise working "at the intersection/s of race, gender and class,"[21] critical race theory shares with Indigenous feminisms this "interlocking" rather than additive approach. Drawing from the work of scholars such as Patricia Hill Collins, Mary Louise Fellows and Sherene Razack explain: "This 'interlocking' effect means that the systems of oppression come into existence in and through one another so that class exploitation could not be accomplished without gender and racial hierarchies; imperialism could not function without class exploitation, sexism, heterosexism, and so on."[22] When applied in the context of front-line feminist organizing, an interlocking or intersectional approach to feminist anti-violence work asserts that shelters and other service agencies "cannot afford to address only the violence inflicted by the batterer; they must also confront the other multilayered and routinized forms of domination that often converge in these women's lives."[23]

Since the late 1980s, then, critical race and Indigenous feminist challenges to mainstream feminist theory and practice have brought questions of "race, nationality, class, ethnicity, and sexuality" to the fore.[24] The effect on the feminist anti-violence service industry has been deeply felt, with community-based providers of crisis, support, and advocacy services working to establish more inclusive policies. For many front-line organizations (including shelters, drop-in centres, and sexual assault centres), this has meant the adoption of anti-oppression service delivery models, mandating intersectional approaches that address gendered violence within broader contexts of social and economic disadvantage.[25] Under the sometimes conflated banner of "multicultural" anti-racist change,[26] staff and volunteer training sessions have thus been developed to "sensitize" anti-violence workers to the social, economic, and racialized facets of gendered violence,[27] while offering strategies toward understanding and responding ethically to factors which may or may not shape front-line workers' own experiences.[28] Taken on its own terms, such programming is grounded in a genuine practical need for services that are appropriate to the women who use them. It is moreover informed by legitimate organizational struggles to confront systemically maintained exclusionary practices. In the discussion that follows, however, I want to discuss some of the tensions that have informed the transition to anti-oppression mandates, and the fraught history of what shelter manager Rita Kohli calls the "intercultural sensitivity training industry."[29]

One major tension in the development of anti-oppression policy has been the "contradiction between mandate and practice."[30] A 1992 handbook in anti-racism service provision, *Developing an Antiracism Action Plan*, discusses how many organizations—despite their stated commitment to serving "all women ... without restriction"—in practice appear only to work "on the basis of a service model suitable to the needs of white women."[31] The handbook goes on to explain this contradiction as an implicit form of "entrenched" racism that is all the more damaging for having surfaced within social justice organizations themselves.[32] I want to analyze this conflict between "inclusive" mandates and exclusionary practices as rooted in what Sarita Srivastava terms a "liberal discourse of equality that denies the systemic nature of racism and its presence in our everyday language and practice."[33] Specifically, I offer a case study analysis of the conflict over anti-racism as it manifested at the Nellie's shelter in Toronto. One of the oldest women's shelters in Canada, Nellie's is perhaps best known for the divisive controversy that erupted there in the early 1990s when several of its staff members formed the Women of Colour Caucus in order to advocate for more accessible services for the women of colour who were fast becoming a larger constituency of Nellie's rapidly changing clientele.[34] These initial efforts toward anti-oppression service delivery were met with resistance and hostility on the part of some well-established white staff and board members who construed the concerns of the Women of Colour Caucus as an "obstruction" that distracted from the shelter's broader service mission.[35] The shelter's mission was to serve all women equally, with "no woman, no matter how difficult the case" being turned away.[36] And yet, as the Caucus would point out, this ostensibly inclusive system was first developed to serve the interests of white, middle-class women.[37]

It is important to note that similar debates about systemic racism and marginalization were taking place in organizations across Canada at this time. While the conflict at Nellie's became a flashpoint for these debates in the feminist service industry of the early 1990s, other Canadian service and cultural industries were likewise engaged in arguments over inclusivity and anti-oppression. In 1992, the same year that the Women of Colour Caucus was formed at Nellie's, the National Action Committee on the Status of Women withdrew its support for Ottawa's panel on violence against women, citing lack of representation for Indigenous women and women of colour.[38] In the writing and publishing industry, conflicts over voice, authority, and systematized exclusion also came to a head when the hegemony of the white literary establishment was challenged by Indigenous writers and writers of colour.[39] In 1992, an ad hoc committee within the Writers Union of Canada began raising issues of access, representation, and marginalization at a historic writer's retreat at Geneva Park, Ontario. This committee would be instrumental in later forming the Racial Minority Writers Committee (RMWC) and in staging the ground-breaking 1994 Writing Thru Race Conference in Vancouver, where prominent writers like Lenore Keeshig-Tobias and Roy Miki would lead participants in some of Canada's first major public debates about voice appropriation and racism in the literary arts.[40] Like the Women of Colour Caucus, the RMWC was received with hostility on the part of many "white writers [who] felt that they were being invaded" as well as censored.[41] However, as Keeshig-Tobias points out in her landmark 1990 *Globe and Mail* editorial, "Stop Stealing Native Stories," the issue is about so much more than "censorship" and the freedom of "artistic imagination:"[42] it is about a broader struggle for social and material justice.[43] Gail Guthrie Valaskakis explains how the focus on censorship and political correctness actually masks "the lived experience and problems of people of colour and people of the First Nations; neglecting the relationship between representation, appropriation and access, and social and political formations which position people of colour and Native North Americans as other and unequal."[44]

Like these contemporaneous debates over voice and representation in national women's organizations and in the publishing industry, the conflict at Nellie's reflects a broader struggle on the part of Indigenous peoples and people of colour to transform racist "social and political formations."[45] The Women of Colour Caucus at Nellie's specifically tried to address, within their own organization, mainstream feminism's "well-documented failure to engage race and acknowledge the complicity of white women in the history of domination."[46] Meanwhile, both internal and public responses to the conflict revealed how "feminist ideals of justice and egalitarian community" aligned with Canadian "national discourses of tolerance, benevolence, and nonracism" in order to disavow white complicity and the reality of ongoing colonial oppression.[47]

The Conflict at Nellie's Shelter

Named for women's rights activist and politician Nellie McClung, Nellie's was incorporated in 1973, making it one of Canada's first women's shelters.[48] The non-profit, community-based organization now operates a thirty-six-bed emergency shelter for women and children, as well as transitional housing and follow-up outreach and support service programs for women who have left the shelter and now live in the community. The shelter program also offers on-site counselling services and provides advocacy for women accessing medical, legal, employment, housing, and education services. Like many feminist front-line agencies today, Nellie's operates these programs under the expressed mission of "an anti-racist, anti-oppression framework."[49] This came about following official "restructuring" in 1998, when a strengthened mission statement was developed to "ensure an integrated feminist, anti-racist, anti-oppression framework" in "all aspects" of the shelter's work.[50] Nellie's "Herstory" states: "We have written a new chapter in Nellie's herstory by paying attention to our past, learning from it, and making changes that have created a new future."

Complicating this progressive narrative of history, in which Nellie's specific history of anti-oppression struggle and debate is effaced, I draw from a number of published news sources and editorials in order to recount the events leading up to and following the height of debate at Nellie's in 1992. My intent is to weave, from among the multiple accounts of the "trouble at Nellie's,"[51] a textually and historically specific example of anti-oppression policy debates. The accounts are in many ways outwardly specific to Nellie's, and yet they reveal much about the broader debates taking place in feminist service agencies and cultural sectors across Canada at the time. In my analysis of these accounts, I consider the principal scripts through which calls for and against anti-racist change were made in the early 1990s, and trouble the narrative of seamless anti-racist progression by which we popularly understand this history today.

From the start, the most public aspects of the conflict at Nellie's revolved around a core disagreement between founding board member and well-known Canadian journalist June Callwood and members of the newly formed Women of Colour Caucus, whose purpose was to advocate for better services for Nellie's racialized clients.[52] At the November 1991 meeting in which the Caucus first raised concerns about the shelter's discriminatory treatment of women of colour and immigrant women, heated discussion reportedly followed. This culminated in an alleged "tirade" from Callwood, who is said to have declared: "Put aside your fucking differences. I don't want to hear that crap."[53] The implication was that Nellie's had a broader feminist mandate to consider, and that the issue of non-discriminatory service provision for women of colour was an unnecessary "obstruction."[54] The on-staff women of colour felt slighted and silenced by this response; in subsequent staff meetings the discussion then quickly moved from broader debates around diversified client services and "who needed Nellie's" most, to more specific discussions about Nellie's "power structure and who calls the shots."[55] The conflict that ensued reflected not only competing priorities in service delivery models, but also mounting tensions around the racialized power asymmetries of the feminist collective. The women of colour contended that their contributions were considered unimportant, and, moreover, that "their white colleagues were refusing to comprehend the extent of the problem"[56]—namely, that the silencing of the Caucus's concerns stemmed not merely from the personal attitudes of individual staff and board members, but also from a system of uneven power relations that implicitly devalued and marginalized women of colour.[57] And so the Nellie's Women of Colour Caucus got to work—first of their own accord, and then with the outside support of the Toronto-based Coalition of Women of Color Working in Women's and Community Services, whose mission it was "to address inequities in the workplace as they affect women of color."[58] The Caucus "wrote letters, brought the subject up at staff meetings and went to the centre's personnel committee."[59] Amid outright expressions of hostility aimed at the Caucus by some white staff members, the issue was brought before the board of directors on December 3, 1991.[60]

There are several competing accounts of what happened at the December board meeting. According to journalist Margaret Cannon's analysis of the Nellie's conflict in *The Invisible Empire: Racism in Canada* (1995), most reports concur on this point: that one-time client and then staff member Joan Johnson, "weeping with emotion," read "a long, rambling, and highly personal letter that she and Karen Hinds, another woman of colour on the Nellie's staff, had written."[61] In this letter, Cannon said, "one cry stands out": Johnson would not be silenced anymore—it was "time for her to be heard."[62] Notably, however, the Coalition itself would later characterize Johnson's speech as a "statement"—not a personal letter. The Coalition also emphasized the speech's primary rhetorical purpose: to persuade the board of the "importance of addressing the problem of racism generally for the sake of all the women Nellie's serves."[63] A published excerpt from the statement appeared in a *Toronto Star* editorial later written by Donna Barker and Carolann Wright on behalf of the Coalition. It read, in part:

> We have to empower these women (residents).... It defeats the purpose to tell them they are equal and then treat them in devaluing and intimidating ways. Our service has to be free from discrimination. The challenge to Nellie's is this: Do we validate the struggle of all women, across the barriers of class, race, sexual orientation and all kinds of oppression, by doing all within our power to eliminate these obstacles? Or do we deny these women and engage systematically in their oppression? We will not be silenced any more.... We are now bringing it to you, the board of directors. Can any of you for a minute put yourselves in our shoes?[64]

Rhetorically, the statement attains a striking balance between the strategic appeal to affective identification and empathy ("Can any of you for a minute put yourselves in our shoes?"), and an uncompromising critique of discriminatory service provision ("It defeats the purpose to tell [women] they are equal and then treat them in devaluing and intimidating ways"). Its selective use of the plural personal pronoun "we" moreover reframes as a *collective responsibility* that which was reportedly dismissed by white staff and board members as divisive and obstructionist: to work "across barriers of class, race, sexual orientation and all kinds of oppression." Through its reflexive use of rhetorical questions, the statement also presents listeners with a stark choice: will workers "validate the struggle of all women," or "engage systematically in their oppression?" Intended to implicate its audience in both the conflict itself, and in its potential resolution, the statement reconstitutes the personal experience of systemic racism within a relational framework of analysis and intervention. As Himani Bannerji explains: "The social signifiers of an oppressive experience can be 'shared' by others who inhabit the same social relations of ruling but benefit from them."[65] Both "white people and non-whites" experience racism; they are just positioned differently by it.[66] As a declaration of protest as well as an invitation to solidarity in anti-racist service provision, the speech names white supremacy but also presumes the necessity of white participation in anti-oppression work. In short, Johnson's statement analyzes her experiential knowledge of racism in the feminist service sector and challenges her colleagues to confront and transform their own complicity with racist structures. When the statement was instead framed as a "rambling, and highly personal letter" in the public debates that followed,[67] its contribution was depoliticized and white complicity was denied.[68] Further to this, patently incredulous responses to Johnson's charge of racism revealed her detractors' trust in a white feminist moral imaginary invested in "benevolence and innocence."[69] Fellows and Razack elaborate on the concept of innocence in the context of feminist solidarity as the "deeply felt belief that each of us, as women, is not implicated in the subordination of other women. When we view ourselves as innocent, we cannot confront the hierarchies that operate among us."[70] The reception of Johnson's statement, both in the board meeting itself and in the public debates that followed, shows how depoliticization and innocence worked in tandem to disavow white experiential knowledge of (and responsibility for) racist oppression.

In the meeting itself, Johnson's speech was met with mixed responses—ranging in tone "from sympathetic to ragingly defensive."[71] Some board members reportedly responded with "the usual comments: 'Thank you for sharing your pain. What can we do?'"[72] By contrast, June Callwood angrily questioned how Johnson—a past recipient of Nellie's services and a woman "whom the staff had harboured, nurtured, [and] given a job"[73]—could possibly accuse the staff of racism. Callwood reminded Johnson that Nellie's had "broken rules" for her,[74] and insinuated that she should be "grateful for the help instead of complaining about racism."[75] To this, Johnson replied: "Do I have to be grateful all my life?"[76] Notably, Callwood's response was considered out of bounds by both staff and board members alike; her remarks effectively outed Johnson as a past resident of the shelter—an egregious breach of confidentiality. Beyond violating Johnson's right to confidentiality, however, Callwood's reaction also revealed something of the power asymmetries which structured the terms on which Johnson entered her testimony "on the record."[77]

Each of the reactions to Johnson's statement—though running the gamut from sympathetic to vociferously incredulous—is arguably rooted in a claim to innocence. For example, in the sympathetic response that would thank Johnson for "sharing [her] pain,"[78] the statement is recast as a personal confession of distress—as "catharsis" rather than critique.[79] As Srivastava's study of anti-racist challenges in feminist organizations suggests, this kind of reaction performs a feminist "ethic of care" that nonetheless denies the listener's possible complicity with racist structures and aligns instead with a "discourse of tolerance," benevolence, and good intentions.[80] Mohawk legal scholar Patricia Monture-Angus discusses the reasons why this position of innocence is problematic despite its ostensibly good intentions: the bewildered offer—"What can I do to help?"—effectively "buys into the 'I am better than you are' routine."[81] It is a position of presumed benevolent superiority that denies white responsibility for the burden of anti-racist action. As Monture-Angus says, "How can you continue to look to me to carry what is your responsibility?"[82] By refusing to acknowledge or change the underlying relation of power, and instead casting Johnson's "pain" as only her own, the sympathetic listener maintains a relative position of innocence—and of power. Meanwhile, in the defensive reaction that would accuse Johnson of being ungrateful, her statement is recast as a personal affront rather than a politically legitimate appeal. In the Coalition's analysis, Callwood's incredulous response bespoke a paternalistic expectation of "gratitude from women of colour"[83]—holding women of colour "hostage to benevolence and missionary-style charity work that requires [them] to be grateful."[84] In this way, whether board members responded with sympathy or with incredulity, this same notion of non-racism—of feminism's inherently "progressive egalitarianism" and innocence—was at work.[85]

In response to Callwood's confrontational outburst, and particularly the violation of Johnson's confidentiality, the board asked Callwood to apologize. According to most sources she did, but Johnson did not accept the apology.[86] Subsequently, some sources have focused on whether or not Callwood's solicited apology was sufficient, and on whether or not it was genuine.[87] Comparatively little attention has been paid to the discursive function the apology itself might have served, and to its potential role in further entrenching the benevolent paternalism that Johnson's speech was calculated to disrupt. Like the example of Canada's official apology for residential schooling, Callwood's apology may outwardly have functioned as a conciliatory expression intended to assure others of her good intentions. However, this gesture simultaneously worked to re-embed the very power asymmetries for which it performed contrition in the first place. In this sense, apology signalled not a definitive break from the paternalism that characterized Nellie's relationship with Johnson in the past, but rather the continuation of this relation. Johnson's pointed refusal—first, to be "grateful for the help instead of complaining about racism,"[88] and second, to be suitably indebted to Callwood's apology—pushed back against her statement's emplacement in a script of painful disclosure and conciliatory redress.

Some thought "the crisis would be over after Callwood apologized."[89] However, the apology served only to deepen the stalemate. As one board member reportedly declared, "This [was] a continuation of racist behavior."[90] In the subsequent fallout from the December board meeting, the Women of Colour Caucus and the Toronto-wide Coalition rallied their efforts once more, this time issuing a "tightly worded list of demands" that would not be confused as a "personal" disclosure of pain.[91] These demands included "improved equity hiring practices, a clear grievance policy, a strong anti-racist mission statement, and new evaluation and training procedures."[92] In hindsight, Callwood herself conceded that many of these demands "were sensible and long-overdue,"[93] though the Caucus's newly phrased requests did not much differ from the previously stated concerns to which Callwood and others had expressed resistance. The Caucus had been asking for the development of an anti-racist mandate all along, and, ironically, it was the lack of a standard grievance policy that led Johnson to appeal to the board of directors for help in the first place. In this now embattled climate following the board meeting, however, the Caucus made one additional demand: the last item on the list called for Callwood's resignation, for being "emotionally and verbally abusive to women of colour on staff and for violating confidentiality as to the history of a former resident."[94] It was at this stage that the conflict at Nellie's became public in a new way. Nellie's gained widespread media attention when, in May of 1992, June Callwood resigned amid charges of racism.

The media storm that ensued at the time of Callwood's resignation predictably characterized the conflict as a battle between well-meaning, white liberal women with undisputed feminist credentials in the mainstream anti-violence movement, and a "small group of power-hungry" women of colour who "wanted to get their hands on the hostel and its jobs and bank accounts."[95] This popular account—although by no means the only interpretation of events in circulation at the time—starkly illustrates the climate of backlash in which the Women of Colour Caucus and other anti-racist organizers were operating. That Callwood could be accused of racism was received with bitter astonishment. As author Pierre Berton quipped without irony: "If Callwood is a racist then so are we all."[96] This sentiment was backed by the many letters of support that cluttered the pages of Toronto newspapers in the weeks and months following the story's break; Callwood's supporters balked at the suggestion that "a woman so committed to doing good could possibly be tossed out on her keester, from a hostel she founded, for being 'racist.'"[97] As Elaine Dewar asserted in her *Toronto Life* account, Callwood's "strength came from the defence of the voiceless. She had always wrapped herself in other people's problems."[98] Dewar further explained: "Racists are people who believe in the supremacy of one race over another and are willing to enforce their ideas by any means, including violence"; they are not "women working in women's services."[99] In short, mainstream journalists and citizen commentators defended Callwood as the one "who has been victimized."[100] By positioning Callwood and white feminists as "victims" in this debate, the media coverage participated in hardening the hierarchical relations of power against which the Caucus was organizing. The coverage insisted upon Callwood's innocence, and thereby further entrenched the notion that "the systems that oppress [women] are unconnected from the ones in which [women] are privileged."[101]

As Akua Benjamin, Judy Rebick, and Amy Go contend in their thoughtful analysis of the Nellie's conflict, "the suggestion that there was something sinister about a group with little power organizing to get more power, is antithetical to everything the women's movement has stood for" and ultimately "aim[s] to maintain a white-dominated status quo"[102] Carolann Wright of the Coalition of Women of Color further remarks that in order for this status quo to change, there must be "a willingness and mental capacity in the people there to give up power, to share it.... Sometimes, white women have to be in the background."[103] Wright's comment offers a relational analysis of oppression, and of solidarity—one that both critiques the retreat to innocence and indicates the strategies by which unearned power and privilege can be undermined. This position holds that white women must take direction and leadership from women of colour in anti-racist organizing; as Harsha Walia similarly notes of Indigenous solidarity organizing, "from an anti-oppression perspective, meaningful support for Indigenous struggles cannot be directed by non-natives."[104] In the case of the Nellie's conflict, however, public accounts continued to re-centre whiteness and protect white privilege, characterizing the debate as a localized conflict between well-intentioned (i.e., legitimate) feminists and a cabal of "hate-mongering" women of colour.[105]

The discord at Nellie's was not a localized event, but was in fact part of a much broader debate taking place across Canada in the late 1980s and early 1990s. This debate, which was fought in the social services industry, in education, and in publishing, spoke to an emergent critical shift toward de-centring the "white-dominated status quo."[106] As Sophie McCall puts it, debates over "the politics of 'voice' and of representation were becoming increasingly heated in a broad range of arenas."[107] Of concern in the publishing industry, for example, "were the material conditions of the publication, distribution, and circulation of texts" and of whose voice was accorded authority.[108] As in the front-line feminist service industry, these debates were often attended by a "motif of reverse racism" and an anxiety about the "tyranny of political correctness."[109] This had the effect of reframing a much-needed discussion about resources, policy, access, and justice as a debate about the prospective exclusion and restraint of white voices. The aforementioned 1994 Writing Thru Race conference is one example of how anti-racist organizing was received with skepticism and outright opposition that re-centred whiteness and claimed innocence from systemic racism. As an earlier example, Manina Jones and others cite the "rift in the editorial board that took place at the Women's Press in 1987 over its policies relating to issues of cultural appropriation. The board of the Toronto-based feminist publishing house had divided in a conflict over the ethics of publishing stories written by white women but articulated from the perspectives of women of colour."[110] Caribbean Canadian writer M. Nourbese Philip argues of the Women's Press debate that underlying issues of access for Indigenous writers and writers of colour were forgotten when the charge of censorship came to the fore; the issue then became "whether White middle class women ought or ought not to be allowed ... to use the voice of traditionally oppressed groups."[111] As a form of cultural theft, voice appropriation is informed by material and political asymmetries;[112] McCall emphasizes how its reframing in terms of censorship actually serves to "sideline" the very "institutional, structural, and material issues" that Philip highlights.

In some cases, debates over racism in Canadian publishing intersected with the front-line feminist service industry in provocative ways. In 1989, members of the Multicultural Women Writers of Canada and Vision 21 demonstrated outside of the 54th PEN Congress (an international group that works on behalf of imprisoned writers) in order to bring attention to the fact that "there was and is a very real problem with racism in writing and publishing here in Canada which, in many instances, serves to silence African, Asian, and First Nations writers."[113] Among those picketing the PEN Congress was M. Nourbese Philip.

When Philip approached then-incoming president of PEN Canada—none other than June Callwood—with a leaflet, Callwood famously told Philip to "fuck off."[114] As Philip later mused, "The irony is that as President of PEN Canada, June Callwood is the head of an organization whose members are sworn to uphold freedom of speech, particularly for writers, the world over."[115] This incident is sometimes seen as indirectly precipitating the conflict at Nellie's that followed.

Following the controversy at Nellie's, the Coalition of Women of Color asked: "What happens when women of color speak up, when we make criticisms or suggestions, when we insist that bad treatment towards us stop and that our voices be heard? Well, the fiasco at Nellie's is a perfect example of what happens."[116] Though the Coalition is referring to the immediate context in which their voices were silenced, this comment also has implications for what happens when politicized appeals get reconstituted as personal disclosures of pain—or when calls to anti-racist solidarity are received with defensive disavowal. Joan Johnson delivered her statement to the board at Nellie's in hopes of galvanizing board members to back formalized anti-racist change—change that did eventually come to Nellie's in the form of an "integrated feminist, anti-racist, anti-oppression framework" for service delivery.[117] The reception and management of Johnson's unsolicited testimony, however, affords some insight into the more subtle and covert ways in which "silencing" might work. The Coalition provocatively stated: "Attempting to silence us will not work."[118] I now want to ask: how do some institutionalized methods for breaking silence, and for hearing dissent, indeed carry within them new and more insidious forms of silencing? I will briefly explore one such strategy, often called the "storytelling" method in anti-oppression training, before then turning to an analysis of Morningstar Mercredi's memoir and the case of its reception.

Storytelling in Anti-Oppression

Like other feminist organizations in the 1990s, Nellie's struggled (and at times failed) to hear the women of colour who were "fighting for equal participation and a voice within the women's movement and agencies."[119] The anti-racist challenge has led front-line feminist agencies like Nellie's to adopt anti-oppression mandates and to include standard "diversity" or "cultural sensitivity" training as part of their staff and volunteer education in anti-oppression frameworks.[120] Redressing the "one-size fits all approach" that characterized earlier organizational attitudes toward anti-violence work,[121] these workshops often institute a form of multicultural pedagogy where women of colour are called upon to communicate their personal knowledge of racism for the educational benefit of their white interlocutors. Such a model does make formal space for discussions about the intersectional contexts of gendered oppression. However, it also re-centres whiteness by prioritizing the educational needs of white staff and volunteers over the possibility of redressing racialized power asymmetries. This approach moreover naturalizes the assumption, now firmly entrenched in liberal education initiatives, that all one needs in order to challenge racism is more knowledge and understanding of "others." As Goli Rezai-Rashti suggests, multicultural education understands racism as "the product of ignorance, which, in turn, is perpetuated by individual prejudice and negative attitudes;"[122] in this model, countering racism means simply learning more about racial "others" and their experiences—often through a one-sided exchange of stories.

Sarita Srivastava calls this the "let's talk" model[123] or "storytelling" approach to organizational reform.[124] This approach uses personal storytelling in group settings as a way to negotiate and potentially diffuse fractious organizational tensions around racism and anti-racist debate. Srivastava's work demonstrates how the "let's talk" model shapes the discussion in ways that "can deflect, suppress and personalize anti-racist change efforts."[125] Wendy Brown terms this deflective move *depoliticization*: in this context, experiential knowledge of racism is received as either "personal and individual, on one hand," or as "natural, religious, or cultural on the other."[126] This is in part because the storytelling method tends to individualize conflict and shift the analysis away from systemically maintained inequitable conditions, but also because it positions Indigenous women and women of colour as objects of allegedly "authentic" cultural knowledge whose experiences of racism can be consumed as an educational exercise. The underlying notion at work is that, by listening to the stories of "other" women, white women will become more "culturally sensitive" and will be better prepared—by virtue of their empathetic encounters with these "native informants"[127]—to carry out anti-racist reform. As Lee Maracle remarks in *I Am Woman*: "White women invite us to speak if the issue is racism or Native people. We are there to teach, to sensitize them or to serve them in some way. We are expected to retain our position well below them, as their servants. We are not, as a matter of course, invited as an integral part of 'their movement'—the women's movement."[128] In this way, a method purportedly designed to legitimize—and to *hear*—about systemic racism has also become the method by which these claims are depoliticized or diffused.

The storytelling strategy of organizational reform can be linked to a broader historical movement in feminist critique wherein experiential understandings of oppression were validated as a political form of knowledge.[129] The storytelling approach is rooted in second-wave feminism's efforts to legitimize personal experience as a politically relevant basis for advancing social analysis and change.[130] Yet, when deployed in the moment of cultural recognition, this method tends to subvert the political efficacy of so-called personal articulations of pain (as when Johnson's appeal was characterized as personal catharsis, rather than politicized critique). Athabaskan critic Dian Million likewise notes connections between the feminist movement's political reconstitution of the "private" or domestic sphere, and the advent of social and therapeutic practices around "consciousness-raising" in the 1970s and '80s.[131] Million points to the affinities between these "talking therapies," originally designed to enable the politicization of white experiences of gendered violence, and the amenability of this storytelling method to Indigenous epistemologies wherein story functions as a crucial site of memory, law, and knowledge.[132]

Million's reading of these affinities reveals the extent to which positivist conceptions of experience have been vital to the project of theorizing personal and communal knowledges among different, historically minoritized subjects.[133] And yet there are crucial distinctions to be made between the particular institutionalized storytelling practices of dominant service agencies, as implemented amid the complex push-pull of colonial imposition and strategic or resistive appropriation, and those practices which are unassimilable to this framework—such as storytelling practices that do not, as Craig Womack puts it, derive authority from "outside" recognition, but rather from "internal" processes of "recognition, practice," and transmission.[134] In drawing from the work of critics whose task has been to theorize storytelling within Indigenous epistemologies, I mean to signal a critical distance between Indigenous knowledges and Eurocentric world views into which they cannot be simply collapsed.[135] Part of this project, then, is to be attentive to those moments in which incommensurable storytelling practices have been uncritically collapsed. Not all instances of storytelling are "culturally intelligible" modes of knowledge production; sometimes this label may also be a means for rendering inscrutable the liberal capturing and recasting of experiential knowledge toward specifically interested ends.

With respect to Indigenous storytelling practices, Chickasaw legal scholar James (Sákéj) Youngblood Henderson suggests: "The key rule is that the listener must accept that regardless of what information he or she *may have requested*, it is an Elder or Storykeeper that determines the best way to tell a story or convey the teaching the story contains."[136] This theorization of storytelling—as a communal practice imbued with responsibility—illuminates the decolonial potential of Indigenous storytelling practices to reframe dominant narratives about colonial violence and absolution: narratives as requested and consumed in the *mise en discours* of cultural recognition become considerably more complicated when the "listener is [made] part of the event too."[137] Listening here comes with responsibilities of interpretation and understanding that go beyond liberal forms of recognition toward a witnessing that is instead, in Beth Brant's words, "intense and intentional."[138] While the storytelling approach has sometimes been applied not as a culturally intelligible mode for the transmission of knowledge about gendered colonial oppression, but rather as a covert strategy for the production of knowledge about racialized others, Indigenous women have wielded the resistive capacity of Indigenous storytelling to reframe listeners' responsibilities. The example of Beverley Jacobs's response to the government's apology for residential schooling is instructive in this regard. In this moment of national redress that would, as Pauline Wakeham suggests, secure the testimony of Indigenous respondents as evidence of the state's "enlightened" capacity to learn from "past" wrongs,[139] Jacobs resists the government's apology as an occasion to seek conciliatory closure on "this sad chapter in our history."[140] Jacobs' request for respect—in return for the government's apology—both reveals and performatively redistributes the uneven power relation structured by the state's public act of contrition. Jacobs's statement then also reconstitutes the status of her testimony—not as a disclosure compelled in the moment of cultural recognition, but as a story meriting reciprocal response. Jacobs said: "Two generations ago, my grandmother, being a Mohawk woman, was beaten, sexually beaten and physically beaten, for being a Mohawk woman."[141] With this, she calls up both the intergenerational and gendered impacts of residential schools, and further states, "Women have taken the brunt of it all."[142] Here, the moment of storytelling works against the grain of multicultural recognition by offering information that, although (and perhaps because) it was not "requested" (to use Henderson's phrase), conveys resistive knowledge toward political ends, opening up a space from which she asks: "What is it that this government is going to do in the future? … What is going to be provided?"[143] Although this story is necessarily produced from within the state's frame of remorse and pardon, it simultaneously works against it.

At this juncture, I want to explore how storytelling might function in a similarly resistive fashion in the literary context of Indigenous women's life writing. In activist and literary sites alike, the personal narrative form has been theorized as "a means for women to employ their own autobiographical accounts as sources of knowledge."[144] This has been the case in both feminist and post-colonial conceptions of autobiography, to the extent that both forms comprise "the coming to voice of previously silenced subjects."[145] As such, I want to expand my discussion of the "storytelling" form from the activist context of anti-violence service agencies to the subject of Indigenous women's life writing—highlighting that in neither the activist nor the literary setting is this "coming to voice" an unmediated or transparent process of resistance. The "let's talk" or storytelling model of anti-oppression pedagogy and "culturally sensitive" reform has been heavily contoured by colonial power asymmetries that necessarily shape the conditions under which some stories get told. The literature of the "still-colonized," as Jo-Ann Episkenew puts it, must likewise be read with consideration for the colonial contexts in which it is written and received.[146] For, just as the "storytelling" model of anti-oppression (with its interest in the personal narratives of so-called "other" women) may risk depoliticizing racial conflict and fetishizing the empathetic identificatory processes taken up by listeners, so too has the life writing of Indigenous women often been received as the "artless" truth of Indigenous women's experiences.[147]

Indigenous Women's Memoir and Reception: *Morningstar: A Warrior's Spirit*

Certainly, this would seem to be the case in the reception of Dene (Chipewyan) activist-writer Morningstar Mercredi's *Morningstar: A Warrior's Spirit* (2006). This memoir is often said to provide readers unmediated access to its author's journey of healing from intergenerational residential school trauma. Recalling "a jigsaw puzzle of pictures," places, and events that shaped her early and adolescent life, Mercredi recounts in the first half of her memoir the "years of moving back and forth between Fort Chipewyan, Uranium City and Edmonton."[148] These years are marked by a lack of stability in home life due to her mother's alcoholism and emotional neglect, and by the trauma of her stepfather's ongoing sexual abuse. Mercredi "sifted like sand through the lives of relatives and friends as [she] tried to fit in";[149] yet, "fearing human contact" and turning often to drugs and alcohol as coping mechanisms, she remains throughout her adolescence largely "detached and unfeeling."[150] Following the birth of her son Matthew at eighteen, she begins a complex process of recovery that involves not only "coming in off the streets" and battling relapse,[151] but also beginning to "face [her] past honestly"[152] by acknowledging her "sexual abuse without shame."[153] Significantly, this means for Mercredi the development of an analysis of her "own issues" in relation to "what wasn't" hers—those "attitudes that were projected onto [her]" as a Native woman.[154] It also entails developing an analysis of herself as a survivor of intergenerational residential school trauma: "I became aware of the links between parent and child that were almost severed," Mercredi reflects, "and of the tragedies of family and community genocide. I finally saw myself as part of the big picture."[155] Seeing herself as part of this "big picture," and arriving at an understanding of how residential schooling in Canada irrevocably shaped her life's story, Mercredi recounts in the final chapters of her memoir the process by which she emerged from the "abyss of rage and confusion" in order to find "peace" and "forgiveness."[156] In researching residential schooling, and in interviewing women who attended the Holy Angels Mission school her mother had attended, Mercredi "realized that the disturbing cycles of abuse and neglect are cohesive to Canadian history and genocide of Aboriginal people."[157] Insofar as the reader is asked to share in this realization, the memoir ultimately politicizes and historicizes what many reviewers have nonetheless insistently characterized as an individualized experience of abuse and recovery.

As one reviewer claims, Mercredi tells, with "brutal honesty," the story of "a woman's difficult journey through racism, poverty and addictions, to eventual recovery and healing."[158] According to another review, the memoir is rendered in an "unadorned style" punctuated with purportedly "simple declarative sentences" that "powerfully convey" the "honest[y]" of this "affecting account."[159] Of course, "style"—"unadorned" or not—would still constitute a calculated stylistic effect. In fact, Mercredi employs a number of aesthetic techniques—including, notably, a shifting between first- and third-person narration, and between italicized and non-italicized typescript, as a way to textually mark a dissociative split in the autobiographical subject's narrativization of traumatic memory. In the opening passages of *A Warrior's Spirit*, for instance, Mercredi relates in third-person italicized script a memory of herself at five years old, engaged in what a reviewer calls a "desperate 21-block flight, barefoot, to find her mother in a bar."[160] In the memoir, this account introduces readers to Mercredi, not from the standpoint of a dominant autobiographical "I"—what Sidonie Smith and Julia Watson call the "sign of the Enlightenment subject, unified, rational, coherent, autonomous, free, but also white, male, Western"[161]—but rather from a limited third-person perspective that confronts the dominant colonial gaze that would fantasize the "Indian as victim" from a position of remove:[162]

> *She runs across the street, startled like a coyote in the oncoming headlights. Pebbles hurt her bare feet, but she doesn't notice the pain. Buses, cars and*

people pass. Some of them glance at her only briefly with curiosity, while others stop for a moment and stare as a five-year-old girl in pyjamas panics past them. Their stares unnerve her.[163]

This opening passage relates the experience of a young Dene girl whose "long walk" up Edmonton's Jasper Avenue is here recalled by the older, more reflexive autobiographical counterpart, Mercredi.[164] As a memory of an unnerving and even traumatic experience—the young girl is in this moment escaping from a babysitter who "hurt us when he touched us, making my sisters cry"[165]—this opening is as much about the fearful knowledge that "her sisters are locked in the basement suite with the babysitter,"[166] as it is about the daunting downtown cityscape that "tower(s) over her" and the sirens that "scream past."[167] However, there exists a subtler subtext to this opening passage—one that conveys not only the trauma of abuse or neglect, or even the "inherited" context "of alcoholism and violence" in which we learn this abuse takes place,[168] but also the colonial gaze that would here consume it. The curiosity of those who watch as "a five-year-old girl in pyjamas panics past"[169] belongs to both the spectators who observe from their cars, and potentially to the readers who now cast their eyes upon the initial pages of this memoir. In this way, Mercredi effectively turns the colonial gaze back on itself, embedding within her narrative's opening passage a subtle address to a dominant readership here represented by the impassive glances and curious stares of passersby. Mercredi relates a yet more direct and unmistakable address to white readers in the memoir's introduction (of which I offer some brief discussion shortly), and in subsequent passages that are likewise formally demarcated from the main body of the narrative by their italicized typescript. In this passage, however, the appeal to a non-Indigenous readership is inferred; the voyeuristic act of *looking*, and the unnerving experience of being *looked at*, are here placed in evocative tension as embodied practices necessarily contoured by the uneven relations of power that condition each subject's position in the storytelling exchange. In this way, the memoir engages the issue of (re)-viewing practices—of the power asymmetries that shape the telling and "hearing" of painful stories—from the outset, refiguring the moment of cultural recognition through a visual metaphor.

The opening passage thus challenges the text's prospective reception as the unmediated "emotion[al]," "rambling," and "intimate"[170] account of "growing up poor and aboriginal while suffering abuse,"[171] in part by inviting (and then overturning) a misrecognition on the part of its imagined readership. Through its performative enactment of a confessional-style narrative in which the silence around childhood abuse is ostensibly broken,[172] the memoir seems to promise a "simple tale" of abuse "suffered" and then overcome through the process of storytelling itself.[173] And yet, the text goes on to complicate these expectations through its strategic reversal of the colonial gaze that would consume this so-called "simple tale" with either the voyeuristic "empathy or violent animosity" afforded by a position of comfortable remove.[174] In this way Mercredi makes manifest the reader's status as "part of the event too."[175] For instance, while reflecting upon how the dominant public receives stories of Indigenous "women who are exploited or abused,"[176] Mercredi addresses her prospective white readership directly: "Don't shame my skin. You don't know what my skin has carried me through. What do you see when you look at me, standing cold and alone on the street?"[177]

Donna Haraway suggests that vision "is *always* a question of the power to see—and perhaps of the violence implicit in our visualizing practices."[178] *A Warrior's Spirit* self-consciously engages and resists the implicit violence of a viewing practice that would position itself outside a relation of reciprocal responsibility. However, like Johnson's statement to the Nellie's board, this process takes place within a complex and uneven terrain of power where speaking "truth to power" does not guarantee an equally self-reflexive and ethical response. For instance, Ken Tingley's review in the *Edmonton Journal* strategically deploys the second-person pronoun as a way to embed the memoir within a frame of metaphorized spectacle to be visually consumed from a safe distance, ironically performing precisely the kind of reviewing practice Mercredi's opening seems calculated to resist. The review, for its part, opens in this way:

> Your car rolls along one of those streets found in every Canadian city. It's night, and people stand in the alleys and shadows. You unconsciously check to ensure that the doors are locked. You don't really look too carefully at

the passing scene, a bit apprehensive about what you might see. You may not want to know the stories behind the faces you ... see in those shadows. Morningstar is one of those stories. It is certainly not a pleasant reading experience, but it is an important one.[179]

The review effectively naturalizes a presumed subject position of privilege for its audience and, through the use of the pronoun "you," positions its readers as embodying a touristic gaze. Like the seemingly ubiquitous trope of the darkened, urban city street to which Christine Welsh's *Finding Dawn* responds in its strategic reframing of Vancouver's Downtown Eastside, Tingley's metaphorized account of reading this memoir can be placed within a broader tradition of social journalism which traffics in what Elizabeth Povinelli calls "guilty glances over ... shoulders into history, or the slum down the block."[180] In this form of reportage, from Blanchard Jerrold and Gustave Doré's forays into the "strange, dark byeways"[181] of London's East End in their 1872 *London: A Pilgrimage*, to journalist Stevie Cameron's recent depiction of Vancouver's Downtown Eastside in *The Pickton File*, the conditions of classed, gendered, and racialized others are documented for the consumption of a mainstream readership whose reading practice is then problematically positioned as a form of socially conscious labour.[182] In Tingley's review, Mercredi's memoir is arguably appropriated as providing a depoliticized account of oppression in which the storytelling subject is individualized, while the reader is positioned comfortably outside a relation of responsibility as a benign (and even benevolent) but ultimately unimplicated viewer. Meanwhile, the "importance" of reading this memoir is positioned as a kind of unpleasant but necessary liberal duty to both recognize and yet move firmly beyond the shame of Canada's colonial past and into the post-colonial future.

Readers of this memoir frequently characterize their reading experience as one of decidedly uncomfortable, unpleasant, but necessary listening. For instance, Laurel Smith remarks on the "litany of horrors" that leaves the reader "feeling somewhat overwhelmed," an effect that, for Smith, produces a "lack of satisfaction with the book as a literary work."[183] Trevor Greyeyes likewise contends that this otherwise worthy "first-person story about an aboriginal woman's experience growing up in Western Canada" in fact "*suffers* from constant references to pseudo-psychiatric jargon and knee-jerk reactions of aboriginals blaming residential schools for everything."[184] However, like Tingley, Smith for her part also concludes: "Mercredi's remains a story that needs to be told."[185] How might we account for this phenomenon, whereby readers feel alienated from and frustrated with this text, but nevertheless insist on the story's inherent social value? Algonquin playwright Yvette Nolan theorizes this critical tendency in terms of an "appetite for Native stories, [and] for Native experience" that is "tempered by a certain set of expectations."[186] These conditional expectations are not unlike those that have tempered recent acts of apology and public recognitions of "subaltern worth"—that is, as Povinelli puts it, "as long as they are not repugnant … as long as they are not, at heart, not-us."[187] Or rather, by extension: as long as they are not angry—as long as that anger is not beyond assimilation into a broader narrative trajectory of colonial relations recounted, lamented, and then overcome. The expression of anger, according to Nolan, disrupts the liberal impulse to assimilate "Native stories" into a palatable script of painful disclosure toward conciliatory redress, but it also provides a justification for offhand dismissal of the kind seen in Greyeyes's review: as Nolan puts it, "Mad is uncomfortable. Mad is threatening. Mad is passé. Get over it."[188] And here, too, we can see at work the same double bind that characterized the board's initial reaction to the challenge posed by Johnson's statement at Nellie's; whether sympathetic—because it has "become fashionable to tell the truth about" and empathize with "Native people"[189]—or defensive—because "mad is threatening"[190]—the consumption of others' stories, and of "Native" stories in particular, becomes not the means by which to "hear" other truths, but rather the means by which to recast the telling of trauma toward hegemonic ends.

In each of the sites I've explored throughout this chapter, whether activist or literary, uncomfortable or threatening challenges to the grand narrative of multicultural tolerance are reconstituted to confirm (rather than disprove) the national imaginary's commitment to reconciliation and healing. In these instances, Indigenous women's stories of colonial violence are afforded a "hearing,"[191] but perhaps only insofar as they can be assimilated into a script of closure and absolution. Whether in the case of Canada's official apology to residential school survivors, in the example of anti-racist reform in feminist agencies, or in the matter of Indigenous women's life writing, the concern with which I began this chapter remains: that the first-person testimony of Indigenous or other racialized subjects is consumed—in the moment of cultural recognition—in ways that are sometimes amenable to (rather than straightforwardly resistant of) colonial strategies of power. For, in whose interests is it that a narrative of colonial violence be received as a story of personal trauma told, and then "overcome"?[192] If this is a text that, by Mercredi's own estimation, contextualizes interpersonal and domestic forms of violence in terms of the broader, colonial context of residential school and its ongoing intergenerational effects, then there are specific political stakes involved in claiming that this "legacy of survival ... allowed her to heal and forgive both herself and those who abused her."[193]

Indeed, while both the reviewing public and the text's marketing overwhelmingly characterize the narrative as telling "one woman's victory over abuse" (back cover), this sits rather uneasily with Mercredi's own public insistence on her memoir as being as much an account of ongoing gendered colonial violence as an individual disclosure of "her own story" of healing and forgiveness.[194] For instance, during her participation on a 2007 panel of creative non-fiction writers at a literary festival session on "truth-telling," Mercredi responded to an audience member's question about "self-examination" and "healing" with the following statement: "I live in a country that is in denial of its own history."[195] Not unlike Jacobs's speech in the House of Commons and Johnson's statement before the board at Nellie's, Mercredi's pronouncement works against her narrative's emplacement in a spectacularized script of trauma disclosed toward conciliatory closure, while moreover drawing attention to the place of literary production in challenging what she terms the country's state of "denial."[196]

In this project, Mercredi's text belongs to a tradition of contemporary Indigenous women's life writing that arguably began with the 1973 publication of Métis author Maria Campbell's *Halfbreed*. Significantly, Campbell's text is prefaced by a statement of pedagogical intent, aimed in part at informing non-Indigenous readers about the material conditions of life for Métis people, and for Métis women in particular: "I write this for all of you, to tell you what it is like to be a Halfbreed woman in our country."[197] Mercredi's memoir is prefaced with a similarly direct appeal to her non-Indigenous readership. In this, she strategically tempers a politically instructive impetus with a call to affective empathy: "Imagine, if you can, a stranger coming to your door to take your children away.... Think the unthinkable.... Do these thoughts anger you, enrage you?"[198] This imperative to *imagine* also recalls Syilx writer Jeannette Armstrong's strategic appeal to non-Indigenous audiences in her 1990 address to the Saskatchewan Writers Guild: "You are writers," Armstrong states. "Imagine it on yourselves and your children. Imagine you and your children and imagine how they would be treated by those who abhorred and detested you, all, as savages without any rights."[199] Like Campbell and Armstrong before her, then, Mercredi asks her readers to engage (if only imaginatively) with the history of colonial violence in Canada. For Campbell, this necessarily involves an account of the processes of colonization that resulted in the displacement of her family and community from both land and aboriginal identity. For Mercredi, this involves an account of her family's history (and, in particular, her mother's history) within a legacy of residential school abuse. Mercredi thus begins her memoir by asserting herself as a "survivor of intergenerational impact of residential schools"[200]—a positioning that is further explored in one of the text's closing chapters when she explains: "I didn't attend the Holy Angels Mission [school]. I wasn't one of the thousands of children over four generations who were forced to. Then again, I didn't have to attend: What Mom, Dad, and Grandma learned—the good, bad, and indifferent—was passed on to me anyway. I remain a survivor of generational indoctrination and abuse."[201] Mercredi articulates the abuse suffered throughout her life as part of a broader context of colonial violence perpetrated by the residential school system. Her life narrative necessitates an understanding of interpersonal violence that is inseparable from state-sanctioned colonial violence. Readers of this memoir are thus challenged to witness interpersonal or "family" violence as a continuation of colonial policy.

Greg Younging (Cree) employs the concept of "blood memory" in order to describe the processes by which intergenerational survivors of residential schools may come to understand their family's experiences within a context of inherited trauma:

Our generation inherited this family history by just being who we are—part of the continuum of our ancestors' legacy right through to the few generations that preceded us. This was not by our own choice, and certainly this was not by our parents' choice as they attempted to shelter us from it, but the truth eventually prevails. Indigenous peoples often refer to our "blood memory," meaning that the experience of those that have gone before us is embedded in our physical and psychological being.[202]

For Younging, blood memory embeds not only experiential knowledges, but also inherited responsibilities. Identifying this as the "Indigenous precept" of both "honouring our ancestors' legacy and safeguarding the rights and well-being of future generations," he explores how the application of this ethic in the case of non-Indigenous Canadians could help to transform broader public understandings of responsibility.[203] Younging elaborates: "In order for this grand concept of reconciliation to work, Canadian people, too, need to inherit the history of those that have gone before them if they are to forge a better path into the future."[204] And this is ultimately what Mercredi recommends, as a first step toward ending violence: that the settler Canadian public stop dissociating themselves from the colonial history and present, and instead begin seeing their responsibility for forging a different set of relations. This is a process, and one which does not have as its prerequisite Indigenous forgiveness, as Rachel Flowers reminds us: "Forgiveness is a gesture reserved for the oppressed to capitulate their resentment to benevolently apologetic structures. In my attempt to gender resentment, I refer to the anger of Indigenous women as righteous; we continue to be the focus of heteropatriarchal colonial policy and practice of domination and dispossession. If we understand forgiveness as the relinquishment of resentment, then my only option as hwulmuhw slheni is refusal to forgive"[205]

A Warrior's Spirit likewise refuses to be reconciled, to "let it go"[206] or to "get over it" as Mercredi provocatively put it,[207] by including in the closing pages of the book—pages otherwise dedicated to a recounting of her "choice to live"[208] and to "move on in life"[209]—a reflection on what she terms a "killing spree in Canada" that targets Indigenous women and girls.[210] This gesture performs the individualized closure readers might expect from a narrative that traces an author's "healing" journey home, to "a new sense of self,"[211] while simultaneously refusing its audience closure on the issue of gendered colonial violence. Although Trevor Greyeyes laments in his review "that aboriginal women ... blame [both] residential schools and white men for all their problems,"[212] Mercredi's memoir pushes back against a frame that would have it reconciled with either, and moreover explores issues of gendered justice as vitally integral to (rather than detracting from) the broader goal of decolonization for both Indigenous and non-Indigenous peoples.[213]

The complication to which I have tried to be attentive, but simultaneously acknowledge I can't solve, is the ambiguity of *Morningstar: A Warrior's Spirit* as a resistive text. The memoir is prefaced with a call to all readers: "Let us ... step out of ignorance and denial to a place where we, as a human race, can understand each other's pain."[214] And yet, the memoir's very reception would seem to belie this possibility. *A Warrior's Spirit* offers a politicized and pedagogical appeal, but one that is often recast as an individualized spectacle, to be taken in from behind locked doors as it were. The memoir is praised for what it can tell us about one woman's task of "moving on" and "getting over" the effects of Canada's colonial past, but where it temporarily obstructs this possibility, turning the reader's gaze back on itself in the colonial present, it is called "bad art," or simply the wrong "kind of story."[215]

Sherene Razack has noted: "Often, women of colour are asked to tell their stories while others do the theorizing and writing up. Yet the chance to speak, to enter your reality on the record, as it were, is as irresistible as it is problematic."[216] Razack refers here to the difficulties involved in storytelling and listening across incommensurable discursive settings, in which the risks of co-optation or suppression are high. This is in many ways like the "irresistibility of speaking truth to power" to which Phil Fontaine referred in his address to the House of Commons. In the context of cultural recognition, this irresistibility signals the doubled meaning of the term as something at once compelled and compelling—and the ambiguous but necessary possibility for resistance within this. As Paula Gunn Allen states: "How does one survive in the face of collective death? Bearing witness is one solution, but it is singularly tearing, for witnessing genocide—as with conversation—requires that someone listen and comprehend."[217]

CHAPTER FOUR

Recognition, Remembrance, and Redress: The Politics of Memorialization in the Cases of Helen Betty Osborne and Anna Mae Pictou-Aquash

This chapter returns our attention to storytelling as a means of remembrance, as a consciousness-raising tool, and as a catalyst toward action. However, while I formerly explored the possibilities and limits of storytelling the "human terms" of violence against Indigenous women,[1] I now turn to the related question of how some anti-violence initiatives, in their work to grant a "human face to the mounting number of victims,"[2] have gravitated toward certain "faces" in particular. Storytelling has emerged as an inveterate strategy of anti-violence campaigns; what, then, of those recurring figures whose individual stories are told and retold? While the telling of individual women's stories is often imagined as a way to both "raise awareness" and promote "recommendations to influence positive change,"[3] I want to explore how certain exemplary cases seem to have circulated more readily as appropriate ambassadors for the cause. In this discussion, I am curious about the intersection between selective memorial practices, and the educative as well as "reparative" functions they ostensibly serve.[4] In exploring the performative links between commemoration, consciousness raising, and the move toward reparation or redress, I hope to trouble what is often assumed to be the unmediated relation between these practices and to question the ironic capacity of these practices to enact the very hierarchization of human life they protest against. And it is precisely because of (rather than in spite of) the urgency and necessity of combating indifference, raising awareness, and promoting social change that I want to unpack the sometimes unforeseen and unintended consequences implied in the valuing of some victims of violence as more illustrative, more affecting, or more instructive than others.

Many anti-violence critics have pointed to the "overexposure to violence and abuse" that results from the systemic marginalization of Indigenous women in the "areas of social engagement, education and economic opportunities, cultural practices, political action, and civil/human rights."[5] Others have critiqued delayed or inadequate media coverage as itself a discursive form of violence. As Laurie McNeill observes, material and discursive forms of marginalization are connected, with many Indigenous women's cases garnering scant attention in the public eye: "As in life, some dead continue to be marginalized."[6] Specifically, McNeill highlights, via Judith Butler's notion of "grievability," the racialized hierarchy of human loss legible in the "gap between official and marginalized" victims of violence.[7] For McNeill, commemoration itself constitutes a particular rhetorical practice in which one can read—in the precise presences and absences it marks—a discerning of just "whose lives count" in so-called "collective memory."[8] Not surprisingly, in these kinds of reckonings, Indigenous women's lives have decidedly counted less.

In resistance to a dominant public discourse characterized by apathetic, indifferent, or even incredulous responses to the social reality of missing and murdered women, various anti-violence campaigns have fashioned for public consumption the stories of certain emblematic figures of victimry—figures who, from the frequency with which they circulate, seem especially capable of revealing "the truth of society's treatment of aboriginal people."[9] This chapter analyzes how and why such figures circulate as archetypal victims of gendered and racial violence, in part by querying the iterative tendency with which their "tragic" trajectories (from life to death) are rehearsed in public acts of remembrance.[10] In earlier chapters I questioned the resistive viability so often afforded the telling of women's stories in the bid to "transform obscure [or marginalized] experience into critical knowledge."[11] Here, I interrogate the assumptions informing the seemingly preferential rehearsal of some women's stories over others: namely, the notion that perhaps certain women's lives and deaths are more likely to garner greater "public recognition" than others.[12] Mourned repeatedly in documentary reportage and film, in poetry and fiction, in public memorials and protest marches, in public inquiries and activist policy critique, two figures in particular—Helen Betty Osborne and Anna Mae Pictou-Aquash—will each be addressed in the space of this chapter. First, I discuss the representation of Helen Betty Osborne in the government of Manitoba's public apology to the Osborne family in July of 2000 and in Cree graphic novelist David Robertson's 2008 commemorative book, *The Life of Helen Betty Osborne*. Next, I turn to a discussion of Anna Mae Pictou-Aquash in Yvette Nolan's 2006 commemorative play *Annie Mae's Movement*. I explore how the memory of each figure is mobilized in projects that would ostensibly "connect the memory of a woman murdered" to a broader "drive for social reparation."[13]

Osborne and Pictou-Aquash share the space of this chapter because their stories have each been told and retold in a range of commemorative anti-violence contexts.[14] And yet, aside from their shared status as victims of gendered colonial violence, the circumstances of their lives and deaths are quite different. At the time of her death in 1975 Pictou-Aquash was, at thirty years old, already a seasoned activist who had participated in some of the American Indian Movement's (AIM) most well-publicized and protracted protests—from the occupation of the Bureau of Indian Affairs head office in the 1972 march on Washington (now dubbed The Trail of Broken Treaties), to the 1973 occupation of Wounded Knee, South Dakota. Conversely, at the time of her death in 1971, Osborne was a nineteen-year-old high school student working toward the goal of becoming a teacher. Pictou-Aquash is now thought to have been murdered by fellow AIM activists who suspected she was an FBI informant; Osborne was murdered by four white men who abducted her from the streets of The Pas, Manitoba. Accordingly, Pictou-Aquash's murder is often attributed to internalized violence in a climate of heightened tension and suspicion intentionally fostered by the FBI's Counter Intelligence Program,[15] while Osborne's is seen as exemplifying the perceived expendability of Indigenous women by dominant Canadian society.[16] Pictou-Aquash's execution-style murder was evidently premeditated and carefully planned; Osborne's murder, while overdetermined by entrenched notions of Indigenous women as disposable, and by a systemically maintained climate of impunity, does not appear to have been premeditated in quite the same way.

Nonetheless, each woman met a violent end that she would not have, had she not been an Indigenous woman. Each of the women was relatively young and ambitious in her own right, and so their deaths are often regarded as all the more "tragic" for having cut short a promising future. As Constance Backhouse remarks of Osborne's murder: "It was a tragic termination to the young woman's dream that she might go to college to become a teacher."[17] Moreover, in each instance, the guilty parties evaded justice for decades; in the case of Pictou-Aquash, twenty-nine years passed before charges were laid,[18] while in Osborne's case sixteen years went by. It is for this reason that both stories are framed as revealing the justice system's failure of Indigenous women: in each case, policing practices and investigation tactics came under public scrutiny, as did the government of Canada's response.

In the *Stolen Sisters* report, the Helen Betty Osborne case serves as a framing narrative and a "stark reminder of the failure of governments to take adequate action to date."[19] The story of Anna Mae Pictou-Aquash—as the story of "one of the most notorious killings of an Indigenous woman from Canada"[20]—forms a transition between the report's section on "Official indifference" and the subsequent case study narratives. While the case studies are themselves meant to illustrate the "indifference of Canadian officials and Canadian society for the welfare and safety of Indigenous women,"[21] the story of Anna Mae Pictou-Aquash substantiates this apathy as a long-standing feature of the government's response. For instance, the report quotes Pictou-Aquash's daughter, Denise Maloney, on the family's "frustration that the Canadian government has done little to support them in their three decade long call for justice."[22] Maloney states: "Any direct contact from any Canadian authorities would be nice. The level of apathy from governmental authorities surrounding my mother's case is disturbing and insulting."[23] In both the cases, the report finds the government's response inadequate. The women's life narratives (though distinct) together offer mutual evidence that the "authorities have failed in their responsibility to protect the rights of Indigenous women in Canada" and to initiate justice in these victims' cases.[24]

In the human rights discourse in which the *Stolen Sisters* report is written, "justice" refers to more than the punishment of guilty parties (in this case, those who have committed violence); it includes also the "public acknowledgment of the crime."[25] To secure broader public acknowledgement for the issue of missing and murdered women, representations of Osborne and Pictou-Aquash often emphasize each figure's relative youth, "innocence" or dignity, and respective commitment to a worthy "helping" cause: Osborne wanted to become a teacher and "[help] her people,"[26] while Pictou-Aquash is often remembered as a "courageous Canadian activist who dedicated her life to helping other Native people."[27] It is in these often-recited details that the figures of Osborne and Pictou-Aquash become exemplary or illustrative victims of violence. A source of frequent appeal among anti-violence activists and writers seeking to spark public recognition and action, these women's stories reveal more than the government's indifference to the issue of violence against Indigenous women in Canada. They in fact speak volumes about who might be considered worthy of public recognition, remembrance, and redress—and why.

In comparing different memorial representations of these women, I don't discount the fact that each had distinct communal ties, that the conditions surrounding their deaths were largely dissimilar, or that each had a very different relationship to the activist concerns to which their deaths are so often framed as having contributed. Rather, I mean to account for how the solicitous rehearsal of some stories, and of some "emplotments of suffering,"[28] may inadvertently value the affective leverage of some lives (and deaths) over others. My concern is that, in pushing back against what Butler terms the "differential allocation of grievability"[29] informing the frequent marginalization of Indigenous women in mainstream public discourse, some memorial practices—be they activist, legislative, or literary—have ironically enacted a differential allocation of their own, whereby some lives and deaths are presented as more illustrative and grievable than others. My goal in this chapter, then, is not to offer a comparative analysis of the Pictou-Aquash and Osborne cases themselves, but rather to analyze the key iterative motifs that emerge in public representations of each.

In the first place, these cases function as synecdochical—figuratively standing in for other "sexual assaults, disappearances and deaths" of Indigenous women across Canada.[30] As Jo-Ann Episkenew explains, "to settlers each one of us is a trope, a living synecdoche, in that one of us inevitably represents the whole."[31] In representations of missing and murdered Indigenous women more specifically, then, these cases are often presented as illustrating broader "patterns of violence that threaten the lives of Indigenous women."[32] These figures are rehearsed as exemplary in both senses of the word: exemplary because they illustrate the ubiquitous threat of violence (and of public indifference) in Indigenous women's lives, and exemplary because they are also appropriate or commendable victims of violence. Feminist linguist Susan Ehrlich terms this the "legitimate or 'believable' victim" of gendered violence—the victim whose qualities in life, and whose circumstances in death, seemingly garner greater public recognition.[33]

In Ehrlich's analysis, such victims—normatively constructed as legitimate or believable (and thus grievable)—often find their legitimacy tied to the status of their victimizers as "legitimate perpetrators": these men are usually "strangers to their victims, carry a weapon, and inflict injury upon their victim"[34] despite her unambiguous efforts to "resist to the utmost."[35] This construction of legitimate victimry applies to Osborne's case in particular, as framed by the Aboriginal Justice Inquiry of Manitoba's findings:

> While walking along Third Street in The Pas on that cold Saturday morning, Betty Osborne was accosted by four men in a car. Houghton, who was driving, stopped the car and Johnston got out, attempting to convince Osborne to go with them to "party." She told them that she did not wish to accompany them. She then was forced into their car and driven away. In the car Osborne was assaulted by Colgan and Johnston as Houghton drove. Johnston ripped at her blouse and Colgan grabbed at her breasts. In spite of her screams and attempts to escape, Osborne was taken to a cabin belonging to Houghton's parents at Clearwater Lake.[36]

Here, Osborne is instantly recognizable as a legitimate victim of violence in Ehrlich's terms: she is "accosted" by four men who were not known to her, and is "forced into their car" where she is assaulted. Moreover, she is unequivocal in her refusals. She declines their initial invitation to "party" and, when abducted, she "screams and attempts to escape."

Clearly, she "resist[s] to the utmost;"[37] the Justice Inquiry's report goes on to state that even while being beaten, she "continued to struggle and scream." Likewise, in David Robertson's commemorative graphic novel *The Life of Helen Betty Osborne*, Osborne utters a firm "No," in reply to her assailant's original invitation to 'party' with them: "I said no!"[38]

I remark on this resolute assertion of Osborne's integrity not because I question Osborne's status as a "legitimate" victim of violence, but because I question the dominant means by which legitimacy is constructed. In the repetitive insistence on Osborne's dignity, there is a subtextual capitulation to normative conceptions of just what constitutes gendered violence in the first place, and moreover what constitutes a victim worthy of remembrance, recognition, and redress. Of course, the emphatic insistence on Osborne's non-consent is in part calculated to counter the historical and ongoing depiction of Indigenous women as inherently "sexually violable"[39] and ultimately disposable. When contending with such racist and sexist stereotypes as those which conditioned Osborne's murder in the first place, it is not surprising that educational and commemorative sources would insist on correcting such egregious misrepresentations. For instance, in Robertson's depiction of Osborne's encounter with her attackers, the third-person narrator notes: "They thought Betty would be easy because they believed Aboriginal women were easy. They were wrong."[40] This narrator's comments typically serve to both advance and annotate the plot; these corrective remarks are overlaid on a panel featuring a close-up of Osborne saying "No." The message is unambiguous: Indigenous women are commonly thought to be illegitimate victims of violence, and this is wrong. And yet, the remedial insistence on Osborne's innocence—on her legitimacy as a victim—is as much about establishing her status as a normatively grievable victim of violence as it is about correcting false assumptions about Indigenous women. In fact, the anxious insistence on her innocence arguably reinscribes the very problematic it purports to overturn: Osborne becomes an exemplary figure of victimry in the bid to raise awareness because she offers a point of entry for the production of public grief that is unencumbered by any nagging questions about her status as a wrongfully injured party.[41]

In the context of anti-violence activism, the legitimate victim of violence fits within a paradoxical teleology wherein her death is both mourned in public acts of commemoration and solemnly celebrated as having occasioned public remembrance and resistance in the first place. In this way, the exemplary victim's death becomes necessary to the cause that would protest it, and her story is reproduced as part of an iterative pattern that is intimately premised upon (even while ostensibly resisting) ongoing gendered colonial violence. The stories of Helen Betty Osborne and Anna Mae Pictou-Aquash require discussion here not only because of the recursive way in which each figure is remembered in academic, activist, and literary sources, but also because certain constructions of their stories retroactively naturalize their deaths as necessary acts of martyrdom. Paradoxically, in this formulation, one's contribution to the activist anti-violence cause is through death. In Osborne's case, her death has been made to signal the urgent need for public acts of recognition and redress. And yet, insofar as her death has occasioned this recognition, it is said not to have been "in vain."[42] In the section that follows, I problematize public representations of Osborne as a grievable martyr whose murder by four white men is presented as positive, insofar as it makes possible certain forms of liberal contrition and redress around violence against Indigenous women in Canada.

Remembering Helen Betty Osborne: The Government of Manitoba's Apology and David Robertson's *The Life of Helen Betty Osborne*

Who was Betty Osborne? In his commemorative biographical graphic novel *The Life of Helen Betty Osborne*, David Robertson says: "She represents the truth of society's treatment of Aboriginal people, but she was also a young woman with real thoughts, emotions and aspirations."[43] For young readers approaching this story for the first time, Osborne is introduced as both a real person and as an emblematic figure whose life (and death) exemplify the justice system's failure of Indigenous people. In this discussion, I explore how Osborne is positioned in government apology and legislation (the Memorial Foundation Act), and in the seeming counter-discourses of commemorative storytelling. In analyzing both the government of Manitoba's public apology and the youth-targeted graphic novel biography, I trouble how her story is mapped onto a progressive narrative about "past" trauma and present efforts toward closure and resolution. I also discuss specific examples of how Osborne emerges as an appropriately "grievable" victim of violence whose death is mobilized retrospectively as having precipitated contemporary public acknowledgements of gendered and racial violence in Canada. Her grievability is tied to this troubling temporality of remembrance and redress: it is because her murder is so senseless and undeserved that it might be marshalled as an exemplary case "worthy" of public remembrance and recognition in the present.[44] Public apology and commemoration are not always curative antidotes to the apathy and injustices of the past, for they are premised upon and occasioned by such injustice. Rather, in public representations of Osborne, "past" injustice offers the necessary antecedent to a contemporary project of white liberal conscience. Public remembrance in this case acknowledges gendered colonial violence, but it is often a remedial, accommodative, and conditional recognition. In this, Osborne's murder is problematically cast as both normatively grievable and as thoroughly past.

In contemporary narrative representations of Osborne's case, her murder and its surrounding circumstances emerge as a point of departure for which both apology and remembrance might offer closure. From her displacement from her home community of Norway House for the purposes of pursuing her education, to her violent murder in The Pas; from the justice system's failure in her case, to the government's eventual apology and legislative "tribute" to her life by "creating a foundation in her memory"[45]—Osborne's story is recounted in a sequential arrangement of events that subtly embeds a retroactive causal logic to her death. This implicitly causal narrative structures the very text of the Government of Manitoba's Memorial Foundation Act itself. The text of the Memorial Foundation Act reads, in part:

> WHEREAS Helen Betty Osborne was an aboriginal woman who left her home community of Norway House to pursue her education with the goal of becoming a teacher;
>
> AND WHEREAS the circumstances surrounding her violent death in 1971 and the events that followed resulted in concerns about the relationship of the justice system to aboriginal people;

AND WHEREAS the Report of the Aboriginal Justice Inquiry published pursuant to *An Act to Establish and Validate the Public Inquiry into the Administration of Justice and Aboriginal People* concluded that events surrounding the murder of Helen Betty Osborne were marked by racism, sexism and indifference;

AND WHEREAS the fact that sixteen years passed before the justice system was able to bring those charged with the murder of Helen Betty Osborne to trial caused immense pain to the Osborne family and created concerns that the justice system failed to do everything it could in this case;

AND WHEREAS paying tribute to the life of Helen Betty Osborne is an important part of the healing process that must follow such a tragedy;

AND WHEREAS creating a foundation in her memory to assist aboriginal students would be a fitting tribute to her life;

THEREFORE HER MAJESTY, by and with the advice and consent of the Legislative Assembly of Manitoba, enacts [the Act] as follows.[46]

In his official apology to Osborne's family in July of 2000, Manitoba Minister of Justice and Attorney General Gord Mackintosh expressed a "profound regret at the way the justice system as a whole responded to the death of Betty,"[47] and announced the Helen Betty Osborne Memorial Foundation Act as a forthcoming piece of legislation that would—in the language of the Act itself—pay "fitting tribute" to her life through the annual provision of financial bursaries, to be awarded to Aboriginal students enrolled in post-secondary study.[48] Toward this end, the government of Manitoba made an initial donation of $50,000 to the Memorial Foundation, the declared purposes of the foundation being "to receive donations," to "provide financial assistance to aboriginal persons residing in Manitoba who are enrolled in post-secondary studies," and to "promote the memory of Helen Betty Osborne" as someone whose own dreams of post-secondary education were tragically cut short.[49] In this way, the very project of official remembrance—that is, of paying tribute to the memory of Osborne through government-issued apology and financial redress—enacts a form of memory making that promotes public recognition of gendered and racial violence only insofar as it can be done by presenting Osborne's murder as unique, as exceptionally "tragic ... senseless, and incomprehensible."[50] Her murder becomes exemplary in its particular tragedy, a tragedy that the apology is then unable or unwilling to acknowledge within the broader context of systemic and ongoing violence against Indigenous women.

As the Cultural Memory Group recalls, the apology came to pass before "a crowded legislature and a throng of ... media."[51] Twenty-nine years after Osborne's murder, the apology was the seeming culmination of a decades-long struggle—both grassroots and government-sponsored—to secure public recognition and legislative redress in this egregious case of historical injustice. The apology was meant to build—in the phrasing of one government press release—"a positive legacy out of tragedy."[52] As a gesture further intended to bring about some measure of "closure"[53] and "healing"[54] to those who had been caused such pain, the apology was—by all public accounts—graciously given and received.[55] Reproduced in a government press release, Mackintosh's statement reads as follows: "On behalf of the Government of Manitoba, I wish to express my profound regret at the way the justice system as a whole responded to the death of Betty, and to apologize for the clear lack of justice in her case.... The examination of her tragic murder through the Aboriginal Justice Inquiry continues to define the path we are following to ensure justice for all Manitobans."[56] The apology was again reiterated by Mackintosh when the Standing Committee on Law Amendments met that following December 2000 in order to hear public presentations on the Helen Betty Osborne Memorial Foundation Act as the proposed measure of legislative redress. At this time, Mackintosh again expressed to Osborne's family, to the members of the standing committee, and to the private witnesses present his "profound regret" for the "clear lack of justice in her case."[57]

As one example among several recent "positive step[s]" towards "resolution" and reconciliation between Indigenous and non-Indigenous peoples in Canada,[58] I cite the government of Manitoba's public apology not only for the broader insight it might afford into the iterative grammars of Canada's contemporary "culture of redress,"[59] but also for the reluctance with which specifically gendered forms of colonial violence are acknowledged therein. Against the conspicuous public characterization of residential schooling as the primary site of colonial injury (and as one that dominant discourse would also locate firmly within Canada's "past"),[60] Manitoba's apology occasions a different way in which to conceive of colonial violence relative to the possibility of reconciliation—one that could but nonetheless fails to bring gendered violence into the discussion.

The recurring trope of closure—discernible in the government of Manitoba's efforts to both "acknowledge" and "move" beyond[61] the "unfortunate mistakes" of the past[62]—calls to mind that other more recent instance of government apology. In the government of Canada's official apology for the residential schools system, the impetus toward closure is similarly legible in statements that cite the "sad chapter in our history"[63] so that we might then "move forward" and beyond this "legacy" together.[64] This coercive movement forward reveals the implicit conditional limits of the apology; through sleight of hand, the apology calls up a colonial past only in order to keep it there. Such a pre-emptive teleology of closure instills problematic "orientations" to temporality and cause.[65] As Jennifer Henderson and Pauline Wakeham suggest in their introduction to the 2010 *ESC* issue on "First Peoples and the Culture of Redress in Canada," "The problem at the level of relations between Indigenous and non-Aboriginal institutions in Canada is not one of inadequate closure but one of repeated, pre-emptive attempts at reaching closure and 'cure.'"[66] In this sense, Manitoba's apology—with its purported end of promoting a "sense of closure," "justice," and healing among those for whom the justice system can only be described as having been unjust[67]—more than signals some provisional capacity on the part of government officials and ordinary citizens to respond at long last to the injustices of the past; it also reveals the concurrent irreconcilability of this reparative gesture with certain realities of Canada's colonial present.

In light of this manner in which apology has recently figured—that is, as so many selective and expedient orchestrations of resolution and redemption—the ongoing social reality of violence against Indigenous women troubles any project that would perform a cordoning-off of colonial violence as "past." Acknowledged only obliquely by the Manitoba apology and in the language of the Memorial Foundation Act, and then arguably not at all by Canada's apology for residential schooling, this violence remains an open site of injury that potentially forestalls Canada's professed commitment to close this "sad chapter in our history."[68] Of the several other irreconcilabilities underpinning Canada's recent attempts at reconciliation more broadly, Gregory Younging has pointed to Canada's former opposition to the UN Declaration on the Rights of Indigenous Peoples, and to its dismal record relative to the UN Commission on Human Rights.[69] Yet others have gestured to that infamous and telling "misstep" when, at a press conference for the 2009 G20 Summit in Pittsburgh, Prime Minister Stephen Harper boasted that Canada has "no history of colonialism."[70] To the extent that these examples would seem to belie Canada's legitimacy on the international stage as a paragon of "progressive," liberal virtue,[71] they do indeed appear fundamentally irreconcilable with the domestic pursuit of reconciliation. And yet, rather than regard such instances as profound aberrations that would "contradict" the sincerity of Canada's liberal and conciliatory cause,[72] we can instead read these "irreconcilabilities" as integral to the selective and historically revisionist discourses by which reconciliation is currently configured. Ongoing violence against women, ongoing violations of Indigenous peoples' rights, and government-authored acts of provisional acknowledgement and erasure relative to its own participation in these realities: these might be productively regarded as instances that would not so much contradict as make possible certain forms of liberal contrition. And herein lies another very troubling teleology.

In turning from the example of government-issued apology, and in looking additionally to remembrance and reconciliation as pursued in works of creative cultural production, one can see the same troubling temporalities unfold. The historical fact of colonial injury—in the Osborne case, an act of gendered and racist violence—is recognized, but in part for what it affords the prospective liberal subject of empathy and conscience: that is, an opportunity to reckon selectively with a grievable "past" and to become a better person in the present for it. In this sense, colonial violence becomes not so much irreconcilable with the goal of reconciled relations—it is in fact the occasion for reconciliation. It signals not the failure of a liberal ideal, but rather provides opportunity for its fulfillment. And it is in this way, too, that colonialism subsists insidiously in our present. It seems like such an innocuous, or perhaps even necessary practice to remember Betty Osborne so that we might, in David Robertson's words, "change, learn, and grow."⁷³ Yet this is a growth that actually requires as its antecedent the murder of an Indigenous woman.

Osborne is "remembered" across multiple sites where the practices of public memory intersect with educative and conciliatory imperatives. In many of these sites, her death is figured as occasioning not only the judicial system's self-examination, but also that of individual citizens of conscience.⁷⁴ Echoing the Aboriginal Justice Inquiry, Minister of Justice Gord Mackintosh stated at the Legislative Assembly of Manitoba's Standing Committee on Law Amendments: "I have looked at the steps that my own department took at the time, and I am far from satisfied that we did everything that we could."⁷⁵ And yet, what does it mean, that the murder of Osborne is figured as the fortunate "catalyst" that would foster such change and make possible the putting "behind us" of this sad history?

David Robertson's commemorative and educational graphic novel *The Life of Helen Betty Osborne* (illustrated by Madison Blackstone) offers some insight into this problematic. The graphic novel was created for and launched by the Helen Betty Osborne Memorial Foundation in 2008, and was published by Portage and Main Press.⁷⁶ In this novel, Osborne's story is focalized through the eyes of a non-Indigenous youth, Daniel. Through a series of mediated flashbacks that punctuate Daniel's present, Osborne's past arrives to readers in part through Daniel's experience of being taught Osborne's "life" story at school,⁷⁷ and through his reading of the Aboriginal Justice Inquiry report itself. For instance, in a series of panels designed to introduce this story to an uninitiated (and likely adolescent) readership, Daniel is seen seated in a classroom, a pensive expression on his face as he listens to his teacher deliver a lesson on Osborne's life.⁷⁸ He is then seen perusing the library shelves while the remarks of his teacher offer a running commentary that carries over from the in-class lesson, while also serving to annotate his present actions. "It was a vicious act of racism that spawned an inquiry into the justice system's treatment of Aboriginals,"⁷⁹ the "voiceover" explains as Daniel reaches down a volume (presumably, the inquiry report) from the library shelf. Daniel's subsequent immersion in the report, as he is shown reading attentively while walking home, signals a transition from the "Present Day"[80] to the early morning hours of "November 13, 1971."[81] A "visual rhyme" is established between these scenes: in paired panels that depict Daniel's present-day walk home against Osborne's own (interrupted) walk, readers are invited to understand both the prospective connection between these characters, and the difference. In Daniel's panel he reads Osborne's narrative intently—his eyes are downcast toward the pages of the AJI report while his feet trace the very steps Osborne likewise followed while "on her way home."[82] The imagery of Osborne's panel is near-identical. The same night-time scene and darkened city street provide the setting for each character's walk, while the same street lamp and railroad crossing feature in the background. In Osborne's panel, however, a car's headlights can be seen approaching just over her left shoulder. Visually, the difference is subtle but striking: Daniel is clearly exempt from the threat of violence that figures so plainly and menacingly for Osborne.

The link between these paired panels, and the ostensibly instructive moment embedded therein, is further clarified by the text of Daniel's frame. With a voiceover from his teacher's in-class lesson, the text in Daniel's panel features the following didactic imperative that signals at once the different circumstances of safety under which each character walks home, and Daniel's responsibility to understand this difference through imaginative empathy: "Imagine walking home afraid because you look different. Worse yet … imagine walking home feeling safe and never making it there."[83] Daniel's burgeoning capacity for empathy is thus established through the interplay of visual and textual cues that rebound off one another in these paired scenes, since his ability to "imagine" another's vulnerability to violence is confirmed by the narrative account of Osborne's abduction that follows. Because this subsequent narrative is actually occasioned by Daniel's learning of it (through his teacher and through the AJI report), this scene becomes the first of many textual markers that indicate his capacity to empathize and moreover to self-reflect on his previously unacknowledged position of privilege and apathy. For instance, after several pages dedicated to the uninterrupted recounting of Osborne's stay in Guy Hill Residential School up until the summer before her move to The Pas, the narrative's temporal focus shifts again to Daniel's present. Gazing into a bathroom mirror, he asks his mother, "Can one thing change you?"[84] Daniel goes on to recount his newfound recognition of his past indifference: "I feel like I was blind before, numb to people like Betty."[85] To the extent that the reader's gaze is focalized through Daniel's perspective—having access to Osborne's story primarily through Daniel's learning of it—the reader is likewise invited to participate in this reflexive practice.

In this way, Daniel's journey is represented as one of learning and of growth that models for readers a meaningful and reflexive way in which to engage with Canada's past acts of "cultural genocide"[86] in a present where "Aboriginal women are *still* in danger."[87] Doubly framed in terms of its "socio-pedagogical function"[88]—first as taught to Daniel within the graphic novel itself, and then also as taught to readers themselves—Osborne's narrative itself occasions this learning and growth. Daniel thus functions as a surrogate of sorts whose capacity for change models the reader's own prospective ability to "learn from the past."[89] One of the ways in which the graphic novel quantifies Daniel's outward change is by tracing his movement from self-justified apathy in the opening (when he chooses to ignore a bullied Indigenous student's request for help), to reflexive empathy and compassion at the end (when he reconciles with the young Indigenous woman to whom he had been previously indifferent). Toward this end, Daniel's understanding of his prior indifference is connected to the broader indifference with which Osborne's murder was met. In a series of panels that visually recall the graphic novel's opening scene, Daniel "look[s] back at things" in light of his newly acquired knowledge of Osborne's case, and "wish[es] [he] would've done something."[90] In the opening panels this reflection is designed visually to recall, Daniel witnesses two male students push a young Indigenous woman into the snow. Their assault is both physical and verbal, calling forth what Emma LaRocque calls the most "dehumanizing" and objectifying term used against Indigenous women: squaw.[91] One of the young men, Mark, shoves her while declaring: "The squaw can't keep her balance. She's so drunk!!"[92] In the following panels, Daniel is seen approaching after the fact—her assailants, meanwhile, have beat an unhurried retreat while casting over their shoulders the additional sexist and racist epithet: "Sleep it off Pocahontas!!!"[93] As Daniel approaches and then passes her, the unnamed young woman remains prone in the snowbank. In one panel, he appears almost to be standing over her while she remains vulnerably posed in the snow, her calf-high boots clearly reminiscent of the boots mentioned so often in accounts of Osborne's murder.[94]

In establishing a visual link between the harassment of the young Indigenous woman in Daniel's present, and the murder of Helen Betty Osborne in the past, Robertson forges a provocative contiguity between these instances of violence as part of an ongoing and systemic problem. In this sense, the graphic novel attempts to negotiate between gendered racism and its resistance at the level of intimate, interpersonal exchanges, and at a broader systemic level. But this is where things get particularly complicated, in terms of the text's representational politics and its capacity for modelling meaningful anti-colonial critique. Daniel's perception of the problem (and of his own past indifference) on an individual scale must also translate to the level of broader social relations in order for the text to depict the systemic and ongoing nature of violence against Indigenous women. The text attempts to accomplish this by positing a visual connection between past and present instances of violence, as well as the indifferent reactions to them. But because the graphic novel is so concerned with indexing Daniel's individual growth from indifference to concern, and with the broader "opportunity for change"[95] this personal growth signifies, the text's delicate negotiation of the past as contiguous with the present is ultimately unable to sustain itself and collapses under the more satisfying dominant temporality of "past" trauma and present recognition and closure.

This temporal mapping of past injury and present redress onto the plot of the graphic novel accounts for how and why it seems to argue, at once, that Indigenous women remain vulnerable to violence today,[96] and that "things have gotten better in The Pas since that time."[97] Indeed, both assertions are sustained in the space of this text: "Aboriginal women are still in danger today,"[98] Daniel learns from his teacher, and yet he nevertheless concludes that the "things that happened back then ... they would never happen now. I think it all goes back to Betty. Just one person caused so much change."[99] As with the irreconcilability of Canada's current project of reconciliation with the material fact of ongoing state-sponsored colonial oppression, I understand this seeming paradox as less the contradiction it appears to be than the logical outcome and fulfillment of liberal ideology, where the recognition of past wrongs is in some ways integral to their deepest disavowal in the present. Of course, it is not always the case that readers of this graphic novel would be necessarily invested in the disavowal of colonial violence. Insofar as this novel was produced for the Helen Betty Osborne Memorial Foundation, and in consultation with "those who knew her best,"[100] the novel (and its memorial function) most certainly signify differently for different readerships, depending on the context in which it is received. My concern here, however, is with a particular kind of readership as prospectively addressed by this novel, especially in its reflexive pedagogical imperative as focalized through a white male youth's eyes. It is through this framework that I read the novel's amenability to reproduce the indifference and disavowal it is intended to resist.

This disavowal is performed in Robertson's novel precisely at those moments in which it can no longer support an analysis of violence against Indigenous women as ongoing and carry forth a narrative of progress that traces the liberal subject of empathy from indifference to recognition. Significantly, in this emplotment, the figure of Helen Betty Osborne emerges as an exemplary and grievable victim whose death is not only individualized—divorced from the systemic racism and sexism that conditioned her murder—but also heralded as having itself uniquely occasioned the change and growth Daniel's character (and, by extension, Canadian society) exhibits. Recall Daniel's reflection, that it "all goes back to Betty":[101] if the conditions that made possible her murder (and the apathy with which it was met) are no longer in effect, and if those "things that happened back then ... would never happen now,"[102] then this is apparently owing to Betty's particular goodness. Indeed, the suggestion is made that "maybe it had to be somebody as good as her to make the difference that she has made."[103] This is not to say that Osborne was anything less than the good person the graphic novel suggests her to be. Moreover, her characterization as "hardworking," good-humoured,[104] and "nurturing" is important to the memorial work of the book.[105] However, the reproduction of these particular qualities is not arbitrary or haphazard; it suggests as much about dominant norms of legitimacy and grievability as it does the worthiness of her memory. In short, it is true that her death is tragic, but certainly it should not be any more so because she was "good."

In the graphic novel, Osborne's "senseless" death is accorded meaning retrospectively: "Nobody can change the past," Daniel's mother reflects, "but we can learn from it. *So maybe it happened for a reason.*"[106] This suggestion is particularly troubling in that it ascribes a fatalistic necessity to Osborne's end. That is, her murder becomes necessary to a broader "progressive" emplotment that moves from white ignorance to enlightenment, from apathy to recognition. Not unlike the movement "forward" coercively plotted by the government of Manitoba's apology to Osborne's family, the graphic novel ultimately invites an understanding of Osborne's death as a fitting causal catalyst for social change. In this sense, the text's pedagogy imparts a model by which the student of Osborne's story might become the liberal citizen of conscience, but the recognition of gendered colonial violence (of both the past and the present) is only invited to go so far, as the very opportunity for change so solemnly celebrated here requires the murder of an Indigenous woman. Senseless though her death might have been, the logic goes, it thankfully brought about the opportunity for change and even perhaps for absolution. In exploring this logic as embedded within acts of selective commemoration, education, and reparation, I have tried to read for the insidious and often unacknowledged conditions that make possible gendered colonial violence in the present. In particular, I have tried to address those instances that would appear outwardly progressive or even liberatory in their politics, while highlighting for whom "progress" often gets made, and for whom such memory-making functions most directly as liberating: the white liberal subject of conscience who might be absolved from reckoning with the violences of the present, so long as he or she witnesses and remembers those of the past.

Remembering Anna Mae Pictou-Aquash: Yvette Nolan's *Annie Mae's Movement*

In her foreword to popular historian Merna Forster's book about one hundred Canadian heroines and their "extraordinary accomplishment[s],"[107] former prime minister Kim Campbell reflects that these biographical stories constitute not only an important "contribution to our understanding of women" in Canada, but also a timely and much-needed "corrective to the standard histories" in which women are chronically under-represented.[108] Campbell further states that "celebrating these one hundred Canadian heroines reminds us that Canadian women do amazing things, and it will be a loss to our whole country if we forget them."[109] Appearing among the one hundred women "recognized and celebrated" for their "extraordinary accomplishments" is the American Indian Movement (AIM) activist Anna Mae Pictou-Aquash.[110] Of her accomplishments, the biographical sketch treats in equal parts Pictou-Aquash's activism and death: "She fought for the rights of Native people," Forster informs her readers—"until someone shot her in the back of the head."[111] Like Osborne's death, Pictou-Aquash's loss is figured as a tragic martyrdom worthy of recognition and remembrance.[112] When read against Campbell's introductory remarks, it is Canada's "loss" to forget her; yet so long as we remember her, her loss presumably becomes Canada's gain.

The final section of this chapter explores how Pictou-Aquash is remembered, looking to the example of Yvette Nolan's play *Annie Mae's Movement*. A one-act play featuring a single female character (Anna Mae), as well as a small cadre of male characters intended to be played by one actor, *Annie Mae's Movement* chronicles the life of a "woman in a man's movement"[113] whose real-life fight for social change during the height of the 1970s Red Power movement was circumscribed not only by racism, but also by the sexism Indigenous women encounter in their contributions to activist politics. In *I Am Woman*, Lee Maracle suggests that sexism was "inherent in the character of the American Indian Movement,"[114] and indeed this seems to have affected the way in which Pictou-Aqaush is remembered. For, against the conspicuous circulation of Pictou-Aquash as a romanticized martyr figure of the Red Power movement, we can also read for her equally conspicuous absence from some of the most canonical works on 1970s AIM activism. As Choctaw scholar Devon Abbot Mihesuah observes of Robert Warrior and Paul Chaat Smith's *Like a Hurricane: The Indian Movement from Alcatraz to Wounded Knee*, "the book mentions only a few women in passing (Anna Mae is mentioned once, and that is to tell us that she was married at Wounded Knee)."[115] In this way, a telling tension has emerged within the representational inventory through which Pictou-Aquash has circulated—one that, between the solicitous rehearsal or excision of her story, points to a broader problematic in gender politics as they relate to Indigenous activist movements. Nolan's play seeks in part to address this problematic by making visible Pictou-Aquash's significant contributions to AIM organizing, fundraising, and activism, while also critiquing the "macho egoism" that characterized some facets of the AIM leadership.[116] The play is thus devoted not only to commemorating Anna Mae's life, but also to analyzing how Indigenous women's activism is circumscribed by colonially derived patriarchal norms that shape the very terms on which women engage in, and are remembered by, activist movements.

With a scene titled "Beginning," Nolan's play opens much as it ends: "*Lights up to reveal Anna Mae, curled in a foetal position [centre stage].*"[117] Compare to this the manner in which the play closes—with a "gunshot": "*She falls, curls into a foetal position, the good red road emanating from her. Blackout.*"[118] Bookended by the simple image of a woman's body curled impassively on its side, Nolan's play performatively engages a trope now well rehearsed in the repertoire of material (both artistic and expository) dedicated to the memory of this activist figure—remembered most often, perhaps, for how she died. As Anthony J. Hall recalls, "the frozen body of this much beloved pillar of AIM ... was found in February of 1976"[119] when, on a remote corner of the Pine Ridge Reservation in South Dakota, a cattle rancher spied what Devon Mihesuah terms "a small indigenous woman [who] lay curled, sleeping it appeared, at the bottom of an embankment."[120] Authorities were notified, and the body was recovered. Following a cursory autopsy that infamously reported the as-yet-unidentified woman as having died of exposure, the body was hastily buried in a local Catholic cemetery.[121] There, as Delaware poet Daniel David Moses imparts in his elegiac "Report on Anna Mae's Remains," "her body sleeps the sleep of the abandoned"[122]—until it was disinterred, some ten days later, at the behest of Pictou-Aquash's belatedly notified family. A second autopsy was then performed, promptly revealing that she had in fact been shot at close range in the back of the head and, moreover, that she had been raped.[123] And with this, Shirley Hill Witt (Mohawk) declared, the women of the Red Power movement had "sadly been given a martyr."[124] "Anna Mae lived and died for all of us," Hill Witt wrote in a commemorative biographical sketch for

Akwesasne Notes later that spring: "The executioners of Anna Mae did not snuff out a meddlesome woman. They exalted a Brave Hearted Woman for all time."[125]

More than commemorative, Hill Witt's remarks appear to have been predictive; far from forgotten, the life of Anna Mae Pictou-Aquash is rehearsed—in mainstream reportage, in alternative and Indigenous-authored periodicals, as well as in literature, performance, and film— with a solicitude matched only by that which is afforded the story of her death. In her biographical treatment, Mihesuah reflects that the "life of Anna Mae Pictou-Aquash demonstrates what it means to be a modern Native woman aggressively fighting racial, cultural, and gender oppression."[126] What, then, of the related demonstrative quality attributed to her death—an event undeniably material in its circumstances and effects, but demanding nonetheless (by virtue of its conspicuous reiteration) critical consideration as to its place in the representational enterprise of memory and history? In her biographical profile, Merna Forster writes: "It is her death that brought great attention to the causes Anna Mae lived and died for";[127] yet, according to journalist Wendy Gillis, "it was her dedication that eventually caused her death."[128] And herein lies a tension to which the play is, in part, addressed: that Pictou-Aquash, a prolific community worker, fundraiser, educator, and veteran of Wounded Knee, is perhaps best remembered not for her substantial contributions to the cause of Indigenous rights but for that final, supplementary act of activism ascribed to her death. The martyrdom of this romanticized figure—so often characterized as epitomizing an ideal in Indigenous women's activism—is thus imbued with an agential quality that forgets, even while remembering, the circumstances under which she died.[129] In representations of Pictou-Aquash's death, the trope of a woman's body curled on its side not only risks aestheticizing the moment of death—what Moses calls that "last jet of breath"[130]—as itself an activist feat meriting solemn celebration; it also assigns a fatalistic or even teleological necessity to Pictou-Aquash's death. "Her path was clear and true," Ellen Klaver declares in her commemorative poem, "So they shot her down and left the body lying in a field."[131] Her untimely death immortalized as part and parcel of her activism in life, this figure of resistance would seem here, like the colonial figure of the "vanishing

Indian," to be exalted in her demise—visually preserved in perpetuity on the threshold of inevitable disappearance.

Thus framed by the image of a woman curled on her side, Nolan's play gestures toward a whole repertoire of commemorative cultural production that has fixated on Pictou-Aquash's death in a romanticized and decontextualized manner. To the extent that this eponymous character revolves through a figurative cycle of death and life with each performance—the seeming inevitability of her violent end having been embedded into the structure of the play itself—the play would appear at first to reinscribe, rather than overturn, this troubling trope. Evocative of the romanticized vision of martyrdom that characterizes so much of the material produced in memory of Pictou-Aquash, the trope cites those instances of commemoration in which her body is effectively severed from the conditions of its violation—the perpetrators having become an "absent referent" whose omission allows her to be celebrated for giving her life to the movement.[132] And yet, as a reflexive means of structuring the audience's engagement with the histories the play tells, this tableau functions in more than one register at once: it not only tells this "most infamous story of a murdered Aboriginal woman in Canadian history,"[133] but also theorizes the significant tensions informing how missing and murdered women are committed to public memory in the first place. In this sense, my interest in the play is here less about its thematic engagement with a particular history of Indigenous resistance from a feminist perspective, and more about the discussion its structuring trope makes possible: a discussion of the politics of representation relative to the issue of violence against Indigenous women.

Nolan deploys the figure of Anna Mae Pictou-Aquash not only in service of exalting a "brave-hearted" woman in death, but also as a means to query where, how, and to what ends this story is told. Far from a mere rehashing of past events, or even a "timely" revisiting of this particular case in light of new evidence, arrests, and trials,[134] *Annie Mae's Movement* is also addressed to a present problematic—both material and discursive—attending the issue of violence against Indigenous women in Canada. Nolan's play interrogates the possibilities and limits of commemorative knowledge making as a means of resisting or transforming the social conditions which make such violence possible. The play's cyclical structure—beginning and ending with Anna Mae's death—thus makes possible a broader conversation about gendered colonial violence and the stakes of its representation.

The reflexive function of the play's structuring trope is to stage both the material fact of a specific act of violence, as well as a complex cultural archive of its representation. For instance, in counterpoint to that ubiquitous image of the fallen Anna Mae curled on her side, Nolan's character instead "*awakens, begins to crawl, then to walk*"[135]—livening her limbs as she prepares to deliver the first of her monologues. "There are all kinds of ways of getting rid of people,"[136] she remarks in her opening lines: "They disappear them by keeping them underfed, keeping them poor, prone to sickness and disease. They disappear them into jails.... They disappear our kids, scoop 'em up, adopt 'em out, they never see their families again."[137] While the trope of Anna Mae curled on her side testifies indelibly to her own "disappearance," these lines establish a context for the systemic "vanishing" of Indigenous people via the broader machinations of ongoing colonial policy. They also analyze the contingent simultaneity of the rhetoric (and reality) of violent disappearance (on one hand), and the heightened visibility with which this character is historically imbued (on the other). In this sense, the opening monologue reflexively queries the resistive viability so often afforded the impetus to counter invisibility with visibility, and puts pressure on the emancipatory promise often ascribed to political or artistic commemorative expression.

To the extent that it addresses this problematic, effectively questioning visibility as a guarantor of progressive or resistive politics, Nolan's play is concerned not only with how best to grant commemorative form to this activist's memory, but also with theorizing the possible limitations of such a project. Yet, the play itself also takes care to detail Pictou-Aquash's life as an organizer in the time immediately leading up to and encompassing her participation in major AIM-led activism. The play's early scenes depict Anna Mae's work as a teacher in the community-run Survival School in Boston and recount her decision to join the siege at Wounded Knee.[138] Tracing this activist's subsequent rise to power in AIM leadership, *Annie Mae's Movement* balances an otherwise realist biographical portrayal of Anna Mae's work (from her fundraising activities, to her work in opening a west coast office in Los Angeles) against the periodic intrusions of a male-embodied threat that hovers menacingly on the edges of the staged action. Described in the stage directions as "the lurker on the other side,"[139] this being appears to the audience as the *Rugaru*. Rugaru is a transformative animal presence believed by some characters to be "a sign that things are gonna change for Indian people,"[140] but whose apparitions in the play warn of the encroachment of malevolent male forces whose political priorities for Indigenous sovereignty are achieved at the expense of women. In this sense, Rugaru signals the potential for Indigenous activism to bring about substantive social change while also foretelling the corruption of the Red Power movement by a militant and patriarchal agenda that dismisses women's labour and targets women dissenters for gendered violence. Charting this male-dominated movement from a woman's perspective, Nolan's play thus employs the figure of the Rugaru as a means of highlighting the historical and ongoing tensions between gendered politics and sovereigntist projects, and in order to analyze lateral violence of colonial origin within Indigenous activist movements.[141]

The Rugaru is to be played by the same male actor who plays versions of the activist allies and foes Anna Mae knew in life, as well as the staged personifications of the "FBI" and the "Law" whose interrogations of Anna Mae in the latter half of the play make her increasingly vulnerable to the mistrust and accusations of those AIM leaders who suspect her of being an FBI informant. In the climate of mistrust deliberately fostered by the FBI Counter Intelligence Program designed to infiltrate and strategically disrupt its targeted organizations,[142] Anna Mae is antagonized by both AIM and the FBI as she becomes inextricably caught in the ongoing conflicts between these organizations. Like the real-life Pictou-Aquash, whose murder took place amid a series of violent conflicts between AIM and the FBI, Nolan's Anna Mae finds herself a target of paranoid aggression at the height of AIM's internal suspicion about prospective infiltrators planted as undercover informers for the FBI. Notably, the play stages this aggression in gendered terms intended to mirror the historical circumstances under which this activist died: in the play's final scene, Anna Mae is raped and then shot by a composite figure comprising male characters from both organizations.[143] The final scene, having culminated in Anna Mae's execution, thus closes the play as it began—with that solitary image of Anna Mae curled in a fetal position, centre stage.

When, with the scene titled "End," Nolan's play brings Anna Mae's "movement" to a close, it extends this character beyond the individualized figure of martyrdom in order to envision her story as instead embedded within a broader intellectual tradition of social critique and change. With a gesture reversely reminiscent of Anishinaabe artist Rebecca Belmore's performance piece *Vigil* (2002), in which Belmore calls out the names of women violently disappeared from Vancouver's Downtown Eastside,[144] this final scene sees Anna Mae recite pieces of her own biography, as well as the names of those she leaves behind as the living:

> My name is Anna Mae Pictou Aquash, Micmac nation from Shubenacadie, Nova Scotia. My mother is Mary Ellen Pictou, my father is Francis Thomas Levi, my sisters are Rebecca Julien and Mary Lafford, my brother is Francis. My daughters are Denise and Deborah. You cannot kill us all. You can kill me, but my sisters live, my daughters live. You cannot kill us all. My sisters live. Becky and Mary, Helen and Priscilla, Janet and Raven, Sylvia, Ellen, Pelajia, Agnes, Monica, Edie, Jessica, Gloria and Lisa and Muriel, Monique, Joy and Tina, Margo, Maria, Beatrice, Minnie, April, Colleen.... You can kill me, but you cannot kill us all. You can kill me. *There is a gunshot. She falls, curls into a foetal position. Blackout.*[145]

More than offering a kind of self-authored obituary, coupled with an effort to document the erasure or occlusion of those unnamed in dominant memory, the character of Anna Mae here gives us the names of those who "live."[146] Placing herself in relation to these names, she then figuratively peoples the stage with those who were, throughout the production, missing from it—the women—and in so doing opens up a space from which to comment on how the individualized iconography of Anna Mae, immortalized in death as an exemplary figure of activism in life, relies to some extent upon the invisibility of others.

Notably, those women who are named as living on metaphorically populate the stage as Anna Mae's relations—as sisters and daughters. Also evoked, however, are the names of Indigenous women activists and writers (from authors Maria Campbell and Beatrice Culleton, to AIM activist and journalist Minnie Two Shoes). In this way, the play's closing extends Anna Mae's legacy beyond her death, demonstrating not only how her activism has influenced others, but also how this activism must itself be understood within a broader context of women's leadership within an intellectual history of Indigenous women's writing. These women's works, like Nolan's play and Belmore's *Vigil*, "reflect a belief in the power of performance," and of storytelling, "as ceremonial and potentially medicinal."[147] Storytelling is thus articulated as a site of critique as well as transformation, accounting for a tradition of Indigenous women's cultural production that theorizes anti-violence as well as the transformative potential of literature in resisting violence. While dominant means of anti-violence intervention (whether in the form of policy critique or legislative reform) have often overlooked the insights of Indigenous women activists and writers, the play asks that we look to contemporary Indigenous women's literature as thoroughly grounded in anti-violence theory and praxis that can help us to imagine beyond these initiatives.

When reflecting on gendered colonial violence and Indigenous invisibility more broadly, Nolan recalls of one of her earliest plays the "very full and attentive audience who had," she says, "come to see a Native woman killed."[148] This expectation she infers from the audience's frustrated reaction when, following the production, some spectators expressed their surprise and displeasure at having watched a play that, contrary to their expectations from an Indigenous playwright writing about gendered violence, had taken up the matter of a murdered white woman. To Nolan, these viewers had rather ironically missed the point—that this play was in fact very much concerned with the *invisibility* of actual Indigenous victims of violence, even while a theatregoing audience had, she says, "paid for Native blood."[149] With *Annie Mae's Movement*, Nolan reflects, the audience is at last given that image of a "Native woman killed"—but to rather different ends than might have been expected. Nolan intends to memorialize the figure of Pictou-Aquash, but also to critically interrogate the affective desire to see this figure meet her end. In this way, *Annie Mae's Movement* intervenes into a broader problematic with respect to public narratives about missing and murdered women—a problematic whereby the presumed progressive imperative to make known some women's stories renders incontestable the means by which this telling occurs. The circumstances of Pictou-Aquash's life and death were indeed specific; her embroilment in the internal politics of AIM amid a period of heightened tension and intrigue make her case exceptional. However, to fetishize the perceived singularity of her death runs the risk of forgetting the place of this case within a broader context of violence against Indigenous women. In this context, the heightened visibility of some victims of gendered violence—deemed appropriately "grievable"[150] by virtue of the professed specificity and "poignancy"[151] of their victimization—is matched by the conspicuous invisibility or elision of others.

Of the theatre's potential to intervene into one way of seeing, while also offering others, Nolan says: "That is my way of witnessing"—of saying "This is so; why is this so?"[152] This chapter set out to ask such questions of those instances in which some victims are deemed more appropriate for public memory than others, while also querying the normative imperatives legible in this hierarchization of victimry. Part of my goal has been to understand such hierarchichal memorial practice as endemic to, rather than signalling a departure from, liberal ideology as informing some anti-violence initiatives and literature. In closing, then, I want to offer a complicating counterpoint to the discussion I've offered of Nolan's play in this chapter, in order to suggest how this play, despite its resistive impulse, may participate nonetheless in the prospective valuing of Anna Mae Pictou-Aquash as normatively grievable and as uniquely worthy of remembrance. For, if the closing monologue manages metaphorically to populate the stage with a living legacy of women who "cannot" all be killed,[153] then Anna Mae notably stands in as their sole embodied representative; ironically, it is through her individualized persona as a martyr for the American Indian Movement, and for Indigenous women more generally, that she is able to evoke the names of others who will proceed her. In this way, the play's reflexive critique of Anna Mae's individualized martyrdom (and of the fatalistic necessity with which it is ascribed) arguably undermines itself in the very moment of its assertion.

If Helen Betty Osborne's case enjoys dominant recognition in part because of her perceived legitimacy as a victim, and because of the possibility for liberal contrition and "progress" her death offers, Anna Mae likewise emerges in Nolan's play as a victim whose death can be solemnly celebrated for what it makes possible in the present: the enduring memory of a "brave-hearted woman"[154] that might then "inspire" others in the activist struggle against the "bitter injustices of racism."[155] In this way, the character of Anna Mae seems designed, in the "End" scene, to both resist and resign to violence in equal measure. By this, I mean that the character both "resist[s] to the utmost,"[156] as the legitimate victim of violence must, *and* resigns to her fate as a gendered martyr whose death figures (retrospectively) as an act of service to the activist movement. This I see as one of the primary ways in which the play attempts to negotiate between accounting for Anna Mae's agency as a figure of activist resistance, and offering a satisfyingly fatalistic account of her life and death. As in the dominant commemorative repertoire through which Osborne circulates, wherein her murder is figured as both "senseless"[157] and as having "happened for a reason,"[158] Anna Mae appears at the end of this play as an agential figure who struggles to her last, *and* as a figure resigned to her fate.

Anna Mae's victimry is anxiously legitimized through the play's emphasis on her resistance to violence, and through the play's positioning of her character in "'respectable' societal roles"—that is, in the role of mother, daughter, and sister.[159] Her vocal resistance to her rape at the end of the play leaves no question as to her non-consent, while the subsequent verbal recitation of her daughters' and sisters' names underscores (if only obliquely, in this instance) the familial commitments she had "willingly give[n] up" for the sake of the movement.[160] For instance, Anna Mae resists the sexual violence that is carried out against her with "agitated, pleading, angry, [and] anguished" protest—repeating the word "don't" over and over again.[161] She is here the clear and unequivocal victim of violence, and her protest is unambiguous. Notably, her assailant is a composite of both AIM-affiliated characters and the "FBI Guy," in order to reflect the suspected historical collusion of both parties in Anna Mae's murder. As this figure of patriarchal malevolence approaches, her 'don'ts' become more "agitated"; and yet, "as he rapes her, she stops begging"[162] and begins instead the commemorative recitation with which the play ends: "My name is Anna Mae Pictou Aquash," she states, before going on to name her family members and all those "sisters" and "daughters" who will carry on—despite (or even because of) her death: "My daughters are Denise and Deborah. You cannot kill us all. You can kill me, but my sisters live, my daughters live."[163]

The line with which the play in fact closes, just prior to the gunshot, reinscribes the very fatalism Nolan elsewhere seems intent to critique. And indeed Anna Mae has been moving toward this very moment since the beginning of the play: "You can kill me, but you cannot kill us all," Anna Mae says—and then, simply, "You can kill me."[164] As experienced in live theatre as an auditory effect, this line—"You can kill me"—would presumably sound as if it were cut off, mid-sentence, by the sound of the gunshot that follows it. And yet, when read as plainly stated on the printed page, the line also comes across as a directive. It is declarative, more than anything, purposefully punctuated in the script by a period rather than a gunshot. Though a possible bid to characterize Anna Mae as agential to the last, the declarative statement creates the subtextual effect of choice where none exists, and moreover ascribes martyr status to Anna Mae's death. For, when read against its qualifying phrase, "but my sisters live, my daughters live," the directive, "you can kill me," becomes an exchange of sorts, where one chooses death so that others might live. In its closing moments, then, *Annie Mae's Movement* cannot sustain an analysis of this murder as part of the ongoing, systemic, and often state-sponsored "disappearing"[165] of Indigenous peoples, though it was with just this sort of analysis that the play began. As with some representations of Helen Betty Osborne, the focus perhaps becomes instead what this individualized and legitimately tragic figure can offer audiences in the present: the memory of a "brave hearted woman," whose death is reassuringly unique, singular, and past.

If, in the dominant rhetoric of recognition and redress, instances of colonial violence remain discrete—embedded within their own contained teleologies of "past" harm and of subsequent remembrance and redress—then we fail irrevocably to see what we must: that history is not past, but rather persists radically in our present. By this I mean to highlight not only how present injustices can be traced to historical colonial policies, but also the yet more insidious means by which the ongoing material reality of colonial violence is alternately evoked and elided in dominant discourses of remembrance. Literature, however, provides an alternative framework through which to reckon with colonial violence against Indigenous women in Canada. In Robertson's commemorative graphic novel, or in Nolan's commemorative play, key problems in popular anti-violence remembrance are revealed. While neither text is without its own limitations, both enable a critical discussion on dominant notions of grievability, on what constitutes a "legitimate" victim of violence, and on the stakes of rehearsing a violent death as both tragic and senseless, on one hand, and as somehow *necessary* to the anti-violence movement, on the other. Through Robertson's and Nolan's texts we can question the instructive or reparative potential of storytelling the lives of missing and murdered women. Through these literary reflections we can see more clearly the problems with ascribing agency and choice to untimely death, and with the public construction of some victims as more worthy of remembrance than others.

CONCLUSION
Thinking beyond the National Inquiry: *A Red Girl's Reasoning*

Every February 14 in communities across Canada, Indigenous women and their allies hold commemorative events in solidarity with the annual Women's Memorial March in Vancouver's Downtown Eastside. In the words of the organizing committee, this march honours the lives of all missing and murdered women—a disproportionate number of whom are Indigenous. Led by Indigenous women's groups and family members of the missing and murdered, the march contests the depoliticization of gendered colonial violence in dominant discourse and affirms the responsibilities of the living in remembrance and protest.

By drawing public attention to the disappearances of women *as violence*, the march counters through communal and embodied acts of gathering, walking, singing, speech making, and prayer the profound erasure of the missing from public memory, and the deeply rooted forms of forgetting and denial this erasure entails. The march thus fulfills a deliberate political purpose: as Amber Dean puts it, "this event has strategically drawn attention to the disappearances and violent deaths of Indigenous women from the neighbourhood and demanded an official response."[1] But the march is more than a strategic bid for recognition or visibility in dominant public culture.[2] It is also a relational practice that requires of its participants a reckoning with what Dean terms "the social circumstances of [these] violent and unjust deaths."[3] Nor can the march do this work for us. As Sharon Rosenberg observes of "remembering for change": "We cannot anticipate that a monument will do the work of remembering for us. We need to do it. Location matters. No one visits a monument empty of history, of life. We all come with what we know and what we cannot bear to know."[4]

It is partly for this reason that visibility in itself is no necessary guarantor of social change, and that the growing public awareness around missing and murdered women has not resulted in decreased rates of violence. Rosenberg reminds us that memory and change are active, relational processes. We are all affected by Canada's colonial history (and present), though we are positioned differently by it. And yet many dominant strategies for raising awareness actually instruct us in the opposite: from public inquiries, human rights reportage, and mainstream anti-violence service providers, we often learn that increased knowledge and awareness lead naturally to social change, that Indigenous women need merely to be better included in dominant paradigms, and that to remember—without a sense of history, location, or responsibility—is enough. In short, we learn that colonialism is a historical phenomenon to learn about, rather than an ongoing set of relationships to be transformed. But Indigenous women's literature tells us otherwise.

From contemporary writers and storytellers we learn not only about the possibilities and limits of public recognition as a pathway to change, but also about the politics of our location as readers, and the relational labour entailed in any reading practice. And this has direct implications for anti-violence activism because, like Rosenberg's monuments, no one visits a literary text empty of history, of life. Both are discursive sites to which we bring the full weight of history; literature can help us to see this more reflexively. As readers, our task is to discern what we are being asked to witness and, depending on our position, to determine our relationships and responsibilities accordingly. In the case of anti-violence activism, there is a danger of subsuming Indigenous struggles within mainstream feminist terms of debate, or of naturalizing the state's assimilationist frameworks of recognition and redress. Reading literature in dialogue with actual sites of anti-violence resistance affords us yet further insight into this problem—emphasizing the incommensurability between Indigenous and Euro-Western strategies of resistance while highlighting the decolonizing recommendations that emerge from the texts themselves.

Harsha Walia recommends, in addition to anti-violence activists taking initiative to educate themselves, that they "take leadership" and direction from those on the front lines.[5] This recommendation emerges in Christine Welsh's *Finding Dawn* when the documentary is read with and against British Columbia's Missing Women Commission of Inquiry. Contrary to the extractive and exclusionary methods of the provincial inquiry, in which the voices of Indigenous, feminist, and sex-work organizations were marginalized, the film draws upon Indigenous women's experiences of violence and of resistance, as well as place-based strategies of response. Through interviews with family members as well as Indigenous anti-violence advocates across western Canada, the film intervenes into how knowledge about missing and murdered women is commonly produced, and argues that we take direction from the very voices the inquiry failed to hear. And yet, when Indigenous women's stories *are* featured in anti-violence awareness and rights campaigns, there is no guarantee of an ethical "hearing" or response. As Robina Anne Thomas says: "For me, there is always the fear of documenting our stories. Will the voices be heard?"[6] This is precisely the complication that Marilyn Dumont's commemorative poetry addresses.

NWAC's Sisters in Spirit Campaign and Amnesty International's *Stolen Sisters* report offer two different examples of how biographical case studies promote awareness and inform policy critique. When read in dialogue with these reports, Dumont's poetry facilitates a critical take on the role of life narratives in rights campaigns. While the case study has become a prominent form in human rights reportage, Dumont explores through her free-verse elegy a different formal approach to the individual "case," one premised upon relational historicity as a responsible remembrance practice. Dumont advocates a politically engaged form of memory for which readers themselves must take responsibility. Naming and historicizing white male violence, exposing the systemic violence of the justice system, and pursuing thorny questions about what constitutes a responsible representation of the missing or murdered, Dumont's commemorative poem suggests that *how* we remember might be as, or more, important than the fact of remembrance itself.

Dumont's intervention instructs readers in the critical vigilance required in our current moment, when national efforts toward reconciliation and redress superficially acknowledge the so-called "historical" violences of colonialism in order to secure settler sovereignty and futurity. Narratives of settler tolerance, benevolence, and inclusivity are central to this dissimulation of colonial power; many Indigenous-authored texts, however, will not "allow the real and symbolic violences of settler colonialism to be overlooked."[7] For instance, Morningstar Mercredi's memoir connects historical and intergenerational traumas to the ongoing experience of gendered colonial violence in the present. This move deliberately troubles the settler reader's prospective retreat to innocence. While some activist and reading practices seek to "reconcile settler guilt and complicity," Mercredi undermines this fantasy as itself a reinscription of colonial relations of power and recommends that readers confront the nation's state of denial.[8]

This confrontation is not always a straightforward process; some texts instruct us in Canada's history of gendered colonial violence but seemingly present this knowledge as something that, once learned, requires of us no further responsibility or structural change. David Robertson's graphic novel, for example, teaches young adult readers about the dehumanizing stereotypes that put Indigenous women and girls at risk of white male violence. And yet, the graphic novel also suggests that such violence is not in vain, as long as settler Canadians learn from it and progress socially as a result. The stories of missing and murdered women are then at risk of becoming a mere proving ground for settler benevolence and for the legitimacy of the settler colonial state. Meanwhile, government-led initiatives have generally not provided new answers or taken meaningful responsibility for change; rather, as Robyn Bourgeois puts it, initiatives like public inquiries allow "the Canadian state to *appear* that it is doing something about violence against women *without ever having to actually do anything.*"[9]

In their collaborative response to calls for a national inquiry, the Families of Sisters in Spirit (FSIS), No More Silence (NMS), and the Native Youth Sexual Health Network (NYSHN) interrogate the limitations of state responses and inquiries while focusing on the strength and knowledge of grassroots organizations and families. Writing in March 2014, they state:

> We have seen how state-led inquiries play out, most recently in British Columbia where the Missing Women's Commission of Inquiry was deemed a sham by families and the communities affected. Of the sixty-three recom-

mendations made only three have been implemented. We have seen less change and improvement from these government initiatives than what is coming from community-based responses; such as the February 14th Women's Memorial March Committee. There have been suggestions on how to make inquiries more inclusive, but we as grassroots organizations, as families who have been through this before, prefer to look to each other for solutions. Where we have seen success has been in engagement with people on the front-lines and in our communities who live these realities everyday and seek change. This is where we draw our strength.[10]

Announced in December 2015, the inquiry officially began its work on September 1, 2016, with promises to offer an "important step towards reconciliation and building a nation-to-nation relationship based on a renewed sense of trust between the Government of Canada and Indigenous peoples in Canada."[11] The collaborative statement by FSIS, NMS, and NYSHN, however, draws attention to the potential for further harm and mistrust—whether resulting from non-inclusive processes, a lack of follow-through on recommendations, or a reliance on colonial structures as the preferred site of anti-violence action (including policing, child welfare, education, and justice systems). For this reason, these grassroots organizations recommend that Indigenous peoples and their consensual allies turn away from solutions that re-embed colonial relations of power and instead look to Indigenous-led initiatives in education, organizing, and creative arts for leadership and direction. Many of these initiatives account for both the strategic necessity and also the pitfalls of engaging "state-led response to deaths and disappearances."[12]

FSIS, NMS, and NYSHN make concrete recommendations for Indigenous-led, resurgence-based practices of resistance, including: critical education and support for communities and families in "understanding the connections between violence in their lives and the bigger political picture"; fostering responsible media arts and other public representations that present Indigenous perspectives; and looking to local, community-based efforts for leadership in change.[13] In closing, I look to Blackfoot/Sami filmmaker Elle-Máijá Tailfeathers's eleven-minute revenge-drama, *A Red Girl's Reasoning* (2012) for its imaginative engagement with these recommendations.

The film begins *in medias res,* opening on the image of a man fleeing through an alleyway. At first, the black-and-white image appears washed out, overexposed; in the foreground, the dark silhouette of a chain-link fence stands in stark contrast to that bleak, bright backdrop of brick alley wall. As the camera pans from left to right, this harsh discord between light and dark gives us the impression of watching from the shadows, unseen, as the fugitive ducks through an opening in the alleyway opposite us and disappears. A cop appears from the left, seconds later, apparently in hot pursuit. A desolate and claustrophobic cityscape then unfolds by way of the chase: a series of fast-cut split screens tracks each figure's progress through a labyrinth of dingy, urban byways, while an accompanying drumbeat sets an unrelenting pace. Abruptly, however, the symmetry of this split-screen foot chase is broken by the introduction of a third figure, fast approaching on a motorcycle. A low-angle shot captures the immaculate, opaque visor of a black helmet. In its shiny surface, we see only the reflections of building tops and lampposts whipping by. We hear the throaty rumble of the motor changing gears. The rider approaches—inscrutable, unremitting.

While the hard-lit, tightly framed aesthetic of the urban foot chase draws unquestionably from film noir and B-movie action stock, the introduction of the rider signals a parallel set of genre conventions: those of the female revenge narrative. As the rider disembarks from the bike and removes the helmet, a woman's dark head of hair is revealed. As she resumes her progress through the alley on foot, a medium shot exposes a young face, a furrowed brow, and a hard stare of purpose and determination. Her pace is swift but measured, unlike the frenetic motion of the men. And when the parallel scenes of chase and pursuit at last converge in confrontation, it is not between men on opposite sides of the law, but rather between the rider herself and the fugitive—simply referred to in the credits as "the hoodlum." The rider is Delia, an epithet for Artemis, Greek goddess of the hunt.

The hoodlum meets her head-on, but Delia dispatches him in short order. Dodging his swipes and disarming him of his switchblade, she then delivers a series of fierce combination punches that see him laid up, prone on a pile of alley refuse in a matter of seconds. Notably, this fight scene is filmed in a series of tight, over-the-shoulder shots in which Delia is a constant. By means of several match cuts, however, the hoodlum and the cop alternate as the object of Delia's wrath: in one shot, Delia's right hook is destined for the cop's face; in the next, it's the hoodlum who recoils from the impact. These taut visual rhymes have the striking effect of implying seamless continuity in action and purpose, but with the following disorienting result: as Delia rains down a punishment from which neither cop nor hoodlum escape, the tidy moral dichotomy of the cold-open chase scene dissolves before our eyes.

In the tradition of revenge narrative, Delia presents an alternative moral universe in which male violence is punished by an avenging heroine-survivor.[14] This is captured visually by the fight scene's dissolution of the white, male, homosocial contest of cops and robbers—a contest which Delia's own revenge supersedes. As she stands over the bruised and bloodied body of the hoodlum, Delia's dispassionate voiceover explains: "I've been on this warpath for six long, lonely years. But white boys have been having their way with Indian girls since contact. Forget what Disney tells you: Pocahontas was twelve when she met John Smith. It's pretty little lies like this that hide the ugly truth."[15]

The film thus establishes at the outset what visual studies scholar Judith Franco calls a "moral alibi" for Delia's actions.[16] This victim-turned-vigilante punishes centuries of gendered colonial violence with a smooth, mechanical efficiency matched by her preferred mode of travel: the gleaming Yamaha cruiser. In this framework for justice, both the individual perpetrators of violence and the system that protects them are under indictment. Delia's voiceover elaborates: "My clients come to me with their requests for justice, when the justice system fails them."[17] Embodied by the cop, the justice system takes as much a beating as the so-called hoodlum. White boys are having their way with Indian girls, the film tells us, and both perpetrators and the law are in on the game.

Indigenous feminist critics have long pointed to the limits of resisting colonial violence within the very structures that have made this violence possible in the first place. The film engages this critique by envisioning an alternative path to justice. This is not to say that the film advocates vigilante action as the only viable solution to the missing and murdered women crisis, but rather that it borrows strategically from the tropes of revenge narrative in order to animate this debate. For instance, critical geographer Sarah Hunt argues that "many of the strategies to address violence have further strengthened broad systems of colonial power, which are themselves inherently violent. We continue to appeal to the Canadian legal system to address physical violence, calling for more policing or better laws, while knowing this system is set up to oppress, rather than help, us."[18] In the context of ongoing settler colonialism, Indigenous women are targets not only of interpersonal violence, but also of colonial policy and law. Rather than seeking improved visibility and recognition within the state's existing legal and political structures, Hunt recommends strategies focused on "rebuilding [Indigenous women's] individual and collective strength."[19]

This entails a profound recentring of Indigenous women's leadership and knowledge in anti-violence action and critique. *A Red Girl's Reasoning* pursues this project implicitly—not only by decentring the state's legal system as a legitimate site of justice, but by exploring Delia's revenge as a form of relationship building between herself and other Indigenous women. These relationships, which Rachel Flowers characterizes as turning "love *inward*,"[20] take place both within the fictional universe of the film itself and within a broader tradition of Indigenous women's resistance writing to which the film refers. In each of these sites, the film enacts a vital form of self-recognition—one that holds a place for politicized anger and resentment and that draws strength from other "warrior women" in resisting gendered colonial violence.[21]

The motorcycle-riding, vengeance-seeking Delia may inspire comparison to The Bride in Quentin Tarantino's *Kill Bill*, and to other heroines of the revenge-exploitation genre whose acts of extrajudicial retribution are motivated by an originary instance of male violence—namely, rape. Yet, Tailfeathers's film is unlike many of its obvious cinematic counterparts in several ways. Feminist critics have debated the extent to which such films are resistive or reactionary in their politics, especially in their tendency to sensationalize sexual violence and to explore female strength as premised upon vulnerability and violation.[22] Tailfeathers avoids some of these more problematic conventions by refusing to depict onscreen Delia's original attack, while still delivering the discomforting oppositional pleasure afforded by the spectacle of redemptive payback at the film's end. This redemption is prefigured in the film's opening scene, in which we first learn of Delia's "long, lonely" search for justice, and is realized in the film's climatic scene of encounter between Delia and her original attacker, Brian. Significantly, however, this path isn't one Delia travels alone. Nor does she seek vengeance solely for herself. Rather, she learns of Brian's whereabouts when his file comes across her desk, so to speak; Delia is in the "business" of revenge, and she conducts her calling through a covert network of other Indigenous women. While *Kill Bill*'s Bride "must step over the bodies of other women, specifically women of color, on her way to her implied equal, a [white] man,"[23] Delia's work is decolonial and relational—"accountable," in Eve Tuck and Wayne Yang's terms, "to Indigenous sovereignty and futures" rather than to the ideal of reconciliation with settlers or with the settler colonial state.[24]

The first scene following the opening finds Delia seated at a bar. Close-up: a half-filled glass is slid across the bar on a cardboard coaster. Delia removes the glass and flips over the coaster to reveal the bartender's scrawled dispatch: simply, "Goldman Industries." Making note of the location, Delia lights first the coaster and then her cigarette. A voiceover from a news broadcast plays softly in the background: "The victim has been identified as an Aboriginal female. Foul play is suspected. But police have yet to name any suspects." Against this backdrop of ineffective or indifferent policing is the reassuring image of Delia at work. The coaster, now alight in her hand, signals the relational and grassroots context in which that work is done—with the help of the bartender.

Cut to the next scene, in which Delia establishes contact with her new client, Nelly. A high-angle shot tracks the tentative footsteps of wedge heels across uneven pavement. A young woman glances nervously over her shoulder and into the shadows cast by non-descript industrial equipment, uttering a startled gasp when Delia makes herself known. Their exchange is brief and professional. Nelly hands Delia a large manila envelope. As Delia shuffles through its contents, an over-the-shoulder shot reveals a candid photo of Nelly's attacker and Delia's latest target: a tall, clean-cut man in a suit and tie. A glimmer of recognition is seen on Delia's face—her jaw tightens at the sight of Brian, her own assailant—but Nelly seems not to notice. Nelly explains: "I took him to court, but they let him walk. Said the damn kit was inconclusive. That my blood showed traces of this, and that. That my lifestyle was high-risk. Like I was fuckin' asking for it."

Nelly's brief discourse works to debunk the victim-blaming rhetoric prevalent in cases of sexual violence against women, and in Indigenous women's cases particularly. As Flowers puts it, when speaking about the February 14th Women's Memorial March, this demonstration offers a "counterdiscourse to the dominant narrative that Indigenous women and girls are 'vulnerable' thereby placing the burden on us to not only protect ourselves by changing our 'risky' behaviors but also to find solutions to ongoing systematic violence and oppression."[25] Nelly's statement likewise counters this narrative, locating dysfunction and responsibility not with Indigenous women but with predatory men and a culture of normalized violence. The glossy photo of Brian does a similar kind of work—that is, by visually naming that which many public commentators are "unwilling to name": white male violence.[26] Sarah Hunt asks: "Why are we so hesitant to name white male violence as a root cause, yet so comfortable naming all the 'risk factors' associated with the lives of Indigenous girls who have died? Why are we not looking more closely at the 'risk factors' that lead to violence in the lives of the perpetrators?"[27] While Brian's particular risk factors—namely, a socially fostered sense of entitlement, impunity, and supremacy—are further explored in his climactic encounter with Delia, the photo is the first information viewers have about Brian's gendered, class-based, and racial privilege.

Contextualized through Nelly's verbal exchange with Delia, the photo also serves in place of a flashback. While this device conventionally offers a rationale for a film's action and the characters' motivations, such backstory is available in Tailfeathers only through Delia's and Nelly's own words, and through such evidentiary documents as Brian's photo. This is a meaningful choice on Tailfeathers's part; her refusal to depict via flashback Brian's original attack on either character means that viewers must take these women at their word. That both Delia and Nelly were assaulted by Brian is not up for debate and requires no visual verification or reproduction. Against the hostile incredulity with which women's allegations of sexual assault are often publicly received, then, the film presumes a viewer's belief and thus spends less time securing it, and more time developing relationships between the women characters themselves.

Before they part ways, Nelly strengthens the reciprocal bond with Delia by offering her a gift of tobacco: "Look, I know you don't take payment, but please: just take these." She hands Delia a pack of cigarettes. This is not an economic exchange, since Delia will not accept payment for the service she provides. As Sami scholar Rauna Kuokkanen says of the gift in the context of Indigenous epistemes, "one does not give primarily in order to receive but rather in order to ensure the balance of the world on which the well-being of the entire social order is contingent."[28] Put another way, Nelly's gift of tobacco is not given to "ensure" or purchase Delia's help, but rather "to actively acknowledge kinship and coexistence in the world."[29] Brian's predation relies on the women's presumed social isolation; he assumes that the women he targets have no relations and behaves as if he had none himself. But Delia, Nelly, and the bartender know different, and the next scene serves to illustrate their network in action.

When the industrial alley dissolves, viewers are returned once more to the bar. Brian, whom we now recognize from the photo, sits alone at the counter, sipping his drink. Enter the bartender from some off-screen location, a baseball bat in hand. She strides across the space with proprietary ease—her polka-dot dress and pleated white apron charmingly incongruous with her casual, studied handling of the bat. The camera follows her, panning left as she replaces the bat next to the register and takes her place behind the bar. When our view cuts back to the counter again, we see that Delia has taken a stool. She leans forward, addressing the bartender brusquely: "Whiskey. Neat." The man turns and regards this new prospect with interest; apparently, he does not recognize her. He addresses Delia without invitation: "Wouldn't take a pretty girl like you to be a whiskey drinker. You from around here?" When she declines to answer, he leans in close, undeterred: "Listen," he says, downing his drink, "I'm gonna run off to the little boys' room. Don't disappear. Maybe I'll buy you a drink."

A close-up of his lips, mere inches from Delia's ear, draws particular attention to the line "don't disappear." Resonant of that nostalgic colonial fantasy of the vanishing Indian, this directive reads ironically against the clichéd pick-up line, "You from around here?" Delia can't help but *be* "from around here," and there's no risk of her disappearing. As

Secwepemc chief Bev Sellars has said, "First Nations people will always be in our territories. We have been here for thousands of years and we will be here for thousands more."[30] This promise is borne out in the wordless exchange that follows between the bartender and Delia: against Brian's sinister proposition, the women conspire to turn his known predatory strategies against him. In his absence, Delia leans forward and raises two fingers. The bartender fills Brian's empty class, into which Delia then empties the contents of a pill-sized capsule. The bartender stirs the drink with her index finger and shares with Delia a wry, conspiratorial smile just seconds before Brian returns. Taking his seat, he is both pleased and amused by Delia's initiative. "So that's how it is," he says, clasping his glass with satisfaction, "Cheers." At this, Delia turns toward him for the first time since taking her seat at the bar. Though she remains silent, she smiles sweetly and raises her glass to his. He throws his drink back in one smooth motion, before Delia takes so much as one sip.

A smash cut transports us abruptly to the film's fourth and final scene—a second-floor open-air landing in yet another abandoned urban alleyway. The blare of a train horn adds to the jarring sense of sudden displacement as a disoriented Brian comes to. He is bound by each wrist, standing with his arms outstretched in a vulnerable pose. He is naked, save for a pair of black briefs. As he begins to stir, his gaze finds Delia stationed a few feet in front of him. Seated in a casual pose, cheek resting in her hand, Delia greets him: "Old habits die hard, hey Brian?" With gloved hands, she then withdraws from her bag a large, glossy photo. "Her name's Nelly," she says, confronting Brian (à la Dexter) with the image of his most recent victim. "What the hell is this?" he asks, anger competing with confusion. Delia merely confronts him with more evidence; she next produces a small ziplock bag of pills, which she tosses to his feet. "Rohypnol. Ruffies, Brian. The asshole that did this to Nelly put one of those in her drink." Now Delia is holding a different photograph—one of Nelly's battered face. "This is crazy," Brian says, indignant in response. "I don't know how they got there." Brian's main concern is to refuse responsibility—not only because he is in a position of temporary vulnerability, but also because his character believes himself entitled to commit violence with impunity. The form this entitlement takes will vary in expression as the scene unfolds. In each case, however, we are asked to interpret this confrontation (and Brian's responses) allegorically. Common public perceptions empty such violence as Brian's of historical context, relations of power, and culpability;[31] in giving us a filmic reality in which the gendered and racial dimensions of Brian's violence are undisputed, Tailfeathers allows us to focus critically on his rhetoric of denial and to experience more fully the implications of Delia's forceful rebuff.

At first, his voice softens: "I'm really sorry about what happened to your friend," Brian says. "That's terrible. But, there's a lot of low lives out there." In this moment, Brian performs the same kind of dismissive recognition that characterizes many official responses to violence in Canada: he acknowledges "what happened" in the same moment that he denies its reality as something for which he is responsible. Like former Prime Minister Stephen Harper's claim in 2014 that violence against Indigenous women is a criminal issue, but not part of a systemic sociological reality,[32] Brian's glib reply places the blame for Nelly's attack with a vague "low life" predator whose actions are explained as individual pathology rather than a centuries-old pattern of subjugation. In the context of the film's narrative and of Delia's personal tribunal, however, his comments come across as absurd. As viewers we already know that Brian is guilty. The phrasing of his denial, familiar to us as the rhetoric of politicians and other commentators, here sounds so hollow as to be insulting. The effect is then twofold, applying to both the world of the film and the social context in which we view it: Tailfeathers refuses an interpretation of colonial violence as interpersonal rather than systemic, and undermines commonplace public expressions of dissociation or disavowal.

As Brian delivers his detached statement of apology, Delia stands and approaches him. Rather than dignify his apology with a response, she simply fixes him with a calm, incredulous stare. In reaction he begins to strain frantically at his bonds. Then, just as suddenly, he changes tack. "Sweetie, if this is about money or something, all you gotta do is ask." Delia replies: "I'm not looking for handouts, Brian." The word choice here is significant. Refiguring Brian's scornful offer of money in the very terms commonly used to "denigrat[e] Aboriginal claims,"[33] Delia reminds Brian (and the audience) of this irreducible fact: it is Canadians and the Canadian state (not Indigenous peoples) that exist in a position of subsidy. Secwepemc leader and legal expert Arthur Manuel could hardly have put it more clearly: "Indigenous peoples basically subsidize the Canadian economy with free land and resources."[34] By free, Manuel means lands and resources falsely constructed by colonial myth and the Doctrine of Discovery as open for European settlement and extraction. As Manuel further explains in *Unsettling Canada*, this doctrine is an outmoded "legal justification for the colonial occupation of our lands and our nations" that has been widely repudiated by legal experts, in the Royal Commission on Aboriginal Peoples (RCAP), and at the UN Permanent Forum on Indigenous Issues.[35] This doctrine provides the foundation for Canada's continued appropriation of lands and resources for "free"—ignoring underlying Aboriginal title and essentially constructing Indigenous peoples as guests in their own territories. Nonetheless the misconception persists that, as Lynda Gray says, it is "First Nations people [who] get most things for free."[36]

As perceived "handouts" in land, housing, education, and tax exemptions, this notion of "free load[ing]" conveniently ignores that many of these "free" things derive, in the first place, from historical agreements and treaties with Indigenous nations—agreements from which Canada directly benefits in land and resources.[37] Toby Rollo reminds other non-Indigenous Canadians that the very "legitimacy of Canada and of Canadians as a people is constituted by historical treaties and agreements that contemporary citizens … benefit from and are obligated to uphold."[38] Misunderstanding the results of these agreements as "handouts" denies Indigenous sovereignty and constructs Indigenous peoples as reliant on the Canadian state (a sentiment which finds its forced legislative equivalent in the Indian Act). In suggesting a mere monetary motivation for Delia's actions, Brian does just this: he denies the legitimacy of her justice-based rationale and seeks to reassert normative colonial relations of power in which he can at once insist upon and resent a manufactured relationship of dependency. In this relation of power, Brian positions himself as a grudging source of benevolent "material redemption":[39] "Sweetie … all you gotta do is ask."

Notably, in no way is Brian's offer meant to admit moral culpability or financial liability for what he has done to Nelly. Brian distances the question of reparations from his own actual culpability by insinuating the unreliability of Delia's claim against him. In this way, Brian's rhetoric is suggestive not only of commonplace dismissals of Indigenous claims, but also of some public responses to the residential schools redress movement more specifically. For instance, as Jennifer Henderson remarks of mainstream newspaper commentary on residential schools redress, "print media addressed to the taxpayer-citizen suggested that government 'giveaways' to residential school survivors were based on an unreliable version of history."[40] Henderson cites Maliseet elder Alma Brooks, whose comments deftly underline the irony of this position: "Taxpayer money, which settlers ultimately derived from Indigenous territory, had funded the 'shock treatment' of residential schools" in the first place.[41]

While Brian's first strategy is to deny the legitimacy of Delia's claims against him, he next admits to but minimizes his violence by placing the blame with Nelly herself. He does this by insinuating Nelly's consent. When Delia refuses his "handouts," Brian replies: "Look. She wanted it. All I did is loosen her up a little." Writing about the deflection of accountability in sexual assault tribunals, feminist scholar Susan Ehrlich explains this as the predictable "discursive means by which a defendant … attempts to represent or construct himself as innocent."[42] In the context of Delia's tribunal, however, Brian's performance of innocence has yet another layer: he affixes to Nelly what Janice Acoose calls the "sexually promiscuous … tawny temptress" stereotype.[43] She "wanted it," Brian assures us—and as a pretext for gendered and racialized violence this concept is centuries old. Mohawk poet Beth Brant attributes its contemporary prevalence to the "ludicrous idea that whitemen are irresistible to Native women," but also traces this fantasy's origins to romanticized accounts of figures like Pocahontas and John Smith.[44] After four hundred years, this story continues to circulate as evidence of Indigenous women's willing subservience to white men: the Indian princess falls in love with and rescues the captured white man from execution, thus helping "colonialists gain a foot-hold in Indian Country."[45] As Brant wryly remarks, "Even Hollywood couldn't improve this tale."[46] And certainly, Delia herself invites the connection between violent subjugation and the stereotypes propagated by "what Disney tells you": "it's pretty little lies like these that hide the ugly truth," she says in the film's opening scene. Cree poet Rosanna Deerchild makes this point yet more explicitly in her poem "We Are Just": "we are just: your disney porn / girl who wears feathers / dances barefoot across / your screens before inviting / you into our tipis."[47] This fantasy of the temptress who invites white sexual aggression is completely overturned in the film's climactic scene—as is the fantasy of Indigenous woman-as-protector. Instead, Delia is Brian's captor, keeper, prosecutor, and judge.

While this long history of violence is embedded in Brian's defence—"She wanted it"—he next characterizes his violence as an isolated event for which he deserves pardon or leniency. "She was the only one," he assures Delia. "The only one," she replies. "Do you remember me?" Brian looks her up and down, then gives the slightest shake to his head. "Let me jog your memory," she offers, hitting him in the face. She then grabs his testicles as he attempts in vain to pull away from her painful grasp. "You and I met seven years ago," she reminds him. "You see, me and Nelly have a few things in common. We both know the dirty things you're capable of, and we've both been screwed over by this country's pathetic excuse of a justice system." With this, she releases her grip and steps back, watching with a bemused smile as Brian gasps for breath and attempts to regain composure. He shifts strategies again, now hanging his head and sniffling: "I'm sorry. I really am." His voice rises an octave as he chokes out his apology through crocodile tears. "I couldn't help it. I just – I'll never do it again. I swear!" As he raises his gaze to meet hers, she addresses him in a falsely gentle tone: "Brian. You've already told me two lies. I'd be a fool to fall for the third, now wouldn't I?"

Brian now realizes the futility of his attempts. He begins calling for help: "Help! Somebody help me! Help! Somebody please, help me!" Meanwhile, Delia casually pulls back a tarp, revealing a can of gasoline. As she douses Brian with gas his calls for help compete with the energetic thrum of A Tribe Called Red's "Electric Pow Wow"—the same song that played during the opening chase scene. He snarls racist epithets as he strains against his bonds, but Delia appears unperturbed. "Dirty fucking squaw," he growls. "You'll never get away with this!" Delia approaches, places a lit cigarette between his lips, and delivers these parting words in Cree: "Just watch me." And as viewers, we do: we don't witness Brian's ultimate decision—either "swallow the cigarette and live with the injury, or drop it and burn to death"—but instead watch a close-up of Delia's bike helmet, lit with the moving reflection of streetlights.[48]

In "Refusal to Forgive: Indigenous Women's Love and Rage," Leey'qsun scholar Rachel Flowers "genders" the discussion of politicized resentment in the context of colonial violence and dispossession. Specifically, she puts Glen Coulthard's work on the colonial politics of recognition into dialogue with Indigenous feminist scholarship of resurgence in order to demonstrate the political legitimacy of women's righteous anger in response to ongoing violence against Indigenous women and girls. *A Red Girl's Reasoning* performs a filmic rejoinder to this critical move: Delia's revenge is positioned not as an individualized form of a pathological return (a refusal to "get over it") but as a reasoned insistence on gendered violence as structurally enjoined by contemporary colonial relations—relations which require resistance and transformation, not reconciliation, for their end. In this, Delia draws strategy and strength from other women in the film, and from a broader tradition of women's resistance writing.

For instance, the film recognizes as one of its ancestors Mohawk poet-performer and critic E. Pauline Johnson (Tekahionwake). Johnson's 1893 short story, "A Red Girl's Reasoning" is an obvious literary antecedent.[49] In the story, Christie, the young bride of a Canadian public servant, argues with and leaves her husband Charlie when he refuses to acknowledge the legitimacy of her parents' marriage upon learning that it was conducted according to her own community's customs rather than by those of the Christian church. In his essay on "A Red Girl's Reasoning," Creek critic Craig Womack analyzes the rhetorical strategies of Christie's righteous response. He also discusses the role of the narrator, whose commentary on the plot and dialogue may seem "clunky" and invasive to contemporary readers, but which serves an important rhetorical function. From the narrator's frequent interjections, Womack infers that "Christie needs an ally."[50] He elaborates: Christie needs "the support of a community of women intellectuals who are notably missing. The narrator's helpless desperation to fill the gap by virtually stepping into the story ... heightens the absence of a group of reasoning women since the only person available for support does not exist—she is a fictional technique."[51] Although Tailfeathers's film differs dramatically in plot, it speaks to Johnson's story in this important respect: the film imagines for Delia (and its viewers) what Christie did not have—a community of reasoning, allied Indigenous women.

Together with its Indigenous women viewers, the film comprises a resistive anti-violence community. Like the statement by FSIS, NMS, and NYSHN, the film advocates that Indigenous women "look to each other for solutions,"[52] a possibility explored at the level of plot and by way of intertextual reference to Johnson's story. In imaginatively enacting this possibility, Tailfeathers affirms what Dory Nason calls the "love that Indigenous women have for their families, their lands, their nations, and themselves as Indigenous people."[53] As a "technique of collective self recognition," the film turns to Johnson's work in order to validate Indigenous women's contemporary practices of resentment and of love in response to gendered violence.[54] In doing so, it links women of different times and spaces in a shared political project of naming interpersonal violence as systemic, of denaturalizing colonial systems of justice and law, and of refusing the redemptive offer of reconciliation in place of decolonial transformation.

The film's engagement with non-Indigenous viewers works quite differently. This is because, as filmmaker Ariel Smith (Nêhiyaw) puts it, Indigenous and non-Indigenous viewers are positioned by the content in very different ways. "As Indigenous women," Smith says, "we are forced to live with the knowledge that we are not safe in this country. We are reminded of this fact constantly, with every missing person poster, every candlelight vigil, every billboard warning us not to hitchhike, every petition demanding an inquiry." By contrast, she says, "Non-Indigenous people do not have to live with this same fear of colonial violence."[55] The film confronts this lived reality of settler privilege by placing Brian in a position of vulnerability and fear. As viewers, Indigenous or not, we likely welcome this ending: the film's narrative logic invites us to derive moral satisfaction from Delia's revenge. And yet this satisfaction is, crucially, imperfect for the settler viewer who cannot identify with Delia-as-deliverer without performing an act of appropriation. To identify with Delia (or her co-conspirators) would be to collapse the very differences which Ariel Smith highlights and which the film is designed to contest. We do not all experience colonial violence, or its resistance, in the same way. Tailfeathers clarifies this distinction in her own comments on the film, in which she differentiates the metaphorical violence visited upon Brian from the actual violence Indigenous women face daily in Canada: "Some people ask how violence solves violence.... But it's metaphorical violence. Indigenous women, particularly in Canada, particularly in Vancouver on the Downtown Eastside—these women live violence on a daily basis. It was interesting to flip that reality."[56] While some non-Indigenous students in my classroom have expressed a discomfort with the film's climactic scene of encounter, I wonder if this discomfort originates from the film's representation of resistance, rather than with its representation of violence against Brian, per se.

After all, Delia's revenge takes place in the absence of non-Indigenous allies. The white characters in the film are all men on the wrong side of justice—the cop, the "hoodlum," and the serial rapist, Brian. Their vigilante resisters—the bartender, Nelly, and Delia herself—operate without assistance from anyone but each other. There is no obvious point of entry for the would-be allied viewer to exercise their solidarity. Not at the level of plot or character, in any case. This is not to say that the film forecloses the possibility of allied resistance, however. Rather, the film simply refuses to imagine for settlers what their solidarity might look like. It invites viewers to do this work for themselves. As Flowers says, "at some point, settlers will need to figure out where to stand without Indigenous peoples marking an 'X' on the ground for them and pointing out clear and plain injustice."[57] *A Red Girl's Reasoning* refuses to mark an X on the ground. It gives viewers the tools to understand gendered colonial violence, but it does not expend any narrative resources in directing settler outrage or in assuaging settler guilt. It exposes colonial injustice, but grants us no character or device through which to escape political responsibility. Ultimately, the film rejects a politics of solidarity performed for the sake of settler reconciliation and recognition—declining to address settler allies at all. Again, as Sharon Rosenberg puts it, we cannot anticipate that the film will "do the work" for us. "We need to do it."[58]

And what does this work entail for non-Indigenous viewers? As directed by the film, this work entails unlearning the justice system as a legitimate site of authority, recognition, and redress. It means rejecting what Hunt calls a "past-tense politics in which we [Indigenous women] only come to matter after we've been victimized."[59] By extension, it means understanding the Canadian nation-state as premised upon violence and displacement—both at the "macro" levels of land theft and oppressive identity policy, and at the "micro" levels of the everyday, where state violence comes home or, in Delia's case, sits beside you at the bar.[60] It means learning the long history of gendered violence to which the film alludes but does not painstakingly explain—as well as the living histories of resistance in the communities where we work and live. It means rethinking what non-Indigenous allies (often self-declared) want or expect from solidarity work. It entails working, learning, and showing up without expectation of approval, recognition, or gratitude. It means taking direction and leadership from Indigenous organizers and communities—a leadership accessible, as this film suggests, in grassroots activism as well as in creative or literary realms.

Tailfeathers models this for all of her viewers, as she takes direction from contemporary anti-violence organizing as well as from a literary ancestor, Pauline Johnson. Arguably, Christie's refusal in "A Red Girl's Reasoning" fuels and emboldens Delia's. That these refusals take place in story does not diminish their application in "real world" scenarios; rather, because they take place in story, they are all the more accessible as precedents for politically consequential work. In "Intense Dreaming: Theories, Narratives, and Our Search for Home," Dian Million explores this connection between story as theory, and story as a form of direct action: "Story *is* Indigenous theory. If these knowledges are couched in narratives, then narratives are always more than telling stories. Narratives seek inclusion, they seek the nooks and crannies of experiences, filling cracks and restoring order. Narratives lay boundaries. Narratives give orphans homes. Narratives both make links and are the links that have been made."[61] That is, story gives shape to what can be thought and done, linking past to present in an unbroken thread. This link restores order to the destruction wrought by colonialism, re-establishing sightlines between generations of women whose thinking, storytelling, and action have made contemporary resistance possible. When poet Marilyn

Dumont looks to her grandmothers, or when playwright Yvette Nolan imagines Anna Mae Pictou-Aquash calling upon her sisters and daughters, these writers model commemoration as political and intellectual work. In seeking new strategies to stop the violence, it is to these voices that we should look.

NOTES

PREFACE

1. Margaret Kovach, *Indigenous Methodologies: Characteristics, Conversations, and Contexts* (Toronto: University of Toronto Press, 2009), 3.
2. Roger Simon, *A Pedagogy of Witnessing: Curatorial Practice and the Pursuit of Social Justice* (Albany: State University of New York Press, 2014), 204.
3. Jeannette Armstrong, "The Disempowerment of First North American Native Peoples and Empowerment through Their Writing," in *An Anthology of Canadian Native Literature in English*, 3rd ed., ed. Daniel David Moses and Terry Goldie (Don Mills, ON: Oxford University Press, 2005), 244.
4. Ibid., 245.
5. Rachel Flowers, "Refusal to Forgive: Indigenous Women's Love and Rage," *Decolonization: Indigeneity, Education and Society* 4, no. 2 (2015): 34.
6. Ibid., 33.
7. See Renate Eigenbrod, "Between 'Colonizer-Perpetrator' and Colonizer-Ally': Toward a Pedagogy of Redress," in *The Oxford Handbook of Indigenous American Literature*, ed. James H. Cox and Daniel Heath Justice (Don Mills, ON: Oxford University Press, 2014), 441–54; Sam McKegney, *Magic Weapons: Aboriginal Writers Remaking Community after Residential School* (Winnipeg: University of Manitoba Press, 2007), 45; Sam McKegney, "Strategies for Ethical Engagement: An Open Letter Concerning Non-Native Scholars of Native Literatures," *Studies in American Indian Literatures* 20, no. 4 (2008): 56–67.

188   Notes to Preface

8 Sarah Hunt, "Why Are We Hesitant to Name White Male Violence as a Root Cause of #MMIW?" *Rabble.ca*, September 4, 2015, http://rabble.ca/news/2014/09/why-are-we-hesitant-to-name-white-male-violence-root-cause-mmiw.

INTRODUCTION

1 Leanne Simpson, *Dancing on Our Turtle's Back: Stories of Nishnaabeg Re-Creation, Resurgence, and a New Emergence* (Winnipeg: Arbeiter Ring, 2011), 101.
2 Ibid., 35.
3 Bonita Lawrence, *"Real" Indians and Others: Mixed-Blood Urban Native Peoples and Indigenous Nationhood* (Vancouver: University of British Columbia Press, 2004), 31.
4 Edward John, in *Missing Women Commission of Inquiry Hearings*, October 12, 2011, 13, http://www.missingwomeninquiry.ca/transcripts/.
5 Native Women's Association of Canada (NWAC), *What Their Stories Tell Us: Research Findings from the Sisters in Spirit Initiative* (Ottawa: NWAC, 2010), i, https://nwac.ca/wp-content/uploads/2015/07/2010-What-Their-Stories-Tell-Us-Research-Findings-SIS-Initiative.pdf.
6 Maryanne Pearce, "An Awkward Silence: Missing and Murdered Vulnerable Women and the Canadian Justice System" (PhD diss., University of Ottawa, 2013), 23, http://dx.doi.org/10.20381/ruor-3344.
7 Inconsistencies and inaccuracies in the official figures suggest that the numbers could be much higher. For further discussion of these statistics in terms of their significance and limitations, see Robert Alexander Innes and Kim Anderson, "Who's Walking with Our Brothers?" in *Indigenous Men and Masculinities: Legacies, Identities, Regeneration*, ed. Robert Alexander Innes and Kim Anderson (Winnipeg: University of Manitoba Press, 2015), 7–9.
8 "Aboriginal Women: A Demographic, Social and Economic Profile" (Ottawa: Indian and Northern Affairs Canada, 1996), quoted in Amnesty International, *Stolen Sisters: A Human Rights Response to Discrimination and Violence against Indigenous Women in Canada* (Ottawa: Amnesty International, 2004), 14, https://www.amnesty.ca/sites/ amnesty/files/amr200032004enstolensisters.pdf.
9 Canada, House of Commons, Standing Committee on the Status of

Women, *Call into the Night: An Overview of Violence against Aboriginal Women*, 3rd sess., 40th Parliament, March 2011, http://www.parl.gc.ca/HousePublications/Publication.aspx?DocId=5056509&Language=E.
10 Ibid.
11 Robyn Gervais, in *Missing Women Commission of Inquiry Hearings*, October 12, 2011, 114.
12 Canada, National Inquiry into Missing and Murdered Indigenous Women and Girls, "Terms of Reference," last modified August 3, 2016, accessed November 6, 2016, https://www.aadnc-aandc.gc.ca/eng/1470422455025/1470422554686.
13 Robyn Bourgeois, "Warrior Women: Indigenous Women's Anti-Violence Engagement with the Canadian State" (PhD diss., University of Toronto, 2014), 11, https://tspace.library.utoronto.ca/bitstream/1807/68238/1/Bourgeois_Robyn_S_201411_PhD_thesis.pdf. Italics in original.
14 Glen Coulthard, *Red Skin, White Masks* (Minneapolis: University of Minnesota Press, 2014), 3.
15 Flowers, "Refusal to Forgive," 35.
16 Dian Million, *Therapeutic Nations: Healing in an Age of Human Rights* (Tucson: University of Arizona Press, 2013), 158.
17 Eve Tuck and K. Wayne Yang, "Decolonization Is Not a Metaphor," *Decolonization: Indigeneity, Education, and Society* 1, no. 1 (2012): 3.
18 Ibid., 35.
19 Ibid., 9.
20 Ibid., 28.
21 Ibid.
22 Sarah Hunt, "More Than a Poster Campaign: Redefining Colonial Violence," in *The Winter We Danced: Voices from the Past, the Future, and the Idle No More Movement*, ed. The Kino-nda-niimi Collective (Winnipeg: Arbeiter Ring, 2014), 190.
23 Cheryl Suzack, "Law, Literature, Location: Contemporary Aboriginal/Indigenous Women's Writing and the Politics of Identity" (PhD diss., University of Alberta, 2004), 32, http://search.proquest.com.ezproxy.library.ubc.ca/docview/305097267?pq-origsite=summon.
24 Joyce Green, "Taking Account of Aboriginal Feminism," in *Making Space for Indigenous Feminism*, ed. Joyce Green (Winnipeg: Fernwood, 2007), 31.

25 Taiaiake Alfred, *Wasáse: Indigenous Pathways of Action and Freedom* (Peterborough: Broadview, 2005), 23.
26 Patricia A. Monture, "Women's Words: Power, Identity, and Indigenous Sovereignty," *Canadian Woman Studies* 26, no. 3/4 (2008): 156, http://cws.journals.yorku.ca/index.php/cws/article/view/22125/20779.
27 Daniel Heath Justice, "Currents of Trans/National Criticism in Indigenous Literary Studies," *American Indian Quarterly* 35, no. 3 (2011): 335–36, doi:10.5250/amerindiquar.35.3.0334.
28 Ibid., 336–37.
29 Craig Womack, *Art as Performance, Story as Criticism: Reflections on Native Literary Aesthetics* (Norman: University of Oklahoma Press, 2009), 96.
30 Justice, "Currents," 337.
31 Jo-Ann Episkenew, "Socially Responsible Criticism: Aboriginal Literature, Ideology, and the Literary Canon," in *Creating Community: A Roundtable on Canadian Aboriginal Literature*, ed. Renate Eigenbrod and Jo-Ann Episkenew (Penticton, BC: Theytus, 2002), 65. Italics in original.
32 Jo-Ann Episkenew, *Taking Back Our Spirits: Indigenous Literature, Public Policy, and Healing* (Winnipeg: University of Manitoba Press, 2009), 4.
33 Kovach, *Indigenous Methodologies*, 39.
34 Simpson, *Dancing*, 20.
35 Kimberly Blaeser, "Native Literature: Seeking a Critical Center," in *Looking at the Words of Our People: First Nations Analysis of Literature*, ed. Jeannette Armstrong (Penticton, BC: Theytus, 1993), 53.
36 Niigonwedom James Sinclair, in Kristina Fagan et al., "Canadian Indian Literary Nationalism? Critical Approaches in Canadian Indigenous Contexts—A Collaborative Interlogue," *Canadian Journal of Native Studies* 29, no. 1–2 (Fall 2009): 22.
37 Andrea Smith, "Beyond the Politics of Inclusion: Violence against Women of Color and Human Rights," *Meridians* 4, no. 2 (2004): 121.
38 Andrea Smith, *Conquest: Sexual Violence and American Indian Genocide* (Cambridge, MA: South End Press, 2005), 1.
39 Julia Emberley, *Defamiliarizing the Aboriginal: Cultural Practices and Decolonization in Canada* (Toronto: University of Toronto Press, 2007), 48.
40 Patricia Monture-Angus, *Thunder in My Soul: A Mohawk Woman Speaks* (Halifax: Fernwood, 1995), 185.

41 Arvin elaborates: "'Whitestream feminism' is a term used by Native feminist Sandy Grande after Claude Denis to draw attention to the whiteness embedded in mainstream discourses that claim to be universal, but often ignore the concerns of Indigenous peoples and communities of color." Maile Arvin, in Hokulani K. Aikau, et al., "Indigenous Feminisms Roundtable," *Frontiers: A Journal of Women Studies* 36, no. 3 (2015): 89, doi:10.5250/fronjwomestud.36.3.0084.
42 Episkenew, *Taking Back*, 8.
43 Ibid., 67.
44 Beverley Jacobs and Andrea J. Williams, "Legacy of Residential Schools: Missing and Murdered Aboriginal Women," in *From Truth to Reconciliation: Transforming the Legacy of Residential Schools*, ed. Marlene Brant Castellano, Linda Archibald, and Mike DeGagné (Ottawa: Aboriginal Healing Foundation, 2008), 121.
45 Section 91(24), Constitution Act 1867 (UK), 30 & 31 Vict., c.3., last modified February 9, 2015, http://laws.justice.gc.ca/eng/Const/page-1.html.
46 Episkenew, *Taking Back*, 28.
47 Joanne Barker, "Gender, Sovereignty, Rights: Native Women's Activism against Social Inequality and Violence in Canada," *American Quarterly* 60, no. 2 (2008): 261, doi:10.1353/aq.0.0002.
48 Lawrence, *"Real" Indians*, 46.
49 Shari M. Huhndorf and Cheryl Suzack, "Indigenous Feminism: Theorizing the Issues," in *Indigenous Women and Feminism: Politics, Activism, Culture*, ed. Cheryl Suzack et al. (Vancouver: University of British Columbia Press, 2010), 5.
50 Joyce Green, "Balancing Strategies: Aboriginal Women and Constitutional Rights in Canada," in *Making Space for Indigenous Feminism*, ed. Joyce Green (Winnipeg: Fernwood, 2007), 145.
51 For an account of the Indian Act's impact on women's access to housing and other community resources, see Janet Silman, *Enough Is Enough: Aboriginal Women Speak Out* (Toronto: Women's Press, 1987). For more information on the gendered impacts of identity legislation, see also Lawrence, *"Real" Indians*, and "Gender, Race, and the Regulation of Native Identity in Canada and the United States," *Hypatia* 18, no. 2 (2003): 3–31, muse.jhu.edu/article/44188.

52 Amnesty International, *Stolen Sisters*, 8.
53 Winona Stevenson, "Colonialism and First Nations Women in Canada," in *Scratching the Surface: Canadian Anti-Racist Feminist Thought*, ed. Enakshi Dua and Angela Robertson (Toronto: Women's Press, 1999), 65.
54 Green, "Balancing Strategies," 149–50.
55 Lawrence, *"Real" Indians*, 51.
56 As the interim report of the Truth and Reconciliation Commission of Canada notes, "What existed prior to 1883 was not a residential school system, but a series of individual church-led initiatives to which the federal government provided grants." In 1883 Sir John A. Macdonald's cabinet "authoriz[ed] the creation of three residential schools for Aboriginal children in the Canadian West," although earlier incarnations of the system certainly existed (fashioned on the existing church-run models as well as the industrial schools system in the United States). Truth and Reconciliation Commission of Canada, *They Came for the Children: Canada, Aboriginal Peoples, and Residential Schools* (Winnipeg: Truth and Reconciliation Commission of Canada, 2012), 6, 5, http://www.myrobust.com/websites/trcinstitution/File/2039_T&R_eng_web[1].pdf.
57 Ibid., 10.
58 Duncan Campbell Scott, quoted in Episkenew, *Taking Back*, 30–31.
59 Truth and Reconciliation Commission of Canada, *They Came*, 17.
60 Ibid., 18.
61 Jacobs and Williams, "Legacy," 126.
62 Stephanie Irlbacher-Fox, *Finding Dahshaa: Self-Government, Social Suffering, and Aboriginal Policy in Canada* (Vancouver: University of British Columbia Press, 2009), 28.
63 Many histories have been written about residential schooling in Canada. See, for example, Roland Chrisjohn and Sherri Young, *The Circle Game: Shadows and Substance in the Indian Residential School Experience in Canada* (Penticton, BC: Theytus, 1997); J.R. Miller, *Shingwauk's Vision: A History of Native Residential Schools* (Toronto: University of Toronto Press, 1996), and J.S. Milloy, *A National Crime: The Canadian Government and the Residential School System, 1879–1986* (Winnipeg: University of Manitoba Press, 1999).
64 Episkenew, *Taking Back*, 65.
65 Raven Sinclair, "Identity Lost and Found: Lessons from the Sixties

Scoop," *First Peoples Child and Family Review* 3, no. 1 (2007): 65, http://journals.sfu.ca/fpcfr/index.php/ FPCFR/article/view/25/63.

66 Ibid., 66.

67 Cindy Blackstock, "Reconciliation Means Not Saying Sorry Twice: Lessons from Child Welfare in Canada," in *From Truth to Reconciliation: Transforming the Legacy of Residential Schools*, ed. Marlene Brant Castellano, Linda Archibald, and Mike DeGagné (Ottawa: Aboriginal Healing Foundation, 2008), 165.

68 For a history of child removal see Suzanne Fournier and Ernie Crey, *Stolen from Our Embrace: The Abduction of First Nations Children and the Restoration of Aboriginal Communities* (Vancouver: Douglas and McIntyre, 1997).

69 Janice Acoose, *Iskwewak--kah' ki yaw ni wahkomakanak: Neither Indian Princesses nor Easy Squaws*, 2nd ed. (Toronto: Women's Press, 2016), 32.

70 See, for example: Andrea Smith, *Conquest: Sexual Violence and American Indian Genocide* (Cambridge, MA: South End Press, 2005); Joyce Green, ed., *Making Space for Indigenous Feminism* (Winnipeg: Fernwood, 2007); Cheryl Suzack et al., eds, *Indigenous Women and Feminism: Politics, Activism, Culture* (Vancouver: University of British Columbia Press, 2010); Mishuana Goeman, *Mark My Words: Native Women Mapping Our Nations* (Minneapolis: University of Minnesota Press, 2013); Robyn Bourgeois, "Warrior Women: Indigenous Women's Anti-Violence Engagement with the Canadian State" (PhD diss., University of Toronto, 2014), https://tspace.library.utoronto.ca/ bitstream/1807/68238/1/Bourgeois_Robyn_S_201411_PhD_thesis.pdf 2014); Amber Dean, *Remembering Vancouver's Disappeared Women: Settler Colonialism and the Difficulty of Inheritance* (Toronto: University of Toronto Press, 2015); and Sarah Deer, *The Beginning and End of Rape: Confronting Sexual Violence in Native America* (Minneapolis: University of Minnesota Press, 2015).

71 Bourgeois, "Warrior Women," 3.

72 Yasmin Jiwani and Mary Lynn Young, "Missing and Murdered Women: Reproducing Marginality in News Discourse," *Canadian Journal of Communications* 31, no. 4 (2006): 896, http://www.cjc-online.ca/index.php/journal/article/view/1825.

73 Sharon D. McIvor and Teressa A. Nahanee, "Aboriginal Women: Invis-

ible Victims of Violence," in *Unsettling Truths: Battered Women, Policy, Politics, and Contemporary Research in Canada*, ed. Kevin Bonnycastle and George S. Rigakos (Vancouver: Collective Press, 1998), 63.
74 Dara Culhane, "Their Spirits Live within Us: Aboriginal Women in Downtown Eastside Vancouver Emerging into Visibility," *American Indian Quarterly* 27, no. 3/4 (2003): 593, doi:10.1353/aiq.2004.0073.
75 Jennifer King, "Sisters in Spirit Research Framework: Reflecting on Methodology and Practice," in *Aboriginal Policy Research Volume 10: Voting, Governance, and Research Methodology*, ed. Jerry P. White et al. (Toronto: Thompson Educational, 2010), 275.
76 Susan Gingell, "Take Action to Show Outrage at Loss of Indigenous Women," *Star Phoenix*, July 4, 2007.
77 A. Smith, *Conquest*, 30.
78 Emma LaRocque, *Violence in Aboriginal Communities* (Ottawa: National Clearing House on Family Violence, Family Violence Prevention Division, Health Programs and Services Branch, Health Canada, 1994), 73–74, http://publications.gc.ca/collections/Collection/H72-21-100-1994E.pdf.
79 Acoose, *Iskwewak*, 31.
80 LaRocque, "Violence," 73.
81 Episkenew, *Taking Back*, 71.
82 Glen Coulthard, "Subjects of Empire: Indigenous Peoples and the 'Politics' of Recognition in Canada," *Contemporary Political Theory* 6 (2007): 438–39; Taiaiake Alfred, "Restitution Is the Real Pathway to Justice for Indigenous Peoples," in *Response, Responsibility, and Renewal: Canada's Truth and Reconciliation Journey*, ed. Gregory Younging, Jonathan Dewar, and Mike DeGagné (Ottawa: Aboriginal Healing Foundation, 2009), 183.
83 Coulthard, *Red Skin*, 155.
84 Linda Tuhiwai Smith, *Decolonizing Methodologies: Research and Indigenous Peoples* (London: Zed, 2012), 35. Italics in original.
85 A. Smith, *Conquest*, 139.
86 Constance Backhouse, "Aboriginal Women Still Waiting for Justice," *Times Colonist*, March 8, 2009.
87 Yvette Nolan, "Selling Myself: The Value of an Artist," in *Aboriginal Drama and Theatre*, ed. Rob Appleford (Toronto: Playwrights Canada Press, 2005), 99.

88 Jiwani and Young, "Missing and Murdered Women," 905.
89 Tuck and Yang, "Decolonization," 3.
90 Episkenew, *Taking Back*, 76.
91 *Oxford English Dictionary*, 3rd ed., s.v. "empathy," accessed November 9, 2016, http://www.oed.com.ezproxy.library.ubc.ca/view/Entry/61284?redirectedFrom=empathy#eid.
92 Meghan Marie Hammond and Sue Kim point out in their introduction to *Rethinking Empathy through Literature*: "The basic yet popular postulation that reading literature necessarily produces empathy and pro-social moral behavior greatly underestimates the complexity of reading, literature, empathy, morality, and society." Meghan Marie Hammond and Sue Kim, "Introduction," in *Rethinking Empathy through Literature*, ed. Meghan Marie Hammond and Sue Kim (New York: Routledge, 2014), 11.
93 Elin Diamond, "The Violence of 'We': Politicizing Identification," in *Critical Theory and Performance*, ed. Janelle Reinelt and Joseph Roach (Ann Arbor: University of Michigan Press, 2010), 403–4.
94 Episkenew, *Taking Back*, 190–91.
95 Tuck and Yang, "Decolonization," 36.
96 Goeman, *Mark My Words*, 27.
97 Ibid., 2.
98 Penny Petrone, *Native Literature in Canada: From the Oral Tradition to the Present* (Toronto: Oxford University Press, 1990), 138.
99 Kristina Fagan et al., "Reading the Reception of Campbell's *Halfbreed*," *Canadian Journal of Native Studies* 29, no. 1 (2009): 257–81.
100 Cheryl Suzack, "Law Stories as Life Stories: Jeanette Lavell, Yvonne Bédard, and *Halfbreed*," in *Tracing the Autobiographical*, ed. Marlene Kadar (Waterloo, ON: Wilfrid Laurier University Press, 2005), 117–41.
101 Acoose, *Iskwewak*, 71.
102 Ibid., 67.
103 Daniel Heath Justice, "Renewing the Fire: Notes toward the Liberation of English Studies," *English Studies Canada* 29, no. 1-2 (2003): 49, https://ejournals.library.ualberta.ca/index.php/ESC/article/view/278.
104 Tomson Highway, "Twenty-One Native Women on Motorcycles: An Interview with Tomson Highway," by Joanne Tompkins and Lisa Male, *Australasian Drama Studies* 24 (1994): 29.

105 Ibid.
106 See Tomson Highway, *Kiss of the Fur Queen* (Toronto: Doubleday Canada, 1998); *The Rez Sisters* (Saskatoon: Fifth House, 1988); and *Dry Lips Oughta Move to Kapuskasing* (Saskatoon: Fifth House, 1989).
107 The reception of Highway's award-winning *Dry Lips Oughta Move to Kapuskasing* is particularly notable in this regard. See Marie Annharte Baker, "Angry Enough to Spit but with Dry Lips It Hurts More Than You Know," *Canadian Theatre Review* 68 (1991): 88–89; Anita Tuharsky, "Play Promotes Racism, Sexism and Oppression," *Windspeaker*, March 12, 1991, 5; Alan Filewod, "Receiving Aboriginality: Tomson Highway and the Crisis of Cultural Authenticity," *Theatre Journal* 46, no. 3 (1994): 363–73.
108 Hunt, "Why Are We Hesitant?"
109 Ibid.
110 King, "Sisters in Spirit," 270.
111 Ibid., 275.
112 Ibid.
113 Susan Ehrlich, *Representing Rape: Language and Sexual Consent* (New York: Routledge, 2001), 91.
114 Nolan, "Selling," 99.

CHAPTER ONE

A portion of this chapter was previously published by the University of Nebraska Press. See Allison Hargreaves, "*Finding Dawn* and Missing Women in Canada: Story-Based Methods in Antiviolence Research and Remembrance," *Studies in American Indian Literatures* 27, no. 3 (Fall 2015): 82–111.

1 *Finding Dawn*, directed by Christine Welsh (Montreal: National Film Board of Canada, 2006), DVD.
2 Barbara Bourrier-Lacroix, review of *Finding Dawn*, directed by Christine Welsh, *Canadian Women's Health Network* 9, no. 3 (2007): 8.
3 Anne Stone and Amber Dean, "Representations of Murdered and Missing Women: Introduction," *West Coast Line 53*, 41, no. 1 (2007): 9.
4 Shauna Ferris, "'The Lone Streetwalker': Missing Women and Sex Work-Related News in Mainstream Canadian Media," *West Coast Line 53*, 41, no. 1 (2007): 16; Jiwani and Young, "Missing and Murdered Women," 899, 902.

5 *Finding Dawn*.
6 Ibid.
7 Fay Blaney further suggests that the tone of acquiescence and closure accompanying some responses to the police investigation into the Vancouver missing women actually ignore the fact that police had "mismanaged these cases for years" and that Indigenous women continue to go missing in BC and across Canada. See Fay Blaney, "Aboriginal Women's Action Network," in *Strong Women Stories: Native Vision and Community Survival*, ed. Kim Anderson and Bonita Lawrence (Toronto: Sumach, 2004), 162. For instance, in the Vancouver Police Department's *Missing Women Investigation Review*, Doug LePard asserts: "The disappearances of the Missing Women began in the mid-1990s and ended when Robert Pickton was arrested in February 2002." Doug LePard, *Vancouver Police Department Missing Women Investigation Review*, Vancouver Police Department, 2010, 18, http://www.cbc.ca/bc/news/bc-100820-vancouver-police-pickton-investigation-review.pdf.
8 Lorraine Crey, quoted in *Finding Dawn*.
9 In addition to its success on the international film circuit—enjoying official selection status at the San Francisco Annual American Indian Film Festival and at the imagineNATIVE Film + Media Arts Festival in Toronto—Welsh's film has been shown at the United Nations headquarters in New York, where it was screened during the fifty-first session of the UN Commission on the Status of Women, as well as in public libraries, lecture halls, and independent theatres across Canada. It is available for streaming through the National Film Board's website and is accompanied online by a thirteen-page *Guide for Teaching and Action* written by anti-violence activist and educator Fay Blaney.
10 NWAC, "Fact Sheet: Missing and Murdered Aboriginal Women and Girls in British Columbia," March 24, 2010, 1, https://nwac.ca/wp-content/uploads/2015/05/2010-Fact-Sheet-British-Columbia-MMAWG.pdf.
11 *Highway of Tears Symposium Recommendations Report*, Lheidli T'enneh First Nation, Carrier Sekani Family Services, Carrier Sekani Tribal Council, Prince George Native Friendship Centre, and Prince George Nechako Aboriginal Employment and Training Association, June 16, 2006, 9, http://www.turtleisland.org/healing/highwayoftears.pdf.
12 Tina Beads, "Aboriginal Feminist Action on Violence against Women,"

interview by Rauna Kuokkanen, in *Making Space for Indigenous Feminism*, ed. Joyce Green (Winnipeg: Fernwood, 2007), 224.

13 As suggested by the Missing Women Commission of Inquiry report on the situations of missing women in northern BC as contrasted with the context of the DTES, "Some participants ... were of the view that the two situations were completely different, because the urban and rural settings were strikingly different and the [Highway of Tears] victims were differently situated with women in the DTES engaged in the survival sex trade." See *Standing Together and Moving Forward: Report on the Pre-Hearing Conference in Prince George and the Northern Community Forums*, Missing Women Commission of Inquiry, February 2012, 13, http://www.missingwomeninquiry.ca/wp-content/uploads/2010/10/Report-on-the-Pre-Hearing-Conference-in-Prince-George-and-the-Northern-Community-Forums-00263779.pdf.

14 Beads, "Aboriginal Feminist," 224.

15 Human Rights Watch, *Those Who Take Us Away: Abusive Policing and Failures in Protection of Indigenous Women and Girls in Northern British Columbia, Canada*, February 13, 2013, https://www.hrw.org/report/2013/02/13/those-who-take-us-away/abusive-policing-and-failures-protection-indigenous-women.

16 Marcel-Eugène LeBeuf, "The Role of the Royal Canadian Mounted Police during the Indian Residential School System," Royal Canadian Mounted Police, 2011, 4, http://publications.gc.ca/collections/collection_2011/grc-rcmp/PS64-71-2009-eng.pdf.

17 Amnesty International, *Stolen Sisters*, 17.

18 Indigenous peoples' relationship with the justice system has been characterized as one of overrepresentation. Yet, as Patricia Monture-Angus emphasizes in her work on Indigenous women and justice in Canada, to say that repressive overrepresentation chiefly characterizes the negative relation between Indigenous people and the justice system is a "drastic simplification of the issue," in part because this does not account for the way in which Indigenous people are simultaneously overpoliced and overrepresented as *offenders*, and drastically underpoliced and underprotected as *victims* of violence. Also, this does not account for the gendered dynamics of these relations relative to the disproportionate "criminalization" and "victimization" of Indigenous people. See

Monture-Angus, *Thunder in My Soul*, 223; Michael Jackson, "Locking Up Natives in Canada," *University of British Columbia Law Review* 23, no. 2 (1989): 215–300; Philip Stenning and Carol LaPrairie. "'Politics by Other Means': The Role of Commissions of Inquiry in Establishing the 'Truth' About 'Aboriginal Justice' in Canada," in *Crime, Truth and Justice: Official Inquiry, Discourse, Knowledge*, ed. George Gilligan and John Pratt (Portland: Willan Publishing, 2004), 138, 150; Jonathan Rudin, "Aboriginal Justice and Restorative Justice," in *New Directions in Restorative Justice: Issues, Practice, Evaluation*, ed. Elizabeth Elliott and Robert M. Gordon (Portland, OR: Willan, 2005), 90–91.

19 Pauline Wakeham, "Settler Colonialism, Slow Violence, and the Time of Idle No More," presentation, Annual Conference of the Native American and Indigenous Studies Association, University of Saskatoon, Saskatoon, June 15, 2013.

20 Karen Warren, quoted in A. Smith, *Conquest*, 17.

21 Sherene H. Razack, *Race, Space, and the Law: Unmapping a White Settler Society* (Toronto: Between the Lines, 2002), 128.

22 Suzack and Huhndorf, "Indigenous Feminism," 12.

23 J. Green, "Taking Account," 21.

24 Ibid., 22.

25 Kim Anderson, "Affirmations of an Indigenous Feminist," in *Indigenous Women and Feminism: Politics, Activism, Culture*, ed. Cheryl Suzack et al. (Vancouver: University of British Columbia Press, 2010), 83.

26 Kovach, *Indigenous Methodologies*, 94.

27 Ibid., 96.

28 Neal McLeod, *Cree Narrative Memory: From Treaties to Contemporary Times* (Saskatoon, SK: Purich, 2007), 7–8.

29 Kovach, *Indigenous Methodologies*, 95.

30 Ibid., 99.

31 Missing Women Commission of Inquiry, *Forsaken: The Report of the Missing Women Commission of Inquiry*, vol. 4, November 19, 2012, 5, http://www.missingwomeninquiry.ca/wp-content/uploads/2010/10/Forsaken-Vol-4-web-RGB.pdf.

32 The signatories to the Open Letter were: the Aboriginal Front Door Society, Amnesty International Canada, Atira Women's Resource Society, B.C. Civil Liberties Association, Battered Women's Support Services,

Carrier Sekani Tribal Council, Downtown Eastside Sex Workers United Against Violence Society, Ending Violence Association of British Columbia, Feb. 14th Women's Memorial March Committee, First Nations Summit, PACE: Providing Alternatives Counselling & Education Society, Pivot Legal Society, Union of B.C. Indian Chiefs, Union Gospel Mission, West Coast LEAF, and WISH Drop-in Centre Society.

33 Aboriginal Front Door Society et al., "Open Letter: Non-Participation in the Policy Forums/Study Commission," April 10, 2012, http://www.fns.bc.ca/pdf/OpenLetterstoMWCI_041012.pdf.

34 Leanne Simpson, "Aboriginal Peoples and Knowledge: Decolonizing Our Processes," *Canadian Journal of Native Studies* 21, no. 1 (2001): 140.

35 Gerald E. Le Dain, "The Role of the Public Inquiry in Our Constitutional System," in *Law and Social Change*, ed. Jacob S. Ziegel (Toronto: Osgoode Hall Law School, 1973), 85.

36 Coulthard, *Red Skin*, 21.

37 Ibid., 119.

38 A. Smith, *Conquest*, 139.

39 Missing Women Commission of Inquiry, *Forsaken*, vol. 4, 3. Emphasis added.

40 Missing Women Commission of Inquiry, *Forsaken*, vol. 1, November 19, 2012, 33, http://www.missingwomeninquiry.ca/wp-content/uploads/2010/10/Forsaken-Vol-1-web-RGB.pdf.

41 LePard, *Vancouver Police Department Missing Women Investigation Review*, 189.

42 Ernie Crey, quoted in *Finding Dawn*.

43 LePard, *Vancouver Police Department Missing Women Investigation Review*, 18–19.

44 "Pickton Victim Families Press for Inquiry," *CBC News*, August 5, 2010, http://www.cbc.ca/beta/news/canada/british-columbia/pickton-victim-families-press-for-inquiry-1.898051.

45 Legally, a public inquiry cannot be held while a police investigation, trial, or appeals process is ongoing.

46 "Missing Women Commission of Inquiry Status Report on Commission Progress," Missing Women Commission of Inquiry, March 3, 2011, http://www.missingwomeninquiry.ca/wp-content/uploads/2010/10/Status-Report-March.pdf.

47 The inquiry's terms of reference are as follows:

> (a) to conduct hearings, in or near the City of Vancouver, to inquire into and make findings of fact respecting the conduct of the missing women investigations;
> (b) consistent with the British Columbia (Attorney General) v. Davies, 2009 BCCA 337, to inquire into and make findings of fact respecting the decision of the Criminal Justice Branch on January 27, 1998, to enter a stay of proceedings on charges against Robert William Pickton of attempted murder, assault with a weapon, forcible confinement and aggravated assault;
> (c) to recommend changes considered necessary respecting the initiation and conduct of investigations in British Columbia of missing women and suspected multiple homicides;
> (d) to recommend changes considered necessary respecting homicide investigations in British Columbia by more than one investigating organization, including the co-ordination of those investigations;
> (e) to submit a final report to the Attorney General or before December 31, 2011.

"Terms of Reference," Missing Women Commission of Inquiry, accessed November 16, 2016, http://www.missingwomeninquiry.ca/terms-of-reference/.

48 *Standing Together and Moving Forward: The Northwest Consultations*, prepared by Linda Locke for The Missing Women Commission of Inquiry, June 2012, 4, http://www.missingwomeninquiry.ca/wp-content/uploads/2010/10/Standing-Together-the-Northwest-Consultations.pdf.

49 Shawn Atleo and Doug Kelly, "Real Inquiry Needed into Pickton Killings," *Times Colonist*, October 28, 2010.

50 In the hearings to determine standing, Commissioner Wally Oppal reminded participants: "We understand the valid concerns of many groups ... who would like to have the terms expanded, but we ... must confine ourselves to the terms that the government has given us." Wally Oppal in *Missing Women Commission of Inquiry Hearings for Standing*, January 31, 2011, 8, http://www.missingwomeninquiry.ca/transcripts/.

51 Hugh Braker, in *Missing Women Commission of Inquiry Hearings for Standing*, 25.

Notes to Chapter One

52 Donald Worme, in *Missing Women Commission of Inquiry Hearings for Standing*, 19.
53 LePard, *Vancouver Police Department Missing Women Investigation Review*, 18.
54 Christine Welsh, quoted in Joanne Bealy, review of *Finding Dawn*, dir. Christine Welsh, *Cahoots* 4 (2006): 33.
55 According to the August 10, 2011, press release: "The two Vancouver-based lawyers, Mr. Jason Gratl, a past president of the BC Civil Liberties Association, and Ms. Robyn Gervais, who previously represented the Carrier Sekani Tribal Council at the Commission, will not represent specific clients. They will work independently of the Commission with a mandate to serve the public interest at the hearings. They are expected to take guidance from unfunded participant groups and affected organizations and individuals. The Commission also announced that two prominent Vancouver lawyers, Mr. Bryan Baynham Q.C. and Mr. Darrell Roberts Q.C., will participate pro bono in the inquiry in support of Ms. Gervais." Robyn Gervais resigned in March 2012, stating that the commission was not making space for the voices of Indigenous women and communities, and was too focused on police witnesses. See "Missing Women Commission Appoints Two Independent Lawyers; Two Others to Participate Pro-Bono," August 10, 2011, http://www.missingwomen inquiry.ca/2011/08/august-10-2011-missing-women-commission-appoints-two-independent-lawyers-two-others-to-participate-pro-bono/; *CBC News*, "Pickton Inquiry Lawyer Quits in Frustration," March 5, 2012, http://www.cbc.ca/news/canada/british-columbia/pickton-inquiry-lawyer-quits-in-frustration-1.1237185.
56 Stacey Edzerza Fox, in *Missing Women Commission of Inquiry Pre-Hearing Conference*, June 27, 2011, 93, http://www.missingwomeninquiry.ca/transcripts/.
57 Fox appeared before the Commission at the Vancouver pre-hearing conference in order to present a joint submission prepared by the Assembly of First Nations, the First Nations Summit, the Union of BC Indian Chiefs, Carrier Sekani Tribal Council, and Native Courtworker and Counselling Association of BC. Ibid., 93.
58 Aboriginal Front Door Society et al., "Open Letter."
59 Nicola Schabus, in *Missing Women Commission of Inquiry Hearings for Standing*, 41.

60 "Missing Women Commission of Inquiry Status Report on Commission Progress."
61 "Study Commission Added to Missing Women Inquiry," *BC Gov News*, March 28, 2011, https://news.gov.bc.ca/stories/study-commission-added-to-missing-women-inquiry.
62 "Northern Community Forums: Frequently Asked Questions," Missing Women Commission of Inquiry, accessed November 11, 2016, http://www.missingwomeninquiry.ca/wp-content/uploads/2011/01/Northern-Community-Forums-FAQ.pdf.
63 Robyn Gervais, in *Missing Women Commission of Inquiry Pre-Hearing Conference*, 175.
64 *Highway of Tears Symposium*, 9. The Highway of Tears Symposium was held March 30–31, 2006, in Prince George, BC. Sponsored by Lheidli T'enneh First Nation, Carrier Sekani Family Services, Carrier Sekani Tribal Council, Prince George Nechako Aboriginal Employment and Training Association, and the Prince George Native Friendship Center, the symposium attracted the participation of five hundred delegates and ninety organizations. The symposium framed its activities as a community-based call for action, and its thirty-three recommendations pertain to victim prevention; emergency planning and team response; victim family counselling and support; and community development and support.
65 Missing Women Commission of Inquiry, *Forsaken*, vol. 1, 29.
66 *Highway of Tears Symposium*, 9.
67 Missing Women Commission of Inquiry, *Forsaken*, vol. 3, November 19, 2012, 118, http://www.missingwomeninquiry.ca/wp-content/uploads/2010/10/Forsaken-Vol-3-web-RGB.pdf.
68 Kendra Milne, quoted in Geordon Omand, "First Nations Groups Urge Caution before Government's Missing Women Inquiry," *Globe and Mail*, November 9, 2015, http://www.theglobeandmail.com/news/british-columbia/first-nations-groups-urge-caution-before-governments-missing-women-inquiry/article27178422/.
69 Millie Percival, quoted in *Standing Together and Moving Forward: The Northwest Consultations*, 13.
70 *Standing Together and Moving Forward: Report on the Pre-Hearing Conference*, 5.
71 Ibid., 8.
72 Ibid., 7.

73 Karen Whonnock, presentation, Kitsumkalum Community Forum, Terrace, September 13, 2011, http://www.missingwomeninquiry.ca/forums/.
74 Ibid.
75 *Standing Together and Moving Forward: Report on the Pre-Hearing Conference*, 4.
76 Tuhiwai Smith, *Decolonizing Methodologies*, 16.
77 *Standing Together and Moving Forward: Report on the Pre-Hearing Conference*, 18.
78 Kovach, *Indigenous Methodologies*, 98.
79 "Northern Community Forums: Questions and Issues for Discussion," Missing Women Commission of Inquiry, accessed November 11, 2016, http://www.missingwomeninquiry.ca/wp-content/uploads/2011/01/Northern-Community-Forums-Questions-and-Issues.pdf.
80 Ibid.
81 Kathleen E. Absolon, *Kaandossiwin: How We Come to Know* (Halifax: Fernwood, 2011), 126.
82 Kovach, *Indigenous Methodologies*, 98–99.
83 James (Sákéj) Youngblood Henderson, *First Nations Jurisprudence and Aboriginal Rights: Defining the Just Society* (Saskatoon: Native Law Centre, University of Saskatchewan, 2006), 159.
84 Tuhiwai Smith, *Decolonizing Methodologies*, 8.
85 Ibid., 11.
86 Simpson, *Dancing*, 34.
87 Leanne Simpson, "Oshkimaadiziig, the New People," in *Lighting the Eighth Fire: The Liberation, Resurgence, and Protection of Indigenous Nations*, ed. Leanne Simpson (Winnipeg: Arbeiter Ring, 2008), 16.
88 Ibid., 20.
89 Taiaiake Alfred, "Opening Words," in *Lighting the Eighth Fire: The Liberation, Resurgence, and Protection of Indigenous Nations*, ed. Leanne Simpson (Winnipeg: Arbeiter Ring, 2008), 10.
90 Absolon, *Kaandossiwi*, 10.
91 Fay Blaney, quoted in *Finding Dawn*.
92 Welsh, quoted in Bealy, review of *Finding Dawn*, 31.
93 Absolon, *Kaandossiwin*, 50.
94 Ibid., 49.
95 Ibid., 50.

96 Ibid., 53.
97 Ibid., 50.
98 *Finding Dawn*.
99 Stephen Berg, "Documentary Traces Plight of Missing Aboriginal Women," *Edmonton Journal*, March 15, 2007, http://www.pressreader.com/canada/edmonton-journal/20070315/281788509604523.
100 Elizabeth Withey, "Discovery of '23rd Woman's' DNA at Pickton Farm Inspires Film," *Edmonton Journal*, March 6, 2007.
101 Shauna Lewis, "Film Remembers Missing and Murdered Women," *Windspeaker* 24, no. 9 (2006): 14.
102 Laura Suthers, "Film Illustrates Hope and Strength," *Windspeaker* 25, no. 2 (2007): 18.
103 Augie Fleras, "*Finding Dawn*," *Visual Anthropology Review* 26, no. 1 (2010): 47, doi:10.1111/j.1548-7458.2010.01053.x.
104 Ibid., 48.
105 *Finding Dawn*.
106 Andrea Smith, "Unsettling the Privilege of Self-Reflexivity," in *Geographies of Privilege*, ed. France Winddance Twine and Bradley Gardener (New York: Routledge, 2013), 265.
107 L. Tuhiwai Smith, *Decolonizing Methodologies*, 27.
108 Gail de Vos, "*Finding Dawn*," *CM: An Electronic Reviewing Journal of Canadian Materials for Young People* 14, no. 10 (2008): 1, http://search.proquest.com.ezproxy.library.ubc.ca/docview/218804516?pq-origsite=summon&accountid=14656; Fleras, "*Finding Dawn*," 47; Jennifer O'Connor, "*Finding Dawn*," *Horizons* 22, no. 3 (2009): 51.
109 Fleras, "*Finding Dawn*," 47.
110 Tuhiwai Smith, *Decolonizing Methodologies*, 146.
111 Gerald Vizenor, "Aesthetics of Survivance: Literary Theory and Practice," in *Survivance: Narratives of Native Presence*, ed. Gerald Vizenor (Lincoln: University of Nebraska Press, 2008), 1.
112 Ibid.
113 Culhane, "Their Spirits," 594.
114 Ibid., 594–95.
115 Ibid., 595.
116 Ibid., 594.
117 Razack, *Race, Space*, 129.

118 LePard, *Vancouver Police Department Missing Women Investigation Review*, 18. Emphasis added.
119 Aboriginal Women's Action Network, "Statement Issued at Press Conference," Vancouver Rape Relief and Women's Shelter, February 8, 2002, http://www.rapereliefshelter.bc.ca/learn/resources/statement-issued-press-conference.
120 *Finding Dawn*.
121 Ibid.
122 Welsh models this principle herself when she reflects at the outset: "Like Dawn," she says, "I too am a Native woman." Welsh clarifies her personal stakes in the research journey, outlining her motive for pursuing this project.
123 Kathleen E. Absolon and Cam Willett, "Putting Ourselves Forward: Location in Aboriginal Research," in *Research as Resistance: Critical, Indigenous and Anti-Oppressive Approaches*, ed. Leslie Brown and Susan Strega (Toronto: Canadian Scholars' Press, 2005), 98.
124 Ibid., 104.
125 Kovach, *Indigenous Methodologies*, 110.
126 Womack, *Art as Performance*, 44.
127 E. Crey, quoted in *Finding Dawn*.
128 Jo-ann Archibald, *Indigenous Storywork: Educating the Heart, Mind, Body, and Spirit* (Vancouver: University of British Columbia Press, 2008), ix, 4.
129 Absolon and Willet, "Putting Ourselves Forward," 111.
130 *Finding Dawn*.
131 Absolon, *Kaandossiwin*, 69.
132 Vizenor, "Aesthetics of Survivance," 1.
133 Elizabeth Cook-Lynn, *Anti-Indianism in Modern America: A Voice from Tatekeya's Earth* (Champaign: University of Illinois, 2007), 179–80.
134 Roger Simon, "Towards a Hopeful Practice of Worrying: The Problematics of Listening and the Educative Responsibilities of Canada's Truth and Reconciliation Commission," in *Reconciling Canada: Historical Injustices and the Contemporary Culture of Redress*, ed. Jennifer Henderson and Pauline Wakeham (Toronto: University of Toronto Press, 2013), 132.
135 Simpson, *Dancing*, 52.
136 Culhane, "Their Spirits," 600.

137 Simpson, *Dancing*, 67.
138 Community search efforts provide a useful contrast to the specialized search for DNA evidence conducted by authorities on the unnamed Pickton farm site at the film's outset. In the film, community searches are depicted as Indigenous-led initiatives that affirm families and communities.
139 Lynne Terbasket, quoted in *Finding Dawn*.
140 Simpson, *Dancing*, 101.
141 Ibid., 102. Simpson further elaborates on this concept by explaining the teaching shared with her by Métis elder Maria Campbell: "She told me that acts of resistance are like throwing a stone into water. The stone makes its initial impact in the water, displacing it and eventually sinking to the bottom. There is the original splash the act of resistance makes.... But there are also more subtle waves of disruption that ripple or echo out from where the stone impacted the water ... [and that] remain in the water long after the initial splash is gone." Ibid., 145.
142 Ibid., 143.
143 *Finding Dawn*.
144 Brenda Wilson, quoted in *Finding Dawn*.
145 Tuhiwai Smith, *Decolonizing Methodologies*, 147.
146 Matilda Wilson, quoted in *Finding Dawn*.
147 Ibid.
148 Simpson, *Dancing*, 49.
149 Audra Simpson, "Settlement's Secret," *Cultural Anthropology* 26, no. 2 (2011): 208, doi:10.1111/j.1548-1360.2011.01095.x.
150 M. Wilson, quoted in *Finding Dawn*.
151 Simpson, *Dancing*, 101.
152 Tuhiwai Smith, *Decolonizing Methodologies*, 147.
153 Ibid., 92.
154 Ibid., 98.
155 *Finding Dawn*.

CHAPTER TWO

1 NWAC, *Voices of Our Sisters in Spirit: A Report to Families and Communities*, Ottawa, 2009, 3, https://nwac.ca/wpcontent/uploads/2015/05/NWAC_Voices-of-Our-Sisters-In-Spirit_2nd-Edition_March-2009.pdf.

2   The five national Aboriginal organizations are: The Assembly of First Nations, the Congress of Aboriginal Peoples, the Métis National Council, the Inuit Tapiriit Kanatami, and the Native Women's Association of Canada.
3   NWAC, "About Us," accessed November 16, 2016, https://www.nwac.ca/home/about-nwac/about-us/.
4   NWAC, *Violations of Indigenous Human Rights: NWAC Submission to the Special Rapporteur Investigating the Violations of Indigenous Human Rights*, December 2002, 3, https://nwac.ca/wp-content/uploads/2016/06/2002-NWAC-Violations-of-Human-Rights-Submission.pdf.
5   NWAC, "Violence against Aboriginal Women and Girls: An Issue Paper," prepared for the National Aboriginal Women's Summit, Corner Brook, June 20–22, 2007, 7, http://www.laa.gov.nl.ca/laa/naws/pdf/nwac-vaaw.pdf.
6   Federal funding for this project was cut in 2010, despite the government's public praise of NWAC's campaign in the 2010 Speech from the Throne. Shari Narine, "Sisters in Spirit Applauded, then Panned by Feds," *Windspeaker* 8, no. 9 (2010): 12.
7   NWAC, *What Their Stories Tell Us*, 2.
8   Ibid., ii.
9   NWAC, *What Their Stories Tell Us*, 30.
10 King, "Sisters in Spirit Research Framework," 272.
11 NWAC, *What Their Stories Tell Us*, 14.
12 King, "Sisters in Spirit Research Framework," 273-4.
13 NWAC, *What Their Stories Tell Us*, 17.
14 King, "Sisters in Spirit Research Framework," 270.
15 Ibid., 276.
16 Ibid., 271.
17 Ibid., 276.
18 Ibid., 270.
19 Ibid., 276.
20 Margaret Kovach, "Emerging from the Margins: Indigenous Methodologies," in *Research as Resistance: Critical, Indigenous, and Anti-Oppressive Approaches*, ed. Leslie Brown and Susan Strega (Toronto: Canadian Scholars' Press, 2005), 30.
21 King, "Sisters in Spirit Research Framework," 270.
22 Robina Anne Thomas, "Honouring the Oral Traditions of My Ancestors

through Storytelling," in *Research as Resistance*, ed. Leslie Brown and Susan Strega (Toronto: Canadian Scholars' Press, 2005), 241–44.
23　Thomas, "Honouring the Oral Traditions," 242.
24　Ibid.
25　Ibid.
26　Ibid., 244.
27　King, "Sisters in Spirit Research Framework," 270.
28　Ibid.
29　NWAC, *What Their Stories Tell Us*, 31.
30　NWAC, *Voices*, 100–103.
31　NWAC, *Community Resource Guide*, Ottawa, 2010, 20, https://nwac.ca/wp-content/uploads/2015/05/2012_NWAC_Community_Resource_Guide_MMAWG.pdf.
32　Ibid., 45.
33　King, "Sisters in Spirit Research Framework," 270.
34　NWAC, *Voices*, 5.
35　Kovach, *Indigenous Methodologies*, 100.
36　King, "Sisters in Spirit Research Framework," 276.
37　Thomas, "Honouring the Oral Traditions," 242.
38　King, "Sisters in Spirit Research Framework," 274.
39　"Key Facts about Amnesty International," Amnesty International Canada, accessed November 17, 2016, http://amnesty.staging.openconcept.ca/about-us/what-we-do/key-facts-about-amnesty-international.
40　"Government Does not Act on Commitment to Improve the Lives of Aboriginal Women," *Canada NewsWire*, February 11, 2005.
41　NWAC, *Voices*, 4.
42　Kay Schaffer and Sidonie Smith, *Human Rights and Narrative Lives: The Ethics of Recognition* (New York: Palgrave Macmillan, 2004), 1.
43　Ibid., 2.
44　Ibid., 17.
45　Ibid., 35.
46　Shari Stone-Mediatore, *Reading across Borders: Storytelling and Knowledges of Resistance* (New York: Palgrave Macmillian, 2003), 4.
47　Ibid., 7.
48　Ibid.
49　Schaffer and Smith, *Human Rights*, 36.

50 Kovach, *Indigenous Methodologies*, 101.
51 Stevenson, "Colonialism," 79.
52 Ibid.
53 Schaffer and Smith, *Human Rights*, 37.
54 Ibid.
55 Ibid.
56 Amnesty International, *Stolen Sisters*, 4.
57 Ibid., 21.
58 Ibid., 4.
59 Ibid., 5.
60 Ibid.
61 Ibid., 3.
62 In the case of the *Stolen Sisters* report, the concepts of safety and security have specific resonances with international human rights discourse, including internationally protected rights to housing and health. This notion of human security is in keeping with the United Nations Development Programme's use of the term; see Connie Deiter and Darlene Rude, "Human Security and Aboriginal Women in Canada" (Ottawa: Status of Women Canada, 2005), 3, http://publications.gc.ca/collections/Collection/SW21-133-2005E.pdf.
63 Amnesty International, *Stolen Sisters*, 4.
64 Ibid., 21.
65 Ibid., 3.
66 Ibid., 2.
67 Ibid., 22.
68 Ibid., 9.
69 Ibid., 10.
70 Ibid.
71 Ibid., 20.
72 Ibid., 22.
73 Ibid.
74 *Report of the Aboriginal Justice Inquiry of Manitoba*, quoted in Amnesty International, *Stolen Sisters*, 22–23.
75 Amnesty International, *Stolen Sisters*, 22.
76 Ibid.
77 Ibid., 22.

78 Ibid., 23.
79 Ibid.
80 Ibid.
81 Ibid.
82 Ibid.
83 *Aboriginal Justice Inquiry*, quoted in Amnesty International, *Stolen Sisters*, 22.
84 Amnesty International, *Stolen Sisters*, 2.
85 Ibid.
86 Ibid., 35.
87 Ibid., 23.
88 Ibid., 35.
89 Ibid., 36.
90 Ibid.
91 Ibid., 35–36.
92 Sidonie Smith, "Narrating the Right to Sexual Well-Being and the Global Management of Misery: Maria Rosa Henson's *Comfort Woman* and Charlene Smith's *Proud of Me*," *Literature and Medicine* 24, no. 2 (2005): 159, doi:10.1353/lm.2006.0013.
93 Smith, "Narrating," 160.
94 Beads, "Aboriginal Feminist," 228; Beads goes on to provide the following example: "I had a good working relationship with one fairly new cop and I asked him what type of training they got for working with women who have been assaulted, and about women and people of a different race. He told me about all the different workshops that are offered as part of their training, and none of them are mandatory anyway. They can choose to take a workshop on cultural sensitivity or Aboriginal people and their issues … but they didn't get paid for that time. There was no incentive to do it. He talked about a lot of his colleagues being pretty unwilling anyway."
95 Amnesty International, *Stolen Sisters*, 4–5.
96 Ibid., 7–8.
97 Human rights discourse is sometimes critiqued for its seeming paternalism and Eurocentrism. Gayatri Spivak, however, cautions that it is "disingenuous to call human rights eurocentric"—in part because this does not actually account for the complex ways that activists (including,

in this case, Indigenous anti-violence activists) engage human rights discourse for their own strategic ends. NWAC's partnership with Amnesty International is an example of this. See Robert Young, "Introduction to Gayatri Spivak," in *Human Rights, Human Wrongs: The Oxford Amnesty Lectures, 2001*, ed. Nicholas Owen (Oxford: Oxford University Press, 2003), 165; Gayatri Spivak, "Righting Wrongs" in *Human Rights, Human Wrongs*, 171.

98 Elizabeth Povinelli, *The Cunning of Recognition: Indigenous Alterities and the Making of Australian Multiculturalism* (London: Duke University Press, 2002), 184. Italics in original.
99 Duncan Ivison, *Postcolonial Liberalism* (Cambridge: Cambridge University Press, 2002), 1.
100 Coulthard, *Red Skin*, 45.
101 Ibid., 45.
102 Leanne Simpson, "Dancing the World into Being: A Conversation with Idle No More's Leanne Simpson," interview by Naomi Klein, *Yes! Magazine*, March 5, 2013, http://www.yesmagazine.org/peace-justice/dancing-the-world-into-being-a-conversation-with-idle-no-more-leanne-simpson.
103 Povinelli, *The Cunning of Recognition*, 13.
104 Coulthard, *Red Skin*, 7.
105 Povinelli, *The Cunning of Recognition*, 12.
106 Million, *Therapeutic Nations*, 38.
107 Ibid., 33.
108 Wendy Brown, "'The Most We Can Hope For …': Human Rights and the Politics of Fatalism," *South Atlantic Quarterly* 102, no. 2/3 (2004): 453, doi:10.1215/00382876-103-2-3-451.
109 Amnesty International, *Stolen Sisters*, 19.
110 Ibid.
111 Million, *Therapeutic Nations*, 38.
112 Simon, "Towards a Hopeful Practice," 133.
113 King, "Sisters in Spirit Research Framework," 282.
114 NWAC, *What Their Stories Tell Us*, 2.
115 Michelle La Flamme, "Revisiting *A Really Good Brown Girl*," *thirdspace* 2, no. 2 (2003), http://journals.sfu.ca/thirdspace/index.php/journal/article/viewArticle/reviews_laflamme/115.

116 Jónína Kirton, quoted in Marilyn Dumont, "Interview with Marilyn Dumont," by Jónína Kirton, *Room*, accessed November 18, 2016, https://roommagazine.com/interview/interview-marilyn-dumont.
117 Dumont, "Interview with Marilyn Dumont."
118 King, "Sisters in Spirit Research Framework," 274.
119 Schaffer and Smith, *Human Rights*, 4.
120 Neal McLeod, "Cree Poetic Discourse," in *Indigenous Poetics in Canada*, ed. Neal McLeod (Waterloo, ON: Wilfrid Laurier University Press, 2014), 89.
121 Marilyn Dumont, "The Pemmican Eaters," in *Indigenous Poetics in Canada*, ed. Neal McLeod (Waterloo, ON: Wilfrid Laurier University Press, 2014), 85.
122 Marilyn Dumont, "Helen Betty Osborne," in *A Really Good Brown Girl* (London: Brick Books, 1996), 1–5. Excerpts reprinted with permission.
123 Acoose, *Iskwewak*, 72.
124 Vizenor, "Aesthetics of Survivance," 1.
125 McLeod, "Cree Poetic," 91.
126 Acoose, *Iskwewak*, 4.
127 Simpson, *Dancing*, 15. Italics in original.
128 Dumont, "Helen Betty Osborne," 12–21.
129 Flowers, "Refusal to Forgive," 42. Italics in original.
130 Hunt, "Why Are We Hesitant?"
131 Amnesty International, *Stolen Sisters*, 20.
132 Ibid., 21.
133 Sherene Razack, *Looking White People in the Eye: Gender, Race, and Culture in Courtrooms and Classrooms* (Toronto: University of Toronto Press, 1998), 83.
134 Joy Mannette, *Elusive Justice: Beyond the Marshall Inquiry* (Halifax: Fernwood, 1992), 65.
135 Razack, *Looking*, 82.
136 Mannette, *Elusive Justice*, 65.
137 Razack, *Looking*, 82.
138 Emma LaRocque, presentation to the Aboriginal Justice Inquiry of Manitoba, February 5, 1990, in *Report of the Aboriginal Justice Inquiry of Manitoba*, vol. 1, ch. 13, 1999, http://www.ajic.mb.ca/volumel/chapter13.html.

139 Dumont, "Helen Betty Osborne," 30.
140 Ibid., 10.
141 Ibid., 29.
142 Acoose, *Iskwewak*, 33.
143 Ibid., 34.
144 Ibid.
145 Ibid., 35.
146 Sylvia Van Kirk, *Many Tender Ties: Women in Fur Trade Society, 1670–1870* (Norman: University of Oklahoma Press, 1980), 1.
147 Acoose, *Iskwewak*, 35.
148 Van Kirk, *Many Tender Ties,* 161.
149 Ibid.
150 Ibid.
151 Shirley Green, "Looking Back, Looking Forward," in *Making Space for Indigenous Feminism*, ed. Joyce Green (Winnipeg: Fernwood, 2007), 162.
152 George Simpson to Governor, Deputy Governor and Committee, May 18, 1821, quoted in Robin Fisher, *Contact and Conflict: Indian-European Relations in British Columbia, 1774–1890*, 2nd ed. (Vancouver: University of British Columbia Press, 1992), 41.
153 Fisher, *Contact and Conflict*, 40.
154 George Simpson, quoted in S. Green, "Looking Back," 164. Emphasis added.
155 Ibid.
156 Dumont, "Helen Betty Osborne," 17.
157 Ibid., 219–21.
158 Crawford was convicted in 1996 for the murders of Eva Taysup, Shelley Napope, and Calinda Waterhen in Saskatoon; prior to this he had served seven years in prison for manslaughter in the killing of Mary Jane Serloin. See Warren Goulding, *Just Another Indian: A Serial Killer and Canada's Indifference* (Saskatoon: Fifth House, 2001); Janice Acoose, *Iskwewak*, 67–68. Gilbert Paul Jordan was responsible for the deaths of at least ten women in Vancouver in the 1970s and 1980s. He deliberately administered fatal amounts of alcohol to his victims, yet was convicted for manslaughter in only one of the cases. See Marie Clements, *The Unnatural and Accidental Women* (Vancouver: Talonbooks, 2005); Michelle La Flamme, "Theatrical Medicine: Aboriginal Performance, Rit-

ual and Commemoration (for Vanessa Lee Buckner)," *Theatre Research in Canada* 31, no. 2 (Fall 2010): 112, https://journals.lib.unb.ca/index.php/TRIC/article/viewFile/18430/19920.
159 Dumont, "Helen Betty Osborne," 24–25.
160 Razack, *Race, Space*, 126.
161 Amnesty International, *Stolen Sisters*, 21.
162 Razack, *Looking*, 36.
163 Ibid.
164 Sarita Srivastava and Margot Francis, "The Problem of 'Authentic Experience': Storytelling in Anti-Racist and Anti-Homophobic Education," *Critical Sociology* 32, no. 2/3 (2006): 282, doi:10.1163/156916306777835330.
165 Razack, *Looking*, 48.
166 Ibid., 52.
167 Amnesty International, *Stolen Sisters*, 22. Human rights reporting often requires that rights violations be established and legitimized according to positivist evidential means. As Inderpal Grewal puts it: "Particular kinds of language, bureaucratic apparatus, surveys, statistical analysis, photographic evidence, and psychological information are all required to make judgments of what or who has suffered human rights abuses." Inderpal Grewal, "Foreword," in *Just Advocacy? Women's Human Rights, Transnational Feminisms, and the Politics of Representation*, ed. Wendy S. Hesford and Wendy Kozol (London: Rutgers University Press, 2005), viii–iv.
168 Beth Brant, "Telling," in *Food and Spirits* (Vancouver: Press Gang, 1991), 13.
169 Dumont, "Helen Betty Osborne," 26–29.
170 Roland Barthes, *Camera Lucida* (New York: Hill and Wang, 1980), 76. Italics in original.
171 Ibid., 106. Italics in original.
172 Ibid., 28.
173 Gail Guthrie Valaskakis, *Indian Country: Essays on Contemporary Native Culture* (Waterloo, ON: Wilfrid Laurier University Press, 2005), 198.
174 Ibid., 197.
175 Ibid.
176 Amnesty International, *Stolen Sisters*, 2.
177 Episkenew, *Taking Back*, 15. Literary scholar Jo-Ann Episkenew uses the term "implicating the audience" to describe Indigenous literature's

socially transformative potential to facilitate readers' reflexive participation in knowledge making about colonial trauma and resistance. Notably, for Episkenew, the process is necessarily inflected by subject position and experiential knowledge. Indigenous readers, she argues, "see their lives and their experiences reflected back to them in the form of narrative." Literature like Dumont's thus "gives voice" to the colonial experience and transforms its Indigenous readers "from individuals often living in isolation to members of a larger community of shared stories." Settler readers, by contrast, undergo a different kind of transformation: witnessing in literature "the structures that sustain White privilege," settler readers are compelled to "examine their position of privilege and their complicity in the continued oppression of Indigenous people." Ibid., 16–17.

178 Paul Farmer, *Pathologies of Power: Health, Human Rights, and the New War on the Poor* (Berkeley: University of California Press, 2003), 31.
179 Amnesty International, *Stolen Sisters*, 21.
180 King, "Sisters in Spirit Research Framework," 274.
181 Ibid.
182 Brant, "Telling," 13.
183 Ibid., 17.
184 Ibid., 14.
185 Ibid., 13.
186 Ibid., 17.
187 Ibid., 16.
188 Ibid.
189 Ibid., 11.
190 Ibid., 17.
191 Ibid., 15.
192 Wendy Brown, *Edgework: Critical Essays on Knowledge and Politics* (Princeton, NJ: Princeton University Press, 2005), 83.
193 Brant, "Telling," 17.
194 Brown, *Edgework*, 84.
195 Razack, *Looking*, 36.
196 Michel Foucault, *The History of Sexuality*, vol. 1: *An Introduction* (New York: Vintage Books, 1990), 60.
197 Amnesty International, *Stolen Sisters*, 21.
198 Povinelli, *The Cunning of Recognition*, 184.

199 Amnesty International, *Stolen Sisters*, 35.
200 Dumont, "Helen Betty Osborne," 5.
201 Ibid., 15.
202 Flowers, "Refusal to Forgive," 44.
203 Dumont, "Helen Betty Osborne," 1. Emphasis added.
204 Ibid., 1–5.
205 Ibid., 22–25.
206 Flowers, "Refusal to Forgive," 35.
207 Dumont, "Helen Betty Osborne," 33.

CHAPTER THREE

A portion of this chapter has been previously published. See Allison Hargreaves, "Compelling Disclosures: Colonial Violence and the Narrative Imperative in Feminist Anti-Violence Discourse and Indigenous Women's Writing," *Canadian Woman Studies* 27, no. 2/3 (2009): 107–13.

1 Beverly Jacobs, quoted in Canada, *House of Commons Debates*, 2nd Session, 39th Parliament of Canada, June 11, 2008, http://www.parl.gc.ca/HousePublications/Publication.aspx?Language=E&Mode=1&Parl=39&Ses=2&DocId=3568890.
2 Ibid.
3 Ibid.
4 Ibid.
5 Jennifer Henderson and Pauline Wakeham, "Colonial Reckoning, National Reconciliation? Aboriginal Peoples and the Culture of Redress in Canada," *English Studies in Canada* 35, no. 1 (2009): 1.
6 Povinelli, *The Cunning of Recognition*, 17.
7 Henderson and Wakeham, "Colonial Reckoning," 2–3.
8 Phil Fontaine, quoted in Canada, *House of Commons Debates*.
9 Foucault, *The History of Sexuality*, 1:60.
10 Andrea Smith and J. Kēhaulani Kauanui, "Native Feminisms Engage American Studies," *American Quarterly* 60, no. 2 (2008): 247, doi:10.1353/aq.0.0001.
11 Povinelli, *The Cunning of Recognition*, 17.
12 *Creating Inclusive Spaces for Women: A Practical Guide for Implementing an Integrated, Anti-Racist, Feminist Service Delivery System*, prepared by

Shara Stone, Rubena Willis Counseling Centre for Assaulted Women and Children, Esther Enyolu, and the Women's Rights Coalition of Durham for the Ontario Association of Interval and Transition Houses (OAITH), 2005, 12, http://www.oaith.ca/assets/files/Publications/CreatingInclusivesSpacesFormatted.pdf.

13 Rita Kohli, "Violence against Women: Race, Class and Gender Issues," *Canadian Women Studies* 11, no. 4 (1991): 14, http://cws.journals.yorku.ca/index.php/cws/issue/view/514.

14 A. Smith and Kauanui, "Native Feminisms," 247.

15 Harsha Walia, "Decolonizing Together: Moving beyond a Politics of Solidarity toward a Practice of Decolonization," in *The Winter We Danced: Voices from the Past, the Future, and the Idle No More Movement*, ed. Kino-nda-niimi Collective (Winnipeg: Arbeiter Ring, 2014), 47.

16 Chandra Talpade Mohanty, *Feminism without Borders: Decolonizing Theory, Practicing Solidarity* (London: Duke University Press, 2003), 110–11.

17 Verna St. Denis, "Feminism Is for Everybody: Aboriginal Women, Feminism and Diversity," in *Making Space for Indigenous Feminism*, ed. Joyce Green (Winnipeg: Fernwood, 2007), 41.

18 Ibid., 40.

19 Ibid.

20 Green, "Taking Account," 23.

21 Agnes Calliste and George Sefa Dei, "Anti-Racist Feminism: Critical Race and Gender Studies," in *Anti-Racist Feminism*, ed. Agnes Calliste and George J. Sefa Dei (Halifax: Fernwood, 2000), 15.

22 Mary Louise Fellows and Sherene Razack, "The Race to Innocence: Confronting Hierarchical Relations among Women," *Journal of Gender, Race, and Justice* 1 (1998): 336.

23 Kimberlé Crenshaw, "Mapping the Margins: Intersectionality, Identity Politics, and Violence against Women of Color," in *Identities: Race, Class, Gender, and Nationality*, ed. Linda Martín Alcoff and Eduardo Mendieta (Malden, MA: Blackwell, 2003), 176.

24 Isabel Altamirano-Jiménez, *Indigenous Encounters with Neoliberalism: Place, Women, and the Environment in Canada and Mexico* (Vancouver: University of British Columbia Press, 2013), 111.

25 See, for example, *Intersectional Feminist Frameworks: A Primer* (Ottawa:

Canadian Research Institute for the Advancement of Women [CRIAW], 2006), http://www.criaw-icref.ca/en/product/intersectional-feminist-frameworks--a-primer; Joanna Simpson, *Everyone Belongs: A Toolkit for Applying Intersectionality* (Ottawa: CRIAW, 2009), http://www.criaw-icref.ca/sites/criaw/files/Everyone_Belongs_e.pdf; OAITH, "Creating Inclusive Spaces."

26 Critics like Goli Rezai-Rashti are concerned to differentiate multiculturalism (with its roots in a "liberal-reformist understanding of racism") from anti-racism (as emerging in the anti-colonial "struggles of racial minorities"). See Goli Rezai-Rashti, "Multicultural Education, Anti-Racist Education, and Critical Pedagogy: Reflections on Everyday Practice," in *Anti-Racism, Feminism, and Critical Approaches to Education*, ed. Roxana Ng, Pat Staton, and Joyce Scane (Westport, CT: Bergin and Garvey, 1995), 6. By contrast, Sarita Srivastava and Margot Francis deliberately use the conflated term "anti-racist multiculturalism" to describe the manner in which liberal discourses of multicultural inclusivity have permeated many feminist organizational efforts toward addressing systemic racism. See Srivastava and Francis, "Troubles with Anti-Racist Multiculturalism: The Challenges of Anti-Racist and Feminist Activism," in *Race and Racism in 21st Century Canada: Continuity, Complexity and Change*, ed. Sean Hier and Singh Bolaria (Peterborough, ON: Broadview, 2007), 291–92.

27 Usha George, "Toward Anti-Racism in Social Work in the Canadian Context," in *Anti-Racist Feminism*, ed. Agnes Calliste and George J. Sefa Dei (Halifax: Fernwood, 2000), 116–17; Fauzia Rafiq, *Developing an Antiracism Action Plan: A Handbook for Workers Working in Service Organizations of Metropolitan Toronto* (Toronto: Women Working with Immigrant Women, 1992), 37.

28 Lisa Barnoff and Ken Moffatt, "Contradictory Tensions in Anti-Oppression Practice in Feminist Social Services," *Affilia: Journal of Women and Social Work* 22, no. 1 (2007): 58, doi:10.1177/0886109906295772; *Creating Inclusive Spaces*, 28.

29 Rita Kohli, "Power or Empowerment: Questions of Agency in the Shelter Movement," in *And Still We Rise: Feminist Political Mobilizing in Contemporary Canada*, ed. Linda Carty (Toronto: Women's Press, 1993), 393.

30 Rafiq, *Developing*, 19.

31 Ibid.
32 Ibid., 20
33 Sarita Srivastava, "'You're Calling Me a Racist?' The Moral and Emotional Regulation of Antiracism and Feminism," *Signs*, 31, no. 1 (2005): 35, doi:10.1086/432738.
34 The once largely white population served by Nellie's was, by 1992, more than half made up of "immigrant, refugee and minority women." See Michele Landsberg, "Callwood Furor Masks Real Racism Struggle at Nellie's," *Toronto Star*, July 18, 1992. See also Margaret Cannon, *The Invisible Empire: Racism in Canada* (Toronto: Random House, 1995), 155; Barbara Wade Rose, "Race and Feminism Trouble at Nellie's," *Globe and Mail,* May 9, 1992.
35 Donna Barker and Carolann Wright, On Behalf of the Coalition of Women of Color Working in Women's and Community Services. "The Women of Color on the Nellie's Saga," *Toronto Star*, September 2, 1992.
36 Cannon, *The Invisible Empire*, 158.
37 A. Smith, *Conquest*, 152; Jeri Dawn Wine and Janice Ristock, "Introduction," in *Women and Social Change: Feminist Activism in Canada*, ed. Jeri Dawn Wine and Janice L. Ristock (Toronto: James Lorimer, 1991), 12.
38 Lynda Hurst, "Controversy Dogs Women's Group," *Windsor Star*, March 16, 1995.
39 Carol Tator, Frances Henry, and Winston Matthis, *Challenging Racism in the Arts: Case Studies of Controversy and Conflict* (Toronto: University of Toronto Press, 1998), 88.
40 Ibid., 92–93.
41 Althea Prince, quoted in Tator, Henry, and Matthis, *Challenging Racism*, 88.
42 Lenore Keeshig-Tobias, "Stop Stealing Native Stories," in *Borrowed Power: Essays on Cultural Appropriation*, ed. Bruce Ziff and Pratima V. Rao (New Brunswick, NJ: Rutgers University Press, 2004), 71.
43 Keeshig-Tobias, "Stop Stealing Native Stories," 72.
44 Gail Guthrie Valaskakis, "Parallel Voices: Indians and Others—Narratives of Cultural Struggle," *Canadian Journal of Communication* 18, no. 3 (1999): 285.
45 Ibid.
46 Sandy Grande, "Whitestream Feminism and the Colonialist Project: A

Review of Contemporary Feminist Pedagogy and Praxis," *Educational Theory* 53, no. 3 (2003): 329, doi:10.1111/j.1741-5446.2003.00329.x.

47 Srivastava, "You're Calling Me," 34.

48 Nellie McClung, known for her celebrated role as one of the "Famous Five" who won the 1929 "Person's Case" for Canadian women, is popularly heralded as having led Canadian women to enfranchisement and personhood. However, McClung's feminist legacy is now often remembered as an ambivalent one because of her support for eugenic legislation and her biologically determinist understandings of both gender and race. That the mainstream feminist debate over anti-racism in the early 1990s should be so often focalized through the events of a shelter named for this "first wave" feminist figure is interesting to note, considering the charges of racism levelled at both Nellie McClung—as an iconic figure of Eurocentric Canadian feminism—and the Nellie's shelter. See Cecily Devereux, *Growing a Race: Nellie L. McClung and the Fiction of Eugenic Feminism* (Montreal and Kingston: McGill-Queen's University Press, 2006), 6.

49 "Mission Statement," *Nellie's*, accessed February 19, 2008, http://www.nellies.org/about/mission-statement/.

50 "Herstory." *Nellie's*, accessed February 19, 2009. http://www.nellies.org/about/herstory/.

51 Wade Rose, "Race and Feminism."

52 Margaret Cannon provides an account of the Nellie's conflict, and the other key events leading up to founding board member June Callwood's resignation at the height of the anti-racism debates. See Cannon, *The Invisible Empire*, 145–60. Throughout May and June of 1992, both the *Toronto Star* and the *Globe and Mail* published several articles and letters about Nellie's; see, for instance, Barbara Wade Rose, "Race and Feminism"; June Callwood, "The Nellie's Furor: June Callwood Tells Her Side," *Toronto Star*, July 23, 1992. The Toronto Coalition of Women of Colour, as the group which helped represent the concerns of the Women of Colour Caucus to the board at Nellie's, told their side of the story in the September 3 edition of the *Toronto Star*. See Barker and Wright, "The Women of Colour."

53 Cannon, *The Invisible Empire*, 159; Barker and Wright, "The Women of Color."

54 Barker and Wright, "The Women of Color."
55 Shirley Brown, quoted in Wade Rose, "Race and Feminism."
56 Wade Rose, "Race and Feminism."
57 Barker and Wright, "The Women of Color."
58 Ibid.
59 Ibid.
60 One example of racist hostility aimed at women of colour is recounted by the Coalition: "At the beginning of a meeting between the coalition and the board, we witnessed one of the board members sticking her tongue out at one of the women of color. This was not only immature, it was a display of the utter and total disrespect for the women of color that goes on there. The individual who did it was the same person who asked a woman of color, 'What do you want us to do? Paint ourselves black?' When told this was a racist remark, she responded by saying that women of color make her racist." Ibid.
61 Cannon, *The Invisible Empire*, 159.
62 Ibid.
63 Barker and Wright, "The Women of Color."
64 Joan Johnson and Karen Hinds, quoted in Barker and Wright, "The Women of Color." Johnson's statement, co-authored with Hinds, was published in excerpted form by Barker and Wright. This is, to my knowledge, the only published version of the statement available.
65 Himani Bannerji, "But Who Speaks For Us? Experience and Agency in Conventional Feminist Paradigms," in *Unsettling Relations: The University as a Site of Feminist Struggles*, ed. Himani Bannerji et al. (Boston: South End Press, 1991), 95.
66 Ibid.
67 Cannon, *The Invisible Empire*, 159.
68 As theorized by Wendy Brown, to depoliticize is to construe "inequality, subordination, marginalization, and social conflict ... as personal and individual. Wendy Brown, *Regulating Aversion* (Princeton, NJ: Princeton University Press, 2006), 15.
69 Srivastava, "You're Calling Me," 33.
70 Fellows and Razack, "The Race to Innocence," 335.
71 Landsberg, "Callwood Furor."
72 Cannon, *The Invisible Empire*, 159.
73 Ibid.

74 Barker and Wright, "The Women of Color."
75 Landsberg, "Callwood Furor."
76 Cannon, *The Invisible Empire*, 160.
77 Razack, *Looking*, 52.
78 Cannon, *The Invisible Empire*, 159.
79 Wade Rose, "Race and Feminism."
80 Srivastava, "You're Calling Me," 35.
81 Monture-Angus, *Thunder in My Soul*, 22.
82 Ibid., 21.
83 Vuyiswa Keyi, quoted in Wade Rose, "Race and Feminism."
84 Barker and Wright, "The Women of Color."
85 Srivastava, "You're Calling Me," 36. By non-racism, Srivastava means a "liberal discourse of equality that denies the systemic nature of racism and its presence in our everyday language and practices." Ibid., 35.
86 Cannon, *The Invisible Empire*, 160; Wade Rose, "Race and Feminism." Callwood later remarked: "I was coerced into this apology.... Only a small part of it is sincere." Callwood, quoted in Landsberg, "Callwood Furor." The Coalition claims that Callwood initially "refused" to apologize at all. See Barker and Wright, "The Women of Color."
87 Callwood, "The Nellie's Furor"; Barker and Wright, "The Women of Color;" Wade Rose, "Race and Feminism."
88 Landsberg, "Callwood Furor."
89 Elaine Dewar, "Wrongful Dismissal," *Toronto Life*, March 1993, 32–45.
90 Landsberg, "Callwood Furor."
91 Cannon, *The Invisible Empire*, 160.
92 Landsberg, "Callwood Furor."
93 Callwood, "The Nellie's Furor."
94 Cannon, *The Invisible Empire*, 160.
95 Ibid.
96 Pierre Berton, "If Callwood Is a Racist Then So Are We All," *Toronto Star*, May 23, 1992.
97 Cannon, *The Invisible Empire*, 147.
98 Dewar, "Wrongful Dismissal."
99 Ibid.
100 Philip Berger, "A Flimsy Case against June Callwood," *Toronto Star*, September 11, 1992.
101 Fellows and Razack, "The Race to Innocence," 352.

102 Akua Benjamin, Judy Rebick, and Amy Go, "Racist Backlash Takes Subtle Form among Feminists," *Toronto Star*, April 30, 1993. Benjamin, Rebick, and Go are responding, in large part, to Elaine Dewar's March 1993 *Toronto Life* article, "Wrongful Dismissal." Typical of the media backlash against the Women of Colour Caucus and anti-racist organizing more broadly, Dewar's article repeatedly characterizes the conflict at Nellie's in terms of an attempted "takeover" by women of colour.
103 Carolann Wright, quoted in Hurst, "Controversy Dogs Women's Group."
104 Walia, "Decolonizing Together," 46.
105 Callwood, "The Nellie's Furor."
106 Benjamin, Rebick, and Go, "Racist Backlash."
107 Sophie McCall, *First Person Plural: Aboriginal Storytelling and the Ethics of Collaborative Authorship* (Vancouver: University of British Columbia Press, 2011), 102.
108 Ibid.
109 Tator, Henry, and Matthis, *Challenging Racism*, 104.
110 Manina Jones,"Coming through Oka: Co-Authorship and Cultural Disturbance in First Nations Auto-Biographies," presentation, TransCanada Two: Literature, Institutions, Citizenship Conference, University of Guelph, Guelph, ON, October 11–14, 2007.
111 M. Nourbese Philip, *Frontiers: Selected Essays and Writings on Racism and Culture: 1984–1992* (Stratford, ON: Mercury Press, 1992), 216.
112 Keeshig-Tobias, "Stop Stealing Native Stories," 72.
113 Philip, *Frontiers*, 136.
114 Cannon, *The Invisible Empire*, 148; Philip, *Frontiers*, 139.
115 Philip, 139.
116 Barker and Wright, "The Women of Color."
117 "Herstory."
118 Barker and Wright, "The Women of Color."
119 Benjamin, Rebick, and Go, "Racist Backlash."
120 Kohli, "Power or Empowerment," 393.
121 Bénita Bunjun et al., *Intersectional Feminist Frameworks: An Emerging Vision* (Ottawa: CRIAW, 2006), 15, http://www.criawicref.ca/images/userfiles/files/Intersectional%20Feminist%20 Frameworks-%20An%20 Emerging%20Vision(2).pdf.
122 Goli Rezai-Rashti, "Multicultural Education," 7.

123 Srivastava, "You're Calling Me," 56.
124 Srivastava and Francis, "The Problem," 275.
125 Srivastava, "You're Calling Me," 57.
126 Brown, *Regulating Aversion*, 15.
127 Sherene Razack, "Your Place or Mine? Transnational Feminist Collaboration," in *Anti-Racist Feminism*, ed. Agnes Calliste and George J. Sefa Dei (Halifax: Fernwood, 2000), 41–44.
128 Lee Maracle, I Am Woman: *A Native Perspective on Sociology and Feminism* (Vancouver: Press Gang, 1996), 18.
129 Srivastava, "You're Calling Me," 62.
130 Srivastava and Francis, "The Problem," 282.
131 Million, *Therapeutic Nations*, 265.
132 Ibid.; Henderson, *First Nations Jurisprudence*, 157–58.
133 Craig Womack states: "The validity of experience, both personal and tribal, becomes one of the key issues in Native studies, if not *the* key issue, because a prevalent reality of postcontact life is that Indians have not had the primary role of representing their own cultures to the outside world; that is, others have reported on their experiences." See Craig Womack, "Theorizing American Indian Experience," in *Reasoning Together: The Native Critics Collective*, ed. Craig Womack, Daniel Heath Justice, and Christopher B. Teuton (Norman: University of Oklahoma Press, 2008), 382.
134 Ibid., 363.
135 Henderson, *First Nations*, 158.
136 Ibid. Emphasis added.
137 Ibid., 159.
139 Beth Brant, *Writing as Witness: Essays and Talk* (Toronto: Women's Press, 1994), 19.
139 Pauline Wakeham, "The Cunning of Reconciliation: Reinventing White Civility in Canada's Culture of Redress," in *Shifting the Ground of Canadian Literary Studies: Nation-State, Indigeneity, Culture*, ed. Smaro Kamboureli and Robert Zacharias (Waterloo, ON: Wilfrid Laurier University Press, 2012), 210.
140 Canada, House of Commons, *Speech from the Throne*, 2nd Session, 39th Parliament of Canada, October 16, 2007, http://www.parl.gc.ca/House Publications/Publication.aspx?Doc=1&Mode=1&Parl=39&Pub=Hansard &Ses=2&Language=E#OOB-2174986.

141 Jacobs, quoted in Canada, *House of Commons Debates*.
142 Ibid.
143 Ibid.
144 Linda Anderson, "Autobiography," in *Encyclopedia of Feminist Theories*, ed. Lorraine Code (New York: Routledge, 2000), 34.
145 Sidonie Smith, and Julia Watson, "Introduction: Situating Subjectivity in Women's Autobiographical Practices," in *Women, Autobiography, Theory: A Reader*, ed. Sidonie Smith and Julia Watson (Madison: University of Wisconsin Press, 1998), 27.
146 Jo-Ann Episkenew, email message to author, November 22, 2007.
147 Doris Sommer, "Sacred Secrets: A Strategy for Survival," in *Women, Autobiography, Theory: A Reader*, ed. Sidonie Smith and Julia Watson (Madison: University of Wisconsin Press, 1998), 198. For an extended discussion of the critical impulse to position Indigenous literature as the honest, artless, and unmediated testimony of the "native informant," see Helen Hoy, "'Nothing but the Truth': Discursive Transparency in Beatrice Culleton," in *In Search of April Raintree*, ed. Cheryl Suzack (Winnipeg: Portage and Main Press, 1999), 273–94.
148 Morningstar Mercredi, *Morningstar: A Warrior's Spirit* (Regina: Coteau, 2006), 42.
149 Ibid., 70.
150 Ibid., 85.
151 Ibid., 110.
152 Ibid., 117.
153 Ibid., 124.
154 Ibid., 126.
155 Ibid., 141.
156 Ibid.
157 Ibid., 147.
158 M.E. Powell Mendenhall, "Review of Morningstar: A Warrior's Spirit, by Morningstar Mercredi," Saskatchewan Publisher's Group, 2006, http://www.skbooks.com/wp-content/uploads/2010/01/3049.pdf.
159 Ken Tingley, "Strong Voice Emerges from the Dark," review of *Morningstar: A Warrior's Spirit*, *Edmonton Journal*, October 29, 2006.
160 Mendenhall, "Review of *Morningstar*," 30.
161 Smith and Watson, "Introduction," 27.

162 Nolan, "Selling," 99.
163 Mercredi, *Morningstar*, 1.
164 Ibid., 2.
165 Ibid., 1.
166 Ibid.
167 Ibid.
168 Laurel Smith, review of "Morningstar: A Warrior's Spirit," Quill and Quire 72, no. 2 (2006): 60.
169 Mercredi, *Morningstar*, 1.
170 Smith, review of "*Morningstar*," 60.
171 Trevor Greyeyes, "A New Age Take on an Old Aboriginal Story," *Winnipeg Free Press*, October 1, 2006.
172 I use the term "confessional" in Rita Felski's sense, as a "type of autobiographical writing which signals its intention to foreground the most personal and intimate details of an author's life." Like consciousness raising, Felski says, the "confessional text makes public that which has been private," disclosing "intimate and often traumatic details of the author's life" in order to "elucidate their broader implications." See Rita Felski. "On Confession," in *Women, Autobiography, Theory: A Reader*, ed. Sidonie Smith and Julia Watson (Madison: University of Wisconsin Press, 1998), 83.
173 Greyeyes, "A New Age."
174 Mercredi, *Morningstar*, 158.
175 Henderson, *First Nations*, 159.
176 Mercredi, *Morningstar*, 158.
177 Ibid., 158–59.
178 Donna Haraway, "The Persistence of Vision," in *Writing on the Body: Female Embodiment and Feminist Theory*, ed. Katie Conboy, Nadia Medina, and Sarah Stanbury (New York: Columbia University Press, 1997), 287–88. Italics in original.
179 Tingley, "Strong Voice."
180 Povinelli, *The Cunning of Recognition*, 184.
181 Blanchard Jerrold and Gustave Doré, *London: A Pilgrimage* [1872] (New York: Dover, 1970), 144.
182 Cameron's account reads, in part: "It was dark by the time I got there, and if it had looked grimy and sinister on my first pass … in bright

sunshine, it was terrifying at night. I snapped the door locks on the Jeep and crawled up and down side streets and along East Hastings, trying to absorb it all: the open-air drug market, thick with muttering dealers and customers; the prostitutes waiting on corners, as drivers inched along in their cars, looking them over; emaciated women lurching along the sidewalks, stooping and hunting in vain for the tiniest crumbs of crack cocaine." See Stevie Cameron, *The Pickton File* (Toronto: Knopf Canada, 2007), 29.

183 Smith, "Rev. of Morningstar," 60.
184 Greyeyes, "A New Age." Emphasis added.
185 Smith, "Review of *Morningstar*," 60.
186 Nolan, "Selling," 97.
187 Povinelli, *The Cunning of Recognition*, 17.
188 Nolan, "Selling," 98.
189 Ibid.
190 Ibid.
191 Deena Rymhs, *From the Iron House: Imprisonment in First Nations Writing* (Waterloo, ON: Wilfrid Laurier University Press, 2008), 65.
192 Smith, "Review of *Morningstar*," 60.
193 Ibid.
194 Tingley, "Strong Voice."
195 Morningstar Mercredi, in "Truth and Lies: Telling Tales in Creative Nonfiction," ed. Gordon Morash. *Aurora*, 2007, http://aurora.icaap.org/index.php/aurora/article/view/72/84.
196 Ibid.
197 Maria Campbell, *Halfbreed* (Toronto: McClelland and Stewart, 1973), 2.
198 Mercredi, *Morningstar*, ii.
199 Armstrong, "Disempowerment," 243.
200 Mercredi, *Morningstar*, iii.
201 Ibid., 150.
202 Gregory Younging, "Inherited History, International Law, and the UN Declaration," in *Response, Responsibility, and Renewal*, 327.
203 Ibid.
204 Ibid.
205 Flowers, "Refusal to Forgive," 47.
206 Mercredi, *Morningstar*, ii.

207 Mercredi, "Truth and Lies."
208 Mercredi, *Morningstar*, 180.
209 Ibid., 178.
210 Ibid., 181.
211 Ibid., 179.
212 Greyeyes, "A New Age."
213 Smith and Kauanui, "Native Feminisms," 247.
214 Mercredi, *Morningstar*, iii.
215 Nolan, "Selling," 99.
216 Razack, *Looking*, 52.
217 Paula Gunn Allen, *The Sacred Hoop: Recovering the Feminine in American Indian Traditions* (Boston: Beacon, 1986), 156.

CHAPTER FOUR

1 Amnesty International, *Stolen Sisters*, 21.
2 Withey, "Discovery."
3 NWAC, *Voices*, 5.
4 Cultural Memory Group, *Remembering Women Murdered by Men: Memorials across Canada* (Toronto: Sumach, 2006), 77.
5 Jacobs and Williams, "Legacy," 135.
6 Laurie McNeill, "Death and the Maidens: Vancouver's Missing Women, the Montreal Massacre, Commemoration's Blind Spots," *Canadian Review of American Studies* 78, no. 3 (2008): 377, doi:10.3138/cras.38.3.375.
7 Ibid., 375.
8 Ibid., 377.
9 David Robertson, *The Life of Helen Betty Osborne: A Graphic Novel*, Illus. Madison Blackstone (Winnipeg: In a Bind Publications, 2008), 6.
10 Stephanie Pyne, "Profile of Helen Betty Osborne," in *Hidden in Plain Sight: Contributions of Aboriginal Peoples to Canadian Identity and Culture*, ed. David Newhouse, Cora Voyageur, and Dan Beavon (Toronto: University of Toronto Press, 2005), 246.
11 Stone-Mediatore, *Reading across Borders*, 3.
12 Ibid., 4.
13 Cultural Memory Group, *Remembering*, 77.
14 For commemorative treatments of Helen Betty Osborne, see: Marie

Annharte Baker, "Penumbra," in *Being on the Moon* (Winlaw, BC: Polestar, 1990), 12; Beth Brant, "Telling"; Marilyn Dumont, "Helen Betty Osborne." For commemorative treatments of Anna Mae Pictou-Aquash, see: Yvette Nolan, *Annie Mae's Movement* (Toronto: Playwrights Canada Press, 2006); Daniel David Moses, "Report on Anna Mae's Remains," in An Anthology of Canadian Native Literature in English, 3rd ed., ed. Daniel David Moses and Terry Goldie (Don Mills: Oxford University Press, 2005), 361–62; Buffy Sainte-Marie, "Bury My Heart at Wounded Knee," in *Coincidence and Likely Stories* (EMI Records, 1992); Joy Harjo, "For Anna Mae Pictou Aqaush, Whose Spirit Is Present Here and in the Dappled Stars," in *The Colour of Resistance: A Contemporary Collection of Writing by Aboriginal Women*, ed. Connie Fife (Toronto: Sister Vision Press, 1993), 78.

15 Ward Churchill and Jim Vander Wall, *The Cointelpro Papers: Documents from the FBI's Secret Wars against Dissent in the United States* (Cambridge, MA: South End Press, 2002), 404.

16 Pyne, "Profile of Helen Betty Osborne," 246.

17 Backhouse, "Aboriginal Women."

18 In February of 2004, former AIM activist Arlo Looking Cloud was convicted of first-degree murder and was sentenced to life in prison for his part in the crime. Two other AIM men, John Graham and Richard Marshall, were also charged in connection to the murder. As recounted by the Associated Press, "prosecutors said Graham and two other AIM members—Arlo Looking Cloud and Theda Clarke—drove Pictou-Aquash from Denver to Rapid City, where she was held against her will and questioned about whether she was an informant. Prosecutors have said she was not working with the government, and allege that Graham raped Pictou-Aquash and later fatally shot her." See "Pictou-Aquash Killing Charges Dropped," *CBC News*, February 4, 2010, http://www.cbc.ca/news/canada/pictou-aquash-killing-charges-dropped-1.916669. A federal jury later found Marshall not guilty, while John Graham was convicted of felony murder in 2011. See "N.S. Woman's Killer in South Dakota Gets Life," *CBC News*, January 24, 2011, http://www.cbc.ca/news/canada/n-s-woman-s-killer-in-south-dakota-gets-life-1.1073080; Bryan Rindfleisch, "'Slaying the Sun Woman': The Legacy of Annie Mae Aquash," *Graduate History Review* 3, no.1 (2011): 89–102, https://journals.uvic.ca/index.php/ghr/article/view/5995/2718.

19 Amnesty International, *Stolen Sisters*, 21.
20 Ibid., 20.
21 Ibid.
22 Ibid.
23 Ibid., 21.
24 Ibid., 3.
25 Ibid., 19.
26 Pat Adamson and Lauree Kopetsky, *Teacher's Guide for The Life of Helen Betty Osborne: A Graphic Novel* (Winnipeg: Portage and Main Press, 2009), 3, http://www.portageandmainpress.com/lesson_plans/plan_260_1.pdf.
27 Merna Forster, "Murder of a Mi'kmaq Activist: Anna Mae Maloney Aquash," in *100 Canadian Heroines: Famous and Forgotten Faces* (Toronto: Dundurn, 2004), 34.
28 Diamond, "The Violence of 'We,'" 405.
29 Judith Butler, *Precarious Life: The Powers of Mourning and Violence* (London: Verso, 2004), xiv.
30 Backhouse, "Aboriginal Women."
31 Episkenew, *Taking Back*, 79.
32 Amnesty International, *Stolen Sisters*, 21.
33 Ehrlich, *Representing Rape*, 20.
34 Ibid.
35 Ibid., 91.
36 *Report of the Aboriginal Justice Inquiry of Manitoba*, vol. 2, ch. 1, http://www.ajic.mb.ca/volumeII/chapter1.html.
37 Ehrlich, *Representing Rape*, 91.
38 Robertson, *The Life of Helen Betty Osborne*, 7.
39 Smith, *Conquest*, 10.
40 Robertson, *The Life of Helen Betty Osborne*, 7.
41 Take, for example, the case of Pamela George. A Saulteux woman of the Sakimay First Nation in Saskatchewan, George was murdered by two white university students in April of 1995 under circumstances which share some commonalities with the case of Helen Betty Osborne. Like Osborne, George was driven to the outskirts of town, was sexually assaulted, and was beaten to death. In George's case, however, her occasional engagement in the sex trade in Regina called into question her

status as a legitimate victim of violence in the subsequent trial. Sherene Razack states that "a number of factors contributed to masking the violence of the two accused and thus diminishing their culpability and legal responsibility for the death of Pamela George. Primarily, I claim that because Pamela George was considered to belong to a space of prostitution and Aboriginality, in which violence routinely occurs, while her killers were presumed to be far removed from this zone, the enormity of what was done to harm her and her family remained largely unacknowledged." See Razack, *Race, Space* 125–26.

42 Adamson and Kopetsky, *Teacher's Guide*, 11.
43 Roberston, *The Life of Helen Betty Osborne*, 6.
44 Ibid., 29.
45 Manitoba, "Helen Betty Osborne Memorial Foundation Act," *Continuing Consolidation of the Statutes of Manitoba* (CCSM c. H38.1), December 15, 2000, http://web2. gov.mb.ca/laws/statutes/ccsm/h038-1e.php.
46 Ibid.
47 "Apology to the Family, Legislation to Honour Osborne," Manitoba government news release, July 14, 2000, http://news.gov.mb.ca/news/index.html?item=24626&posted=2000-07-14.
48 Manitoba, "Helen Betty Osborne Memorial Foundation Act."
49 Ibid.
50 Gord Mackintosh, in the Legislative Assembly of Manitoba, The Standing Committee on Law Amendments, 2nd Session, 37th Legislature, December 11, 2000, 9. http://www.gov.mb.ca/legislature/hansard/37th_2nd/hansardpdf/la1.pdf.
51 Cultural Memory Group, *Remembering*, 84.
52 "Helen Betty Osborne Foundation Board Appointments and New Web Site Announced," Manitoba government news release, January 31, 2003, http://news.gov.mb.ca/news/print,index.html?item=26296&posted=2003-01-31.
53 Mackintosh, Legislative Assembly, 9.
54 Manitoba, "Helen Betty Osborne Memorial Foundation Act."
55 "Manitoba Says Sorry for Actions in Osborne Case," *Toronto Star*, July 15, 2000; David Kuxhaus, "Province Apologizes for Role in Probe of Osborne Murder," *Winnipeg Free Press*, July 15, 2000; Tammy Marlowe, "Helen's Dream Lives On," *Winnipeg Sun*, July 15, 2000.
56 "Apology to the Family, Legislation to Honour Osborne."

57 Mackintosh, Legislative Assembly, 9–10.
58 "Apology to the Family, Legislation to Honour Osborne."
59 Henderson and Wakeham, "Colonial Reckoning," 1.
60 Reconciliation cannot be "about residential schools alone; this long history did not exist in a vacuum and cannot be addressed as if it did" (341). Gregory Younging, Jonathan Dewar, and Mike DeGagné, "Conclusion," in *Response, Responsibility, and Renewal*, 341.
61 "Manitoba Says Sorry."
62 Eric Robinson, Legislative Assembly, 7.
63 "Canada's Statement of Apology," in *Response, Responsibility, and Renewal*, 357.
64 Ibid., 359; For a discussion of the trope of closure as deployed in contemporary discourse around redress, and in the government of Canada's apology particularly, see Pauline Wakeham's "The Cunning of Reconciliation: Reinventing White Civility in the Age of Apology," 16–17.
65 Henderson and Wakeham, "Colonial Reckoning," 7
66 Ibid.
67 Mackintosh, Legislative Assembly, 9.
68 "Canada's Statement," 357.
69 Younging, "Inherited History," 331–33.
70 Jorge Barrera, "Prime Minister Needs to Apologize for Colonialism Denial, Native Groups Say," *CanWest News*, September 30, 2009.
71 Henderson and Wakeham, "Colonial Reckoning," 3.
72 Jorge Barrera, "Prime Minister Needs to Apologize."
73 Robertson, *The Life of Helen Betty Osborne*, 1.
74 Pyne, "Profile of Helen Betty Osborne," 247.
75 Mackintosh, Legislative Assembly, 9.
76 Notably, Portage and Main Press specializes in educational books and resources for teachers. The Portage and Main *Teacher's Guide* by Pat Adamson and Lauree Kopetsky suggests the graphic novel as a "teachable" resource in the Manitoba curriculum. The guide itself lists points of "curriculum correlation" for Manitoba high schools, including in the English Language Arts, the Manitoba Residential School Survivors Social Studies Project, Social Studies units on Diversity and Pluralism, and in the History of First Nations, Métis, and Inuit peoples in Canada. Adamson and Kopetsky, *Teacher's Guide*, 3.
77 Robertson, *The Life of Helen Betty Osborne*, 5.

78 Ibid., 6.
79 Ibid.
80 Ibid., 1.
81 Ibid., 7.
82 Ibid.
83 Ibid., 6.
84 Ibid., 15.
85 Ibid.
86 Ibid., 12.
87 Ibid., 6. Emphasis added.
88 Episkenew, *Taking Back*, 11.
89 Adamson and Kopetsky, *Teacher's Guide*, 10.
90 Robertson, *The Life of Helen Betty Osborne*, 15.
91 LaRocque, "Violence," 73–74.
92 Robertson, *The Life of Helen Betty Osborne*, 1.
93 Ibid.
94 As the Aboriginal Justice Inquiry reports, "her clothing, other than her boots, was removed and hidden over 30 metres away, below some rocks on the breakwater which extends some 45 metres out into the lake." Osborne's boots are also seen depicted in the graphic novel, when her body is discovered. *Report of the Aboriginal Justice Inquiry of Manitoba*, vol. 2, ch. 3, http://www.ajic.mb.ca/volumell/chapter3.html.
95 Robertson, *The Life of Helen Betty Osborne*, 26.
96 Ibid., 6.
97 Ibid., 19.
98 Ibid., 6.
99 Ibid., 19.
100 Ibid., 28.
101 Ibid., 19.
102 Ibid.
103 Ibid., 29.
104 Ibid., 18.
105 Ibid., 29.
106 Ibid., 15. Emphasis added.
107 Kim Campbell, "Foreword," in *100 Canadian Heroines: Famous and Forgotten Faces*, by Merna Forster (Toronto: Dundurn, 2004), 13.

108 Ibid., 15.
109 Ibid.
110 Ibid., 19.
111 Forster, "Murder of a Mi'kmaq Activist," 31.
112 Ibid., 34.
113 Yvette Nolan, *Annie Mae's Movement* (Toronto: Playwrights Canada Press, 2006), back cover.
114 Maracle, *I Am Woman*, 107.
115 Devon Abbott Mihesuah, *Indigenous American Women: Decolonization, Empowerment, Activism* (Lincoln: University of Nebraska Press, 2003), 12.
116 M. Annette Jaimes, "Review of *Lakota Woman*, by Mary Crow Dog," *American Indian Culture and Research Journal* 15, no. 1 (1991): 110.
117 Yvette Nolan, *Annie Mae's Movement*, 3. This is the stage direction with which the 2006 Playwrights Canada Press edition begins. An earlier version of the play varies slightly on this detail. The original 1999 Playwrights Union of Canada Press edition begins with Anna Mae "isolated in a pool of light," "doing karate moves." See Nolan, "Selling," 102. Both editions of the play end with a "gunshot," and leave the audience with the image of Anna Mae curled in a fetal position. Unless otherwise stated, I refer to the 2006 edition of the play. Although I am here making specific reference to the play's print history, its production history is briefly recounted by Canadian theatre scholar Michelle La Flamme. See La Flamme, "Theatrical Medicine," 109–10.
118 Nolan, *Annie Mae's Movement*, 53.
119 Anthony J. Hall, "Imperialism, Conquest, Indigenous Peoples, Aboriginal Title, Treaties, and International Law: The Occupation of BC, Iraq, and the West Bank, the Extradition Cases of Sitting Bull, Leonard Peltier, James Pitawanakwat, and John Graham," presentation, University of Lethbridge, Lethbridge, AB, March 3, 2004.
120 Mihesuah, *Indigenous American Women*, 123.
121 Johanna Brand, *The Life and Death of Anna Mae Aquash* (Toronto: James Lorimer, 1993), 15–16.
122 Daniel David Moses, "Report on Anna Mae's Remains," 361.
123 Brand, *The Life and Death of Anna Mae Aquash*, 20–21; Mihesuah, *Indigenous American Women*, 124.

124 Shirley Hill Witt, "The Brave-Hearted Women," *Akwesasne Notes* 8, no. 2 (1976): 17.
125 Ibid.
126 Mihesuah, *Indigenous American Women*, 115.
127 Forster, "Murder of a Mi'kmaq Activist," 34.
128 Wendy Gillis, "SNTC Play Recalls Aboriginal Heroine," *Star Phoenix*, May 9, 2008.
129 For example, Shannon M. Collins's lyrics to the commemorative song "I'd Do It Again in a Heartbeat" problematically assign agency and choice to Pictou-Aquash's death—in part by deploying the first-person pronoun: "But remember what went into my name when I died for you. / And I'd do it again in a heartbeat. / I'm Anna Mae Pictou." Collins, quoted in Mihesuah, *Indigenous American Women*, 115.
130 Moses, "Report on Anna Mae's Remains," 361.
131 Ellen Klaver, "Daughter of the Earth: Song for Anna Mae Aquash," in *Agents of Repression: The FBI's Secret Wars against the Black Panther Party and the American Indian Movement*, by Ward Churchill and Jim Vander Wall (Boston: South End Press, 1988), vii.
132 Smith, *Conquest*, 22.
133 La Flamme, "Theatrical Medicine," 109.
134 Lynn Mitges, "Celebrating Human Spirit: Plays Deal with Constant Struggles of Aboriginal Women," *The Province*, October 11, 2006.
135 Nolan, *Annie Mae's Movement*, 3.
136 Ibid., 4.
137 Ibid., 3.
138 As Julie Davis recounts, the Minneapolis and St. Paul survival schools grew out of AIM activism in education and child welfare. Established in 1972 as an Indigenous-run urban alternative to the public schools system, the survival schools promoted Indigenous self-determination in education. Julie Davis, *Survival Schools: The American Indian Movement and Community Education in the Twin Cities* (Minneapolis: University of Minnesota Press, 2013), 6.
139 Nolan, *Annie Mae's Movement*, 32.
140 Ibid., 7.
141 Warren Cariou distinguishes between European and Indigenous conceptions of the Rugaru or *rigoureau*: "A Michif word, derived from the

French 'lou-garou,' the frightening figure in a series of wolf folk tales that are common in Quebec, France, and Louisiana," the rigoureau emerges in Métis stories as a "heroic figure." These stories are connected to "Cree and Anishinaabe transformation stories, in which people are gifted with the ability to change themselves into certain creatures and sometimes animals are able to turn themselves into humans." This tradition stands in contrast to the European one, in which the loup-garou is "virtually always a symbol of terror"; representative of irrationality and an "unstable humanity," the loup-garou is also a "topism for purity and a commensurate stigmatization of all kinds of hybridity." Warren Cariou, "Dances with Rigoureau," in *Troubling Tricksters: Revisioning Critical Conversations*, ed. Deanna Reder and Linda M. Morra (Waterloo, ON: Wilfrid Laurier University Press, 2010), 159–61.

142 Churchill and Vander Wall, *The Cointelpro Papers*, 404.

143 This is one way in which Nolan's play captures the initial conflict over who killed Pictou-Aquash and negotiates this conflict's expression in AIM politics. As Bryan Rindfleisch recounts, "At first, AIM accused the FBI of collaborating with the Pine Ridge reservation tribal chairman, Dick Wilson, and his vigilante police force (GOON squad) in Aquash's assassination. Further, AIM alleged that the federal government conspired to cover-up the murder. The FBI, on the other hand, suspected that AIM was responsible for Aquash's death. For the next three decades, the federal government and AIM traded accusations over who was to blame for Aquash's murder." Bryan Rindfleisch, "'Slaying the Sun-Woman,'" 89–90.

144 Belmore's website describes the performance piece: "Performing on a street corner in the Downtown East Side, Belmore commemorates the lives of missing and murdered aboriginal women who have disappeared from the streets of Vancouver. She scrubs the street on hands and knees, lights votive candles, and nails the long red dress she is wearing to a telephone pole. As she struggles to free herself, the dress is torn from her body and hangs in tatters from the nails, reminiscent of the tattered lives of women forced onto the streets for their survival in an alien urban environment. Once freed, Belmore, vulnerable and exposed in her underwear, silently reads the names of the missing women that she has written on her arms and then yells them out one by one. After each name

is called, she draws a flower between her teeth, stripping it of blossom and leaf, just as the lives of these forgotten and dispossessed women were shredded in the teeth of indifference. Belmore lets each woman know that she is not forgotten: her spirit is evoked and she is given life by the power of naming." Rebecca Belmore, *Vigil*, accessed November 18, 2016, http://www.rebeccabelmore.com/video/Vigil.html.

145 Nolan, *Annie Mae's Movement*, 53.
146 Ibid.
147 La Flamme, "Theatrical Medicine," 108.
148 Nolan, "Selling," 99.
149 Ibid.
150 McNeill, "Death and the Maidens," 386.
151 Mitges, "Celebrating Human Spirit."
152 Nolan, "Selling," 104.
153 Nolan, *Annie Mae's Movement*, 53.
154 Ibid., 26.
155 Natasha Joachim, "Profile of Anna Mae Pictou-Aquash: Mi'kmaq, Aboriginal Rights Activist," in *Hidden in Plain Sight*, 215.
156 Ehrlich, *Representing Rape*, 91.
157 Eric Robinson, Legislative Assembly, 9.
158 Robertson, *The Life of Helen Betty Osborne*, 15.
159 Jiwani and Young, "Missing and Murdered Women," 903.
160 Nolan, *Annie Mae's Movement*, 25.
161 Ibid., 53.
162 Ibid.
163 Ibid.
164 Ibid.
165 Ibid., 3.

CONCLUSION

1 Amber Dean, *Remembering*, 139.
2 Dara Culhane, "Their Spirits," 595.
3 Amber Dean, *Remembering*, 140.
4 Sharon Rosenberg, "Distances and Proximities: (Not) Being There," *West Coast Line 53*, 41, no. 1 (2007): 63.
5 Harsha Walia, "Decolonizing Together," 46.

6   Thomas, "Honouring the Oral Traditions," 242.
7   Tuck and Yang, "Decolonization," 2.
8   Ibid., 3.
9   Robyn Bourgeois, "National Inquiry on Missing, Murdered Women Not Best Answer," *Huffpost British Columbia*, December 21, 2012, http://www.huffingtonpost.ca/robyn-bourgeois/missing-women-inquiry-report-vancouver-pickton_b_2333262.html. Italics in original.
10 Families of Sisters in Spirit (FSIS), No More Silence (NMS), and the Native Youth Sexual Health Network (NYSHN), "Supporting the Resurgence of Community-Based Responses to Violence," *Nations Rising*, March 14, 2014, http://nationsrising.org/it-starts-with-us/.
11 Canada, "Final Report of the Pre-Inquiry Engagement Process," last modified May 19, 2016, https://www.aadnc-aandc.gc.ca/eng/1463677554486/1463677615622.
12 FSIS, NMS, and NYSHN, "Supporting."
13 Ibid.
14 See Carol Clover, *Men, Women, and Chain Saws: Gender in the Modern Horror Film* (Princeton, NJ: Princeton University Press, 1992), 16; Jamaluddin Aziz, *Transgressing Women: Space and the Body in Contemporary Noir Thrillers* (Newcastle: Cambridge Scholars Publishing, 2012), 103.
15 *A Red Girl's Reasoning*, directed by Elle-Máijá Tailfeathers (Vancouver: Crazy8s Film Society, 2012), DVD.
16 Judith Franco, "Gender, Genre and Female Pleasure in the Contemporary Revenge Narrative: *Baise moi* and *What It Feels Like for a Girl*," *Quarterly Review of Film and Video* 21, no. 1 (2004), 5.
17 *A Red Girl's Reasoning*.
18 Sarah Hunt, "More Than a Poster Campaign," 191.
19 Ibid., 192.
20 Flowers, "Refusal to Forgive," 40. Italics in original.
21 Bourgeois, "Warrior Women," 2–4.
22 See Carol Clover, *Men, Women and Chain Saws*; Judith Franco, "Gender, Genre and Female Pleasure"; Jacinda Read, *The New Avengers: Feminism, Femininity and the Rape-Revenge Cycle* (Manchester: Manchester University Press, 2000); Alison Young, *The Scene of Violence: Cinema, Crime, Affect* (New York: Routledge, 2009).

23 Angelina Rodriquez, "Revenge Is a Dish Best Served ... Not at All?" *Bitch Flicks*, April 21, 2014, http://www.btchflcks.com/2014/04/revenge-is-a-dish-best-served-not-at-all.html#.WKkY1-u3A8A.
24 Tuck and Yang, "Decolonization," 35.
25 Flowers, "Refusal to Forgive," 39.
26 Hunt, "Why Are We Hesitant?"
27 Ibid.
28 Rauna Kuokkanen, *Reshaping the University: Responsibility, Indigenous Epistemes, and the Logic of the Gift* (Vancouver: University of British Columbia Press, 2008), 33.
29 Ibid., 38.
30 Bev Sellars, *They Called Me Number One: Secrets and Survival at an Indian Residential School* (Vancouver: Talonbooks, 2012), 189–90.
31 Razack, "Gendered Racial Violence," 128.
32 Alex Boutilier, "Native Teen's Slaying a 'Crime,' Not a 'Sociological Phenomenon,' Stephen Harper Says," *Toronto Star*, August 21, 2014, https://www.thestar.com/news/canada/2014/08/21/native_teens_slaying_a_crime_not_a_sociological_phenomenon_stephen_harper_says.html.
33 Roland Chrisjohn and Tanya Wasacase, "Half-Truths and Whole Lies: Rhetoric in the 'Apology' and the Truth and Reconciliation Commission," in *Response, Responsibility, and Renewal*, 220.
34 Arthur Manuel, "Until Canada Gives Indigenous People Their Land Back, There Can Never Be Reconciliation," *Rabble.ca*, January 18, 2017, http://rabble.ca/blogs/bloggers/views-expressed/2017/01/until-canada-gives-indigenous-people-their-land-back-there-ca.
35 Arthur Manuel, *Unsettling Canada: A National Wake-Up Call* (Toronto: Between the Lines, 2015), 108.
36 Lynda Gray, *First Nations 101: Tons of Stuff You Need to Know about First Nations People* (Vancouver: Adaawx, 2013), 207.
37 Ibid.
38 Toby Rollo, "I Am Canadian! (Because of Treaties with Indigenous Nations)," in *The Winter We Danced*, 228.
39 Irlbacher-Fox, *Finding Dahshaa*, 2.
40 Jennifer Henderson, "Residential Schools and Opinion-Making in the Era of Traumatized Subjects and Taxpayer-Citizens," *Journal of Canadian Studies* 49, no. 1 (Winter 2015): 24.
41 Ibid., 26.

42 Susan Ehrlich, "The Discursive Reconstruction of Sexual Consent," *Discourse and Society* 9, no. 2 (1998): 150.
43 Acoose, *Iskwewak*, 43.
44 Brant, *Writing as Witness*, 85–86.
45 Ibid., 83.
46 Ibid., 84.
47 Rosanna Deerchild, "We Are Just," *Puritan* 30 (Summer 2015): 5–9, http://puritan-magazine.com/we-are-just/.
48 Katelyn Verstraten, "For Indigenous Women, Radical Art as a Last Resort," *The Tyee*, June 22, 2013, https://thetyee.ca/ArtsAndCulture/2013/06/22/Radical-Art/.
49 E. Pauline Johnson, "A Red Girl's Reasoning," in *Tekahionwake: E. Pauline Johnson's Writing on Native North America*, ed. Margery Fee and Dory Nason (Peterborough, ON: Broadview, 2016), 163–77.
50 Womack, *Art as Performance*, 62.
51 Ibid.
52 FSIS, NMS, and NYSHN, "Supporting."
53 Dory Nason, "We Hold Our Hands Up: On Indigenous Women's Love and Resistance," in *The Winter We Danced*, 186–87.
54 Flowers, "Refusal to Forgive," 40.
55 Ariel Smith, "Indigenous Cinema and the Horrific Reality of Colonial Violence," *Decolonization: Indigeneity, Education, and Society*, February 13, 2015, https://decolonization.wordpress.com/2015/02/13/indigenous-cinema-and-the-horrific-reality-of-colonial-violence/.
56 Elle-Máijá Tailfeathers, quoted in Verstraten, "For Indigenous Women."
57 Flowers, "Refusal to Forgive," 37.
58 Rosenberg, "Distances and Proximities," 63.
59 Sarah Hunt, "Violence, Law and the Everyday Politics of Recognition: Comments on Glen Coulthard's *Red Skin, White Masks*, presentation, Annual Conference of the Native American and Indigenous Studies Association, Washington, DC, June 6, 2015, 7.
60 Ibid., 4–5.
61 Dian Million, "Intense Dreaming: Theories, Narratives, and Our Search for Home," *American Indian Quarterly* 35, no. 3 (Summer 2011): 322, muse.jhu.edu/article/447049. Italics in original.

BIBLIOGRAPHY

A Red Girl's Reasoning. DVD. Directed by Elle-Máijá Tailfeathers. Vancouver: Crazy8s Film Society, 2012.

Aboriginal Front Door Society, Amnesty International Canada, Atira Women's Resource Society, B.C. Civil Liberties Association, Battered Women's Support Services, Carrier Sekani Tribal Council, Downtown Eastside Sex Workers United Against Violence Society, Ending Violence Association of British Columbia, Feb. 14th Women's Memorial March Committee, First Nations Summit, PACE: Providing Alternatives Counselling & Education Society, Pivot Legal Society, Union of B.C. Indian Chiefs, Union Gospel Mission, West Coast LEAF, and WISH Drop-in Centre Society. "Open Letter: Non-Participation in the Policy Forums/Study Commission." April 10, 2012. http://www.fns.bc.ca/pdf/OpenLetterstoMWCI_041012.pdf.

Aboriginal Women's Action Network. "Statement Issued at Press Conference." Vancouver Rape Relief and Women's Shelter, February 8, 2002. http://www.rapereliefshelter.bc.ca/learn/resources/statement-issued-press-conference.

Absolon, Kathleen E. *Kaandossiwin: How We Come to Know*. Halifax: Fernwood, 2011.

Absolon, Kathleen E., and Cam Willett. "Putting Ourselves Forward: Location in Aboriginal Research." In *Research as Resistance: Critical, Indigenous and Anti-Oppressive Approaches*, edited by Leslie Brown and Susan Strega, 97–126. Toronto: Canadian Scholars' Press, 2005.

Acoose, Janice. *Iskwewak--kah' ki yaw ni wahkomakanak: Neither Indian Princesses Nor Easy Squaws*, 2nd ed. Toronto: Women's Press, 2016.

Adamson, Pat, and Lauree Kopetsky. *Teacher's Guide for The Life of Helen Betty Osborne: A Graphic Novel*. Winnipeg: Portage and Main Press, 2009. http://www.portageandmainpress.com/lesson_plans/plan_260_1.pdf.

Aikau, Hokulani K., Maile Arvin, Mishuana Goeman, and Scott Morgensen. "Indigenous Feminisms Roundtable." *Frontiers: A Journal of Women Studies* 36, no. 3 (2015): 84–106. doi:10.5250/fronjwomestud.36.3.0084.

Alfred, Taiaiake. "Opening Words." In *Lighting the Eighth Fire: The Liberation, Resurgence, and Protection of Indigenous Nations*, edited by Leanne Simpson, 9–11. Winnipeg: Arbeiter Ring, 2008.

———. "Restitution is the Real Pathway to Justice for Indigenous Peoples." In *Response, Responsibility, and Renewal: Canada's Truth and Reconciliation Journey*, edited by Gregory Younging, Jonathan Dewar, and Mike DeGagné, 181–87. Ottawa: Aboriginal Healing Foundation, 2009.

———. *Wasáse: Indigenous Pathways of Action and Freedom*. Peterborough, ON: Broadview Press, 2005.

Allen, Paula Gunn. *The Sacred Hoop: Recovering the Feminine in American Indian Traditions*. Boston: Beacon Press, 1986.

Altamirano-Jiménez, Isabel. *Indigenous Encounters with Neoliberalism: Place, Women, and the Environment in Canada and Mexico*. Vancouver: University of British Columbia Press, 2013.

Amnesty International. *Stolen Sisters: A Human Rights Response to Discrimination and Violence against Indigenous Women in Canada*. Ottawa: Amnesty International, 2004. https://www.amnesty.ca/sites/amnesty/files/amr200032004enstolensisters.pdf.

Anderson, Kim. "Affirmations of an Indigenous Feminist." In *Indigenous Women and Feminism: Politics, Activism, Culture*, edited by Cheryl Suzack, Shari M. Huhndorf, Jeanne Perreault, and Jean Barman, 81–91. Vancouver: University of British Columbia Press, 2010.

Anderson, Linda. "Autobiography." In *Encyclopedia of Feminist Theories*, edited by Lorraine Code, 34–35. New York: Routledge, 2000.

"Apology to the Family, Legislation to Honour Osborne." Manitoba government news release, July 14, 2000. http://news.gov.mb.ca/news/index.html?item=24626&posted=2000-07-14.

Archibald, Jo-ann. *Indigenous Storywork: Educating the Heart, Mind, Body, and Spirit*. Vancouver: University of British Columbia Press, 2008.

Armstrong, Jeannette. "The Disempowerment of First North American Native Peoples and Empowerment through Their Writing." In *An Anthology of Canadian Native Literature in English*, 3rd ed., edited by Daniel David

Moses and Terry Goldie, 242–45. Don Mills, ON: Oxford University Press, 2005.

Atleo, Shawn, and Doug Kelly. "Real Inquiry Needed into Pickton Killings." *Times Colonist*, October 28, 2010.

Aziz, Jamaluddin. *Transgressing Women: Space and the Body in Contemporary Noir Thrillers*. Newcastle: Cambridge Scholars Publishing, 2012.

Backhouse, Constance. "Aboriginal Women Still Waiting for Justice." *Times Colonist,* March 8, 2009.

Baker, Marie Annharte. "Angry Enough to Spit but with Dry Lips It Hurts More Than You Know." *Canadian Theatre Review* 68 (1991): 88–89.

———. *Being on the Moon*. Winlaw, BC: Polestar, 1990.

Bannerji, Himani. "But Who Speaks for Us? Experience and Agency in Conventional Feminist Paradigms." In *Unsettling Relations: The University as a Site of Feminist Struggles*, edited by Himani Bannerji, Linda Carty, Kari Dehli, Susan Heald, and Kate McKenna, 67–108. Boston: South End Press, 1991.

Barker, Donna, and Carolann Wright, On Behalf of the Coalition of Women of Color Working in Women's and Community Services. "The Women of Color on the Nellie's Saga." *Toronto Star,* September 2, 1992.

Barker, Joanne. "Gender, Sovereignty, Rights: Native Women's Activism against Social Inequality and Violence in Canada." *American Quarterly* 60, no. 2 (2008): 259–66. doi:10.1353/aq.0.0002.

Barnoff, Lisa, and Ken Moffatt. "Contradictory Tensions in Anti-Oppression Practice in Feminist Social Services." *Affilia: Journal of Women and Social Work* 22, no. 1 (2007): 56–70. doi:10.1177/0886109906295772.

Barrera, Jorge. "Prime Minister Needs to Apologize for Colonialism Denial, Native Groups Say." *CanWest News*, September 30, 2009.

Barthes, Roland. *Camera Lucida*. New York: Hill and Wang, 1980.

Beads, Tina. "Aboriginal Feminist Action on Violence against Women." By Rauna Kuokkanen. In *Making Space for Indigenous Feminism*, edited by Joyce Green, 221–32. Winnipeg: Fernwood, 2007.

Bealy, Joanne. Review of *Finding Dawn*, directed by Christine Welsh. *Cahoots* 4 (2006): 31–33.

Belmore, Rebecca. *Vigil*. Accessed November 18, 2016. http://www.rebeccabelmore.com/video/Vigil.html.

Benjamin, Akua, Judy Rebick, and Amy Go. "Racist Backlash Takes Subtle Form among Feminists." *Toronto Star,* April 30, 1993.

Berg, Stephen. "Documentary Traces Plight of Missing Aboriginal Women." *Edmonton Journal*, March 15, 2007. http://www.pressreader.com/canada/edmonton-journal/20070315/281788509604523.

Berger, Philip. "A Flimsy Case against June Callwood." *Toronto Star*, September 11, 1992.

Berton, Pierre. "If Callwood Is a Racist Then So Are We All." *Toronto Star*, May 23, 1992.

Blackstock, Cindy. "Reconciliation Means Not Saying Sorry Twice: Lessons from Child Welfare in Canada." In *From Truth to Reconciliation: Transforming the Legacy of Residential Schools*, edited by Marlene Brant Castellano, Linda Archibald, and Mike DeGagné, 163–75. Ottawa: Aboriginal Healing Foundation, 2008.

Blaeser, Kimberly. "Native Literature: Seeking a Critical Center." In *Looking at the Words of Our People: First Nations Analysis of Literature*, edited by Jeannette Armstrong, 51–62. Penticton, BC: Theytus, 1993.

Blaney, Fay. "Aboriginal Women's Action Network." In *Strong Women Stories: Native Vision and Community Survival*, edited by Kim Anderson and Bonita Lawrence, 156–70. Toronto: Sumach, 2004.

———. *Finding Dawn: A Guide for Teaching and Action*. National Film Board of Canada, 2009. http://www.onf-nfb.gc.ca/sg/100567.pdf.

Bourgeois, Robyn. "National Inquiry On Missing, Murdered Women Not Best Answer." *Huffpost British Columbia*, December 21, 2012. http://www.huffingtonpost.ca/robyn-bourgeois/missing-women-inquiry-report-vancouver-pickton_b_2333262.html.

———. "Warrior Women: Indigenous Women's Anti-Violence Engagement with the Canadian State." PhD diss., University of Toronto, 2014. https://tspace.library.utoronto.ca/bitstream/1807/68238/1/Bourgeois_Robyn_S_201411_PhD_thesis.pdf.

Bourrier-Lacroix, Barbara. Review of *Finding Dawn*, directed by Christine Welsh. *Canadian Women's Health Network*, 9, no. 3 (2007): 8–9.

Boutilier, Alex. "Native Teen's Slaying a 'Crime,' not a 'Sociological Phenomenon,' Stephen Harper Says." *Toronto Star*, August 21, 2014. https://www.thestar.com/news/canada/2014/08/21/native_teens_slaying_a_crime_not_a_sociological_phenomenon_stephen_harper_says.html.

Brand, Johanna. *The Life and Death of Anna Mae Aquash*. Toronto: James Lorimer, 1993.
Brant, Beth. *Food and Spirits*. Vancouver: Press Gang Publishers, 1991.
———. *Writing as Witness: Essays and Talk*. Toronto: Women's Press, 1994.
Brown, Wendy. *Edgework: Critical Essays on Knowledge and Politics*. Princeton, NJ: Princeton University Press, 2005.
———. "'The Most We Can Hope For ...': Human Rights and the Politics of Fatalism." *South Atlantic Quarterly* 102, no. 2/3 (2004): 451–63. doi: 10.1215/00382876-103-2-3-451.
———. *Regulating Aversion*. Princeton, NJ: Princeton University Press, 2006.
Bunjun, Bénita, Jo-Anne Lee, Suzanne Lenon, Lise Martin, Sara Torres and Marie-Katherine Waller. *Intersectional Feminist Frameworks: An Emerging Vision*. Ottawa: Canadian Research Institute for the Advancement of Women, 2006. http://www.criawicref.ca/images/userfiles/files/Intersectional%20Feminist%20 Frameworks-%20An%20Emerging%20 Vision(2).pdf.
Butler, Judith. *Precarious Life: The Powers of Mourning and Violence*. London: Verso, 2004.
Calliste, Agnes, and George Sefa Dei. "Anti-Racist Feminism: Critical Race and Gender Studies." In *Anti-Racist Feminism*, edited by Agnes Calliste and George J. Sefa Dei, 11–18. Halifax: Fernwood, 2000.
Callwood, June. "The Nellie's Furor: June Callwood Tells Her Side." *Toronto Star*, July 23, 1992.
Cameron, Stevie. *The Pickton File*. Toronto: Knopf Canada, 2007.
Campbell, Kim. "Foreword." In *100 Canadian Heroines: Famous and Forgotten Faces*, edited by Merna Forster, 13–15. Toronto: Dundurn, 2004.
Campbell, Maria. *Halfbreed*. Toronto: McClelland and Stewart, 1973.
Canada. British Columbia. Missing Women Commission of Inquiry. *Forsaken: The Report of the Missing Women Commission of Inquiry*. Victoria: Distribution Centre, 2012. http://www.missingwomeninquiry.ca/obtain-report/.
———. British Columbia. Missing Women Commission of Inquiry. *Missing Women Commission of Inquiry Hearings*, October 12, 2011. http://www.missingwomeninquiry.ca/transcripts/.
———. British Columbia. Missing Women Commission of Inquiry. *Missing Women Commission of Inquiry Hearings for Standing*, January 31, 2011. http://www.missingwomeninquiry.ca/transcripts/.

———. British Columbia. Missing Women Commission of Inquiry. *Missing Women Commission of Inquiry Pre-Hearing Conference*, June 27, 2011. http://www.missingwomeninquiry.ca/transcripts/.

———. British Columbia. Missing Women Commission of Inquiry. *Standing Together and Moving Forward: Report on the Pre-Hearing Conference in Prince George and the Northern Community Forums*. February 2012. http://www.missingwomeninquiry.ca/wp-content/uploads/2010/10/Report-on-the-Pre-Hearing-Conference-in-Prince-George-and-the-Northern-Community-Forums-00263779.pdf.

———. British Columbia. Missing Women Commission of Inquiry. *Standing Together and Moving Forward: The Northwest Consultations*. Prepared by Linda Locke for the Missing Women Commission of Inquiry, June 2012. http://www.missingwomeninquiry.ca/wpcontent/uploads/2010/10/Standing-Together-the-Northwest-Consultations.pdf.

———. British Columbia. Missing Women Commission of Inquiry. "Terms of Reference." Accessed November 16, 2016. http://www.missingwomeninquiry.ca/terms-of-reference/.

———. Manitoba. "Helen Betty Osborne Memorial Foundation Act." *Continuing Consolidation of the Statutes of Manitoba* (CCSM c. H38.1), December 15, 2000. http://web2. gov.mb.ca/laws/statutes/ccsm/h038-1e.php.

———. Manitoba. Legislative Assembly of Manitoba. The Standing Committee on Law Amendments, 2nd Session, 37th Legislature, December 11, 2000, 9. http://www.gov.mb.ca/legislature/hansard/37th_2nd/hansardpdf/la1.pdf.

Canada. Manitoba. Aboriginal Justice Inquiry of Manitoba. *Report of the Aboriginal Justice Inquiry of Manitoba*. Winnipeg, 1991. http://www.ajic.mb.ca/volume.html.

———. National Inquiry into Missing and Murdered Indigenous Women and Girls. *Final Report of the Pre-Inquiry Engagement Process*. Last modified May 19, 2016. https://www.aadnc-aandc.gc.ca/eng/1463677554486/1463677615622.

———. National Inquiry into Missing and Murdered Indigenous Women and Girls. "Terms of Reference." Last modified August 3, 2016. https://www.aadnc-aandc.gc.ca/eng/1470422455025/1470422554686.

———. Parliament. House of Commons. *Debates*. 2nd Session, 39th Parliament of Canada, June 11, 2008. http://www.parl.gc.ca/HousePublications/

Publication.aspx?Language=E&Mode=1&Parl=39&Ses=2&DocId= 3568890.

———. Parliament. House of Commons. *Speech from the Throne.* 2nd Session, 39th Parliament of Canada, October 16, 2007. http://www.parl.gc.ca/HousePublications/Publication.aspx?Doc=1&Mode=1&Parl=39&Pub=Hansard&Ses=2&Language=E#OOB-2174986.

———. Parliament. House of Commons. Standing Committee on the Status of Women. *Call into the Night: An Overview of Violence against Aboriginal Women.* 3rd Session, 40th Parliament, March 2011. http://www.parl.gc.ca/HousePublications/Publication.aspx?DocId=5056509&Language=E.

"Canada's Statement of Apology." In *Response, Responsibility, and Renewal: Canada's Truth and Reconciliation Journey,* edited by Gregory Younging, Jonathan Dewar, and Mike DeGagné, 357–71. Ottawa: Aboriginal Healing Foundation, 2009.

Cannon, Margaret. *The Invisible Empire: Racism in Canada.* Toronto: Random House, 1995.

Cariou, Warren. "Dances with Rigoureau." In *Troubling Tricksters: Revisioning Critical Conversations,* edited by Deanna Reder and Linda M. Morra, 157–68. Waterloo, ON: Wilfrid Laurier University Press, 2010.

Chrisjohn, Roland and Sherri Young. *The Circle Game: Shadows and Substance in the Indian Residential School Experience in Canada.* Penticton, BC: Theytus, 1997.

Chrisjohn, Roland, and Tanya Wasacase. "Half-Truths and Whole Lies: Rhetoric in the 'Apology' and the Truth and Reconciliation Commission." In *Response, Responsibility, and Renewal,* edited by Gregory Younging, Jonathan Dewar, and Mike DeGagné, 219–29. Ottawa: Aboriginal Healing Foundation, 2009.

Churchill, Ward, and Jim Vander Wall. *The Cointelpro Papers: Documents from the FBI's Secret Wars against Dissent in the United States.* Cambridge, MA: South End Press, 2002.

Clements, Marie. *The Unnatural and Accidental Women.* Vancouver: Talonbooks, 2005.

Clover, Carol. *Men, Women, and Chain Saws: Gender in the Modern Horror Film.* Princeton, NJ: Princeton University Press, 1992.

Constitution Act 1867 (UK), 30 & 31 Vict., c.3. Last modified February 9, 2015. http://laws.justice.gc.ca/eng/Const/page-1.html.

Cook-Lynn, Elizabeth. *Anti-Indianism in Modern America: A Voice from Tatekeya's Earth*. Champaign: University of Illinois, 2007.

Coulthard, Glen. *Red Skin, White Masks*. Minneapolis: University of Minnesota Press, 2014.

———. "Subjects of Empire: Indigenous Peoples and the 'Politics' of Recognition in Canada." *Contemporary Political Theory* 6 (2007): 437–60.

Creating Inclusive Spaces for Women: A Practical Guide for Implementing an Integrated, Anti-Racist, Feminist Service Delivery System. Prepared by Shara Stone, Rubena Willis Counseling Centre for Assaulted Women and Children, Esther Enyolu, and the Women's Rights Coalition of Durham for the Ontario Association of Interval and Transition Houses (OAITH), 2005. http://www.oaith.ca/assets/files/Publications/CreatingInclusivesSpacesFormatted.pdf.

Crenshaw, Kimberlé. "Mapping the Margins: Intersectionality, Identity Politics, and Violence against Women of Color." In *Identities: Race, Class, Gender, and Nationality*, edited by Linda Martín Alcoff and Eduardo Mendieta, 175–200. Malden, MA: Blackwell, 2003.

Culhane, Dara. "Their Spirits Live within Us: Aboriginal Women in Downtown Eastside Vancouver Emerging into Visibility." *American Indian Quarterly* 27, no. 3/4 (2003): 593–606. doi:10.1353/aiq.2004.0073.

Cultural Memory Group. *Remembering Women Murdered by Men: Memorials across Canada*. Toronto: Sumach Press, 2006.

Davis, Julie. *Survival Schools: The American Indian Movement and Community Education in the Twin Cities*. Minneapolis: University of Minnesota Press, 2013.

Dean, Amber. *Remembering Vancouver's Disappeared Women: Settler Colonialism and the Difficulty of Inheritance*. Toronto: University of Toronto Press, 2015.

Deer, Sarah. *The Beginning and End of Rape: Confronting Sexual Violence in Native America*. Minneapolis: University of Minnesota Press, 2015.

Deerchild, Rosanna. "We Are Just." *Puritan* 30 (Summer 2015): 5-9. http://puritan-magazine.com/we-are-just/.

Deiter, Connie, and Darlene Rude. "Human Security and Aboriginal Women in Canada." Ottawa: Status of Women Canada, 2005. http://publications.gc.ca/collections/Collection/SW21-133-2005E.pdf.

Devereux, Cecily. *Growing a Race: Nellie L. McClung and the Fiction of Eugenic*

Feminism. Montreal and Kingston: McGill-Queen's University Press, 2006.
de Vos, Gail. "*Finding Dawn.*" *CM: An Electronic Reviewing Journal of Canadian Materials for Young People* 14, no. 10 (2008): 1.
Dewar, Elaine. "Wrongful Dismissal." *Toronto Life*, March 1993, 32–45.
Diamond, Elin. "The Violence of 'We': Politicizing Identification." In *Critical Theory and Performance*, edited by Janelle Reinelt and Joseph Roach, 403–12. Ann Arbor: University of Michigan Press, 2010.
Dumont, Marilyn. "Interview with Marilyn Dumont." By Jónína Kirton. *Room.* Accessed November 18, 2016. https://roommagazine.com/interview/interview-marilyn-dumont.
———. "The Pemmican Eaters." In *Indigenous Poetics in Canada*, edited by Neal McLeod, 83–88. Waterloo, ON: Wilfrid Laurier University Press, 2014.
———. *A Really Good Brown Girl.* London: Brick Books, 1996.
Ehrlich, Susan. "The Discursive Reconstruction of Sexual Consent," *Discourse and Society* 9, no. 2 (1998): 149–71.
———. *Representing Rape: Language and Sexual Consent.* New York: Routledge, 2001.
Eigenbrod, Renate. "Between 'Colonizer-Perpetrator' and Colonizer-Ally': Toward a Pedagogy of Redress." In *The Oxford Handbook of Indigenous American Literature*, edited by James H. Cox and Daniel Heath Justice, 441–54. Don Mills, ON: Oxford University Press, 2014.
Emberley, Julia. *Defamiliarizing the Aboriginal: Cultural Practices and Decolonization in Canada.* Toronto: University of Toronto Press, 2007.
Episkenew, Jo-Ann. "Socially Responsible Criticism: Aboriginal Literature, Ideology, and the Literary Canon." In *Creating Community: A Roundtable on Canadian Aboriginal Literature,* edited by Renate Eigenbrod and Jo-Ann Episkenew, 51–68. Penticton, BC: Theytus, 2002.
———. *Taking Back Our Spirits: Indigenous Literature, Public Policy, and Healing.* Winnipeg: University of Manitoba Press, 2009.
Fagan, Kristina, Daniel Heath Justice, Keavy Martin, Sam McKegney, Deanna Rider, and Niigonwedom James Sinclair. "Canadian Indian Literary Nationalism? Critical Approaches in Canadian Indigenous Contexts—A Collaborative Interlogue." *Canadian Journal of Native Studies* 29, no. 1–2 (Fall 2009): 19–44.

Fagan, Kristina, Stephanie Danyluk, Bryce Donaldson, Amelia Horsburgh, Robyn Moore, and Martin Winquist. "Reading the Reception of Maria Campbell's *Halfbreed*." *Canadian Journal of Native Studies* 29, no. 1 (2009): 257–81.

Families of Sisters in Spirit (FSIS), No More Silence (NMS), and the Native Youth Sexual Health Network (NYSHN). "Supporting the Resurgence of Community-Based Responses to Violence." *Nations Rising*, March 14, 2014. http://nationsrising.org/it-starts-with-us/.

Farmer, Paul. *Pathologies of Power: Health, Human Rights, and the New War on the Poor*. Berkeley: University of California Press, 2003.

Fellows, Mary Louise, and Sherene Razack. "The Race to Innocence: Confronting Hierarchical Relations among Women." *Journal of Gender, Race, and Justice* 1 (1998): 335–52.

Felski, Rita. "On Confession." In *Women, Autobiography, Theory: A Reader*, edited by Sidonie Smith and Julia Watson, 83–95. Madison: University of Wisconsin Press, 1998.

Ferris, Shauna. "'The Lone Streetwalker': Missing Women and Sex Work–Related News in Mainstream Canadian Media." *West Coast Line 53*, 41, no. 1 (2007): 14–24.

Filewod, Alan. "Receiving Aboriginality: Tomson Highway and the Crisis of Cultural Authenticity." *Theatre Journal* 46 (1994): 363–73. doi:10.2307/3208612.

Finding Dawn. DVD. Directed by Christine Welsh. Montreal: National Film Board of Canada, 2006.

Fisher, Robin. *Contact and Conflict: Indian–European Relations in British Columbia, 1774–1890*. 2nd ed. Vancouver: University of British Columbia Press, 1992.

Fleras, Augie. "*Finding Dawn*." *Visual Anthropology Review* 26, no. 1 (2010): 47–48. doi:10.1111/j.1548-7458.2010.01053.x.

Flowers, Rachel. "Refusal to Forgive: Indigenous Women's Love and Rage." *Decolonization: Indigeneity, Education and Society* 4, no. 2 (2015): 32–49.

Forster, Merna. *100 Canadian Heroines: Famous and Forgotten Faces*. Toronto: Dundurn, 2004.

Foucault, Michel. *The History of Sexuality*, vol. 1: *An Introduction*. New York: Vintage, 1990.

Fournier, Suzanne, and Ernie Crey. *Stolen from Our Embrace: The Abduction of First Nations and the Restoration of Aboriginal Communities.* Vancouver: Douglas and McIntyre, 1997.

Franco, Judith. "Gender, Genre and Female Pleasure in the Contemporary Revenge Narrative: *Baise moi* and *What It Feels Like for a Girl.*" *Quarterly Review of Film and Video* 21, no. 1 (2004): 1–10. doi:10.1080/10509200490262415.

George, Usha. "Toward Anti-Racism in Social Work in the Canadian Context." In *Anti-Racist Feminism*, edited by Agnes Calliste and George J. Sefa Dei, 111–22. Halifax: Fernwood, 2000.

Gillis, Wendy. "SNTC Play Recalls Aboriginal Heroine." *Star Phoenix*, May 9, 2008.

Gingell, Susan. "Take Action to Show Outrage at Loss of Indigenous Women." *Star Phoenix,* July 4, 2007.

Goeman, Mishuana. *Mark My Words: Native Women Mapping Our Nations.* Minneapolis: University of Minnesota Press, 2013.

Goulding, Warren. *Just Another Indian: A Serial Killer and Canada's Indifference.* Calgary: Fifth House, 2001.

"Government Does Not Act on Commitment to Improve the Lives of Aboriginal Women." *Canada NewsWire*, February 11, 2005.

Grande, Sandy. "Whitestream Feminism and the Colonialist Project: A Review of Contemporary Feminist Pedagogy and Praxis." *Educational Theory* 53, no. 3 (2003): 329–46. doi:10.1111/j.1741-5446.2003.00329.x.

Gray, Lynda. *First Nations 101: Tons of Stuff You Need to Know about First Nations People.* Vancouver: Adaawx, 2013.

Green, Joyce. "Balancing Strategies: Aboriginal Women and Constitutional Rights in Canada." In *Making Space for Indigenous Feminism*, edited by Joyce Green, 140–59. Winnipeg: Fernwood, 2007.

———. "Taking Account of Aboriginal Feminism." In *Making Space for Indigenous Feminism*, edited by Joyce Green, 20–32. Winnipeg: Fernwood, 2007.

Green, Shirley. "Looking Back, Looking Forward." In *Making Space for Indigenous Feminism*, edited by Joyce Green, 160–73. Winnipeg: Fernwood, 2007.

Grewal, Inderpal. "Foreword." In *Just Advocacy? Women's Human Rights, Transnational Feminisms, and the Politics of Representation*, edited by Wendy S. Hesford and Wendy Kozol, vii–ix. London: Rutgers University Press, 2005.

Greyeyes, Trevor. "A New Age Take on an Old Aboriginal Story." *Winnipeg Free Press,* October 1, 2006.

Hall, Anthony J. "Imperialism, Conquest, Indigenous Peoples, Aboriginal Title, Treaties, and International Law: The Occupation of BC, Iraq, and the West Bank, the Extradition Cases of Sitting Bull, Leonard Peltier, James Pitawanakwat, and John Graham." Presentation at the University of Lethbridge, Lethbridge, AB, March 3, 2004.

Hammond, Meghan Marie, and Sue J. Kim, eds. *Rethinking Empathy through Literature*. New York: Routledge, 2014.

Haraway, Donna. "The Persistence of Vision." In *Writing on the Body: Female Embodiment and Feminist Theory,* edited by Katie Conboy, Nadia Medina, and Sarah Stanbury, 283–95. New York: Columbia University Press, 1997.

Hargreaves, Allison. "Compelling Disclosures: Colonial Violence and the Narrative Imperative in Feminist Anti-Violence Discourse and Indigenous Women's Writing." *Canadian Woman Studies* 27, no. 2/3 (2009): 107–13.

———. "*Finding Dawn* and Missing Women in Canada: Story-Based Methods in Antiviolence Research and Remembrance." *Studies in American Indian Literatures* 27, no. 3 (2015): 82–111.

Harjo, Joy. "For Anna Mae Pictou Aqaush, Whose Spirit Is Present Here and in the Dappled Stars." In *The Colour of Resistance: A Contemporary Collection of Writing by Aboriginal Women,* edited by Connie Fife, 77–78. Toronto: Sister Vision Press, 1993.

"Helen Betty Osborne Foundation Board Appointments and New Web Site Announced." Manitoba government news release, January 31, 2003, http://news.gov.mb.ca/news/print,index.html?item=26296&posted=2003-01-31.

Henderson, James (Sákéj) Youngblood. *First Nations Jurisprudence and Aboriginal Rights: Defining the Just Society*. Saskatoon: Native Law Centre, University of Saskatchewan, 2006.

Henderson, Jennifer. "Residential Schools and Opinion-Making in the Era of Traumatized Subjects and Taxpayer-Citizens." *Journal of Canadian Studies* 49, no. 1 (Winter 2015): 5–43.

Henderson, Jennifer, and Pauline Wakeham. "Colonial Reckoning, National Reconciliation? Aboriginal Peoples and the Culture of Redress in Canada." *English Studies in Canada* 35, no. 1 (2009): 1–26.

"Herstory." *Nellie's*. Accessed February 19, 2009. http://www.nellies.org/about/herstory/.

Highway of Tears Symposium Recommendations Report. Lheidli T'enneh First Nation, Carrier Sekani Family Services, Carrier Sekani Tribal Council, Prince George Native Friendship Centre, and Prince George Nechako Aboriginal Employment and Training Association, June 16, 2006. http://www.turtleisland.org/healing/highwayoftears.pdf.

Highway, Tomson. *Dry Lips Oughta Move to Kapuskasing.* Saskatoon: Fifth House, 1989.

———. *Kiss of the Fur Queen.* Toronto: Doubleday, 1998.

———. *The Rez Sisters.* Saskatoon: Fifth House, 1988.

———. "Twenty-One Native Women on Motorcycles: An Interview with Tomson Highway." By Joanne Tompkins and Lisa Male. *Australasian Drama Studies* 24 (1994): 13–28.

Hoy, Helen. "'Nothing but the Truth': Discursive Transparency in Beatrice Culleton." In *In Search of April Raintree*, edited by Cheryl Suzack, 273–94. Winnipeg: Portage and Main Press, 1999.

Huhndorf, Shari M., and Cheryl Suzack. "Indigenous Feminism: Theorizing the Issues." In *Indigenous Women and Feminism: Politics, Activism, Culture*, edited by Cheryl Suzack, Shari M. Huhndorf, Jeanne Perreault, and Jean Barman, 1–17. Vancouver: University of British Columbia Press, 2010.

Human Rights Watch. *Those Who Take Us Away: Abusive Policing and Failures in Protection of Indigenous Women and Girls in Northern British Columbia, Canada.* February 13, 2013. https://www.hrw.org/report/2013/02/13/those-who-take-us-away/abusive-policing-and-failures-protection-indigenous-women.

Hunt, Sarah. "More Than a Poster Campaign: Redefining Colonial Violence." In *The Winter We Danced: Voices from the Past, the Future, and the Idle No More Movement*, edited by the Kino-nda-niimi Collective, 190–92. Winnipeg: Arbeiter Ring, 2014.

———. "Violence, Law and the Everyday Politics of Recognition: Comments on Glen Coulthard's *Red Skin, White Masks*. Presentation at the Annual Conference of the Native American and Indigenous Studies Association, Washington, DC, June 6, 2015.

———. "Why Are We Hesitant to Name White Male Violence as a Root Cause of #MMIW?" *Rabble.ca*, September 4, 2015. http://rabble.ca/news/2014/09/why-are-we-hesitant-to-name-white-male-violence-root-cause-mmiw.

Hurst, Lynda. "Controversy Dogs Women's Group." *Windsor Star*, March 16, 1995.

Innes, Robert Alexander, and Kim Anderson. "Who's Walking with Our Brothers?" In *Indigenous Men and Masculinities: Legacies, Identities, Regeneration*, edited by Robert Alexander Innes and Kim Anderson, 4–15. Minneapolis: University of Minnesota Press, 2015.

Intersectional Feminist Frameworks: A Primer. Ottawa: Canadian Research Institute for the Advancement of Women, 2006. http://www.criaw-icref.ca/en/product/intersectional-feminist-frameworks--a-primer.

Irlbacher-Fox, Stephanie. *Finding Dahshaa: Self-Government, Social Suffering, and Aboriginal Policy in Canada.* Vancouver: University of British Columbia Press, 2009.

Ivison, Duncan. *Postcolonial Liberalism.* Cambridge: Cambridge University Press, 2002.

Jackson, Michael. "Locking Up Natives in Canada." *University of British Columbia Law Review* 23, no. 2 (1989): 215–300.

Jacobs, Beverley, and Andrea J. Williams. "Legacy of Residential Schools: Missing and Murdered Aboriginal Women." In *From Truth to Reconciliation: Transforming the Legacy of Residential Schools*, edited by Marlene Brant Castellano, Linda Archibald, and Mike DeGagné, 119–40. Ottawa: Aboriginal Healing Foundation, 2008.

Jaimes, M. Annette. "Review of *Lakota Woman*, by Mary Crow Dog." *American Indian Culture and Research Journal* 15, no. 1 (1991): 109–12.

Jerrold, Blanchard, and Gustave Doré. *London: A Pilgrimage* [1872]. New York: Dover, 1970.

Jiwani, Yasmin, and Mary Lynn Young. "Missing and Murdered Women: Reproducing Marginality in News Discourse." *Canadian Journal of Communications* 31, no. 4 (2006): 895–917.

Joachim, Natasha. "Profile of Anna Mae Pictou-Aquash: Mi'kmaq, Aboriginal Rights Activist." In *Hidden in Plain Sight: Contributions of Aboriginal Peoples to Canadian Identity and Culture*, edited by David R. Newhouse, Cora J. Voyageur, and Dan Beavon, 215–17. Toronto: University of Toronto Press, 2005.

Johnson, Pauline. "A Red Girl's Reasoning." In *Tekahionwake: E. Pauline Johnson's Writing on Native North America*, edited by Margery Fee and Dory Nason, 163–77. Peterborough, ON: Broadview Press, 2016.

Jones, Manina. "Coming through Oka: Co-Authorship and Cultural Disturbance in First Nations Auto-Biographies." Presentation at the TransCanada Two: Literature, Institutions, Citizenship Conference, University of Guelph, Guelph, ON, October 11–14, 2007.

Justice, Daniel Heath. "Currents of Trans/National Criticism in Indigenous Literary Studies." *American Indian Quarterly* 35, no. 3 (2011): 334–52. doi:10.5250/ amerindiquar.35.3.0334.

———. "Renewing the Fire: Notes toward the Liberation of English Studies." *English Studies Canada* 29, no. 1-2. (2003): 45–54. https://ejournals .library.ualberta.ca/index.php/ESC/article/view/278.

Keeshig-Tobias, Lenore. "Stop Stealing Native Stories." In *Borrowed Power: Essays on Cultural Appropriation*, edited by Bruce Ziff and Pratima V. Rao, 71–73. New Brunswick, NJ: Rutgers University Press, 2004.

"Key Facts about Amnesty International." Amnesty International Canada. Accessed November 17, 2016. http://amnesty.staging.openconcept.ca/ about-us/what-we-do/key-facts-about-amnesty-international.

King, Jennifer. "Sisters in Spirit Research Framework: Reflecting on Methodology and Practice." In *Aboriginal Policy Research Volume 10: Voting, Governance, and Research Methodology*, edited by Jerry P. White, Julie Peters, Dan Beavon, and Peter Dinsdale, 269–85. Toronto: Thompson Educational Publishing, 2010.

Klaver, Ellen. "Daughter of the Earth: Song for Anna Mae Aquash." In *Agents of Repression: The FBI's Secret Wars against the Black Panther Party and the American Indian Movement*, edited by Ward Churchill and Jim Vander Wall, vii. Boston: South End Press, 1988.

Kohli, Rita. "Power or Empowerment: Questions of Agency in the Shelter Movement." In *And Still We Rise: Feminist Political Mobilizing in Contemporary Canada*, edited by Linda Carty, 387–425. Toronto: Women's Press, 1993.

———. "Violence against Women: Race, Class and Gender Issues." *Canadian Women Studies* 11, no. 4 (1991): 13–14. http://cws.journals.yorku.ca/ index.php/cws/issue/view/514.

Kovach, Margaret. "Emerging from the Margins: Indigenous Methodologies." In *Research as Resistance: Critical, Indigenous, and Anti-Oppressive Approaches*, edited by Leslie Brown and Susan Strega, 19–36. Toronto: Canadian Scholars' Press, 2005.

———. *Indigenous Methodologies: Characteristics, Conversations, and Contexts*. Toronto: University of Toronto Press, 2009.

Kuokkanen, Rauna. *Reshaping the University: Responsibility, Indigenous Epistemes, and the Logic of the Gift*. Vancouver: University of British Columbia Press, 2008.

Kuxhaus, David. "Province Apologizes for Role in Probe of Osborne Murder." *Winnipeg Free Press*. July 15, 2000.

La Flamme, Michelle. "Revisiting *A Really Good Brown Girl*." thirdspace 2, no. 2 (March 2003). http://journals.sfu.ca/thirdspace/index.php/journal/article/viewArticle/reviews_laflamme/115.

———. "Theatrical Medicine: Aboriginal Performance, Ritual and Commemoration (for Vanessa Lee Buckner)." *Theatre Research in Canada* 31, no. 2 (2010): 107–17. https://journals.lib.unb.ca/index.php/tric/article/view/18430/19919.

Landsberg, Michele. "Callwood Furor Masks Real Racism Struggle at Nellie's." *Toronto Star*, July 18, 1992.

LaRocque, Emma. Presentation to the Aboriginal Justice Inquiry of Manitoba, February 5, 1990. In *Report of the Aboriginal Justice Inquiry of Manitoba*, vol. 1, ch. 13, 1991. http://www.ajic.mb.ca/volumel/chapter13.html.

———. *Violence in Aboriginal Communities*. Ottawa: National Clearing House on Family Violence, Family Violence Prevention Division, Health Programs and Services Branch, Health Canada, 1994. http://publications.gc.ca/collections/Collection/H72-21-100-1994E.pdf.

Lawrence, Bonita. "Gender, Race, and the Regulation of Native Identity in Canada and the United States." *Hypatia* 18, no. 2 (2003): 3–31, muse.jhu.edu/article/44188.

———. *"Real" Indians and Others: Mixed-Blood Urban Native Peoples and Indigenous Nationhood*. Vancouver: University of British Columbia Press, 2004.

LeBeuf, Marcel-Eugène. "The Role of the Royal Canadian Mounted Police during the Indian Residential School System." Royal Canadian Mounted Police, 2011. http://publications.gc.ca/collections/collection_2011/grc-rcmp/PS64-71-2009-eng.pdf.

Le Dain, Gerald E. "The Role of the Public Inquiry in our Constitutional System." In *Law and Social Change*, edited by Jacob S. Ziegel, 79–97. Toronto: Osgoode Hall Law School, 1973.

LePard, Doug. *Vancouver Police Department Missing Women Investigation Review*. Vancouver Police Department, 2010. http://www.cbc.ca/bc/news/bc-100820-vancouver-police-pickton-investigation-review.pdf.

Lewis, Shauna. "Film Remembers Missing and Murdered Women." *Windspeaker* 24, no. 9 (2006): 14–15.

"Manitoba Says Sorry for Actions in Osborne Case." *Toronto Star* July 15, 2000.

Mannette, Joy. *Elusive Justice: Beyond the Marshall Inquiry*. Halifax: Fernwood, 1992.

Manuel, Arthur. *Unsettling Canada: A National Wake-Up Call*. Toronto: Between the Lines Press, 2015.

———. "Until Canada Gives Indigenous People Their Land Back, There Can Never Be Reconciliation." *Rabble.ca*, January 18, 2017. http://rabble.ca/blogs/bloggers/views-expressed/2017/01/until-canada-gives-indigenous-people-their-land-back-there-ca.

Maracle, Lee. *I Am Woman: A Native Perspective on Sociology and Feminism*. Vancouver: Press Gang Publishers, 1996.

Marlowe, Tammy. "Helen's Dream Lives On." *Winnipeg Sun*, July 15, 2000.

McCall, Sophie. *First Person Plural: Aboriginal Storytelling and the Ethics of Collaborative Authorship*. Vancouver: University of British Columbia Press, 2011.

McIvor, Sharon D., and Teressa A. Nahanee. "Aboriginal Women: Invisible Victims of Violence." In *Unsettling Truths: Battered Women, Policy, Politics, and Contemporary Research in Canada*, edited by Kevin Bonnycastle and George S. Rigakos, 63–70. Vancouver: Collective Press, 1998.

McKegney, Sam. *Magic Weapons: Aboriginal Writers Remaking Community after Residential School*. Winnipeg: University of Manitoba Press, 2007.

———. "Strategies for Ethical Engagement: An Open Letter Concerning Non-Native Scholars of Native Literatures." *Studies in American Indian Literatures* 20, no. 4 (2008): 56–67.

McLeod, Neal. *Cree Narrative Memory: From Treaties to Contemporary Times*. Saskatoon: Purich, 2007.

———. "Cree Poetic Discourse." In *Indigenous Poetics in Canada*, edited by Neal McLeod, 89–104. Waterloo, ON: Wilfrid Laurier University Press, 2014.

McNeill, Laurie. "Death and the Maidens: Vancouver's Missing Women, the

Montreal Massacre, Commemoration's Blind Spots." *Canadian Review of American Studies* 78, no. 3 (2008): 375–98. doi:10.3138/cras.38.3.375.

Mendenhall, M.E. Powell. "Review of *Morningstar: A Warrior's Spirit*, by Morningstar Mercredi." Saskatchewan Publisher's Group, 2006. http://www.skbooks.com/wp-content/uploads/2010/01/3049.pdf.

Mercredi, Morningstar. *Morningstar: A Warrior's Spirit*. Regina: Coteau, 2006.

———. "Truth and Lies: Telling Tales in Creative Nonfiction." *Aurora* (2007), edited by Gordon Morash. http://aurora.icaap.org/index.php/aurora/article/view/72/84.

Mihesuah, Devon Abbott. *Indigenous American Women: Decolonization, Empowerment, Activism*. Lincoln: University of Nebraska Press, 2003.

Miller, James Rodger. *Shingwauk's Vision: A History of Native Residential Schools*. Toronto: University of Toronto Press, 1996.

Million, Dian. "Intense Dreaming: Theories, Narratives, and Our Search for Home." *American Indian Quarterly* 35, no. 3 (Summer 2011): 313–33. muse.jhu.edu/article/447049.

———. *Therapeutic Nations: Healing in an Age of Human Rights*. Tucson: University of Arizona Press, 2013.

Milloy, John S. *A National Crime: The Canadian Government and the Residential School System, 1879 to 1986*. Winnipeg: University of Manitoba Press, 1999.

"Missing Women Commission Appoints Two Independent Lawyers; Two Others to Participate Pro Bono." Missing Women Commission of Inquiry, August 10, 2011. www.missingwomeninquiry.ca/2011/08/august-10-2011-missing-women-commission-appoints-two-independent-lawyers-two-others-to-participate-pro-bono/.

"Missing Women Commission of Inquiry Status Report on Commission Progress." Missing Women Commission of Inquiry. March 3, 2011. http://www.missingwomeninquiry.ca/wp-content/uploads/2010/10/Status-Report-March.pdf.

"Mission Statement." *Nellie's*. Accessed February 19, 2008. http://www.nellies.org/about/mission-statement/.

Mitges, Lynn. "Celebrating Human Spirit: Plays Deal with Constant Struggles of Aboriginal Women." *The Province*, October 11, 2006.

Mohanty, Chandra Talpade. *Feminism without Borders: Decolonizing Theory, Practicing Solidarity*. London: Duke University Press, 2003.

Monture-Angus, Patricia. *Thunder in My Soul: A Mohawk Woman Speaks.* Halifax: Fernwood, 1995.

———. "Women's Words: Power, Identity, and Indigenous Sovereignty." *Canadian Woman Studies* 26, no. 3/4 (2008): 154–59. http://cws.journals.yorku.ca/index.php/cws/article/view/22125/20779.

Moses, Daniel David. "Report on Anna Mae's Remains." In *An Anthology of Canadian Native Literature in English*, edited by Daniel David Moses and Terry Goldie, 361–62. Oxford: Oxford University Press, 2005.

Narine, Shari. "Sisters in Spirit Applauded, then Panned by Feds." *Windspeaker* 28, no. 9 (2010): 8. http://www.ammsa.com/publications/windspeaker/sisters-spirit-applauded-then-panned-feds.

Nason, Dory. "We Hold Our Hands Up: On Indigenous Women's Love and Resistance." In *The Winter We Danced: Voices from the Past, the Future, and the Idle No More Movement*, edited by the Kino-nda-niimi Collective, 186–90. Winnipeg: Arbeiter Ring, 2014.

Native Women's Association of Canada. "About Us." Accessed November 16, 2016. https://nwac.ca/home/about-nwac/about-us/.

———. *Community Resource Guide*. Ottawa: Native Women's Association of Canada, 2010. https://www.nwac.ca/wp-content/uploads/2015/05/2012_NWAC_Community_Resource_Guide_MMAWG.pdf.

———. "Fact Sheet: Missing and Murdered Aboriginal Women and Girls in British Columbia." Ottawa: Native Women's Association of Canada, 2010. https://nwac.ca/wp-content/uploads/2015/05/2010-Fact-Sheet-British-Columbia-MMAWG.pdf.

———. *Violations of Indigenous Human Rights: NWAC Submission to the Special Rapporteur Investigating the Violations of Indigenous Human Rights.* Ottawa: Native Women's Association of Canada, 2002. https://nwac.ca/wp-content/uploads/2016/06/2002-NWAC-Violations-of-Indigenous-Human-Rights-Submission.pdf.

———. "Violence against Aboriginal Women and Girls: An Issue Paper." Prepared for the National Aboriginal Women's Summit. Corner Brook, June 20–22, 2007. http://www.laa.gov.nl.ca/laa/naws/pdf/nwac-vaaw.pdf.

———. *What Their Stories Tell Us: Research Findings from the Sisters in Spirit Initiative.* Ottawa: Native Women's Association of Canada, 2010. https://nwac.ca/wp-content/uploads/2015/07/2010-What-Their-Stories-Tell-Us-Research-Findings-SIS-Initiative.pdf.

———. *Voices of Our Sisters in Spirit: A Report to Families and Communities*. Ottawa: Native Women's Association of Canada, 2009. https://nwac.ca/wpcontent/uploads/2015/05/NWAC_Voices-of-Our-Sisters-In-Spirit_2nd-Edition_March-2009.pdf.

Nolan, Yvette. *Annie Mae's Movement*. Toronto: Playwrights Canada Press, 2006.

———. "Selling Myself: The Value of an Artist." In *Aboriginal Drama and Theatre*, edited by Rob Appleford, 95–105. Toronto: Playwrights Canada Press, 2005.

"Northern Community Forums: Frequently Asked Questions." Missing Women Commission of Inquiry. Accessed November 11, 2016. http://www.missingwomeninquiry.ca/wp-content/uploads/2011/01/Northern-Community-Forums-FAQ.pdf.

"Northern Community Forums: Questions and Issues for Discussion." Missing Women Commission of Inquiry. Accessed November 11, 2016, http://www.missingwomeninquiry.ca/wp-content/uploads/2011/01/Northern-Community-Forums-Questions-and-Issues.pdf.

"N.S. Woman's Killer in South Dakota Gets Life," *CBC News*, January 24, 2011. http://www.cbc.ca/news/canada/n-s-woman-s-killer-in-south-dakota-gets-life-1.1073080.

O'Connor, Jennifer. "*Finding Dawn*." *Horizons* 22, no. 3 (2009): 51.

Omand, Geordon. "First Nations Groups Urge Caution before Government's Missing Women Inquiry." *Globe and Mail*, November 9, 2015. http://www.theglobeandmail.com/news/british-columbia/first-nations-groups-urge-caution-before-governments-missing-women-inquiry/article27178422/.

Pearce, Maryanne. "An Awkward Silence: Missing and Murdered Vulnerable Women and the Canadian Justice System." PhD diss., University of Ottawa, 2013. http://dx.doi.org/10.20381/ruor-3344.

Petrone, Penny. *Native Literature in Canada: From the Oral Tradition to the Present*. Toronto: Oxford University Press, 1990.

Philip, M. Nourbese. *Frontiers: Selected Essays and Writings on Racism and Culture: 1984–1992*. Stratford, ON: Mercury Press, 1992.

"Pickton Inquiry Lawyer Quits in Frustration." *CBC News*, March 5, 2012. http://www.cbc.ca/news/canada/british-columbia/pickton-inquiry-lawyer-quits-in-frustration-1.1237185.

"Pickton Victim Families Press For Inquiry." *CBC News*, August 5, 2010. http://www.cbc.ca/beta/news/canada/british-columbia/pickton-victim-families-press-for-inquiry-1.898051.

"Pictou-Aquash Killing Charges Dropped." *CBC News*, February 4, 2010. http://www.cbc.ca/news/canada/pictou-aquash-killing-charges-dropped-1.916669.

Povinelli, Elizabeth. *The Cunning of Recognition: Indigenous Alterities and the Making of Australian Multiculturalism*. London: Duke University Press, 2002.

Pyne, Stephanie. "Profile of Helen Betty Osborne." In *Hidden in Plain Sight: Contributions of Aboriginal Peoples to Canadian Identity and Culture*, edited by David Newhouse, Cora Voyageur, and Dan Beavon, 246–48. Toronto: University of Toronto Press, 2005.

Rafiq, Fauzia. *Developing an Antiracism Action Plan: A Handbook for Workers Working in Service Organizations of Metropolitan Toronto*. Toronto: Women Working with Immigrant Women, 1992.

Razack, Sherene H. *Looking White People in the Eye: Gender, Race, and Culture in Courtrooms and Classrooms*. Toronto: University of Toronto Press, 1998.

———. *Race, Space, and the Law: Unmapping a White Settler Society*. Toronto: Between the Lines, 2002.

———. "Your Place or Mine? Transnational Feminist Collaboration." In *Anti-Racist Feminism*, edited by Agnes Calliste and George J. Sefa Dei, 39–53. Halifax: Fernwood, 2000.

Read, Jacinda. *The New Avengers: Feminism, Femininity and the Rape-Revenge Cycle*. Manchester: Manchester University Press, 2000.

Rezai-Rashti, Goli. "Multicultural Education, Anti-Racist Education, and Critical Pedagogy: Reflections on Everyday Practice." In *Anti-Racism, Feminism, and Critical Approaches to Education*, edited by Roxana Ng, Pat Staton, and Joyce Scane, 3–19. Westport, CT: Bergin and Garvey, 1995.

Rindfleisch, Bryan. "'Slaying the Sun Woman': The Legacy of Annie Mae Aquash." *Graduate History Review* 3, no. 1 (2011): 89–102. https://journals.uvic.ca/ index.php/ghr/article/view/5995/2718.

Robertson, David. *The Life of Helen Betty Osborne: A Graphic Novel*. Illustrated by Madison Blackstone. Winnipeg: In a Bind Publications, 2008.

Rodriquez, Angelina. "Revenge Is a Dish Best Served … Not at All?" *Bitch Flicks*, April 21, 2014. http://www.btchflcks.com/2014/04/revenge-is-a-dish-best-served-not-at-all.html#.WKkY1-u3A8A.

Rollo, Toby. "I Am Canadian! (Because of Treaties with Indigenous Nations)." In *The Winter We Danced: Voices from the Past, the Future, and the Idle No More Movement*, edited by the Kino-nda-niimi Collective, 226–30. Winnipeg: Arbeiter Ring, 2014.

Rosenberg, Sharon. "Distances and Proximities: (Not) Being There." *West Coast Line 53*, 41, no. 1 (2007): 60–63.

Rudin, Jonathan. "Aboriginal Justice and Restorative Justice." In *New Directions in Restorative Justice: Issues, Practice, Evaluation*, edited by Elizabeth Elliott and Robert M. Gordon, 89–114. Portland, OR: Willan, 2005.

Rymhs, Deena. *From the Iron House: Imprisonment in First Nations Writing*. Waterloo, ON: Wilfrid Laurier University Press, 2008.

Sainte-Marie, Buffy. "Bury My Heart at Wounded Knee." *Coincidence and Likely Stories*. EMI Records, 1992.

Schaffer, Kay, and Sidonie Smith. *Human Rights and Narrative Lives: The Ethics of Recognition*. New York: Palgrave Macmillan, 2004.

Sellars, Bev. *They Called Me Number One: Secrets and Survival at an Indian Residential School*. Vancouver: Talonbooks, 2012.

Silman, Janet. *Enough Is Enough: Aboriginal Women Speak Out*. Toronto: Women's Press, 1987.

Simon, Roger. *A Pedagogy of Witnessing: Curatorial Practice and the Pursuit of Social Justice*. Albany: State University of New York Press, 2014.

———. "Towards a Hopeful Practice of Worrying: The Problematics of Listening and the Educative Responsibilities of Canada's Truth and Reconciliation Commission." In *Reconciling Canada: Historical Injustices and the Contemporary Culture of Redress*, edited by Jennifer Henderson and Pauline Wakeham, 129–42. Toronto: University of Toronto Press, 2013.

Simpson, Audra. "Settlement's Secret." *Cultural Anthropology* 26, no. 2 (2011): 205–17. doi:10.1111/j.1548-1360.2011.01095.x.

Simpson, Joanna. *Everyone Belongs: A Toolkit for Applying Intersectionality*. Ottawa: Canadian Research Institute for the Advancement of Women, 2006. http://www.criaw-icref.ca/sites/criaw/files/Everyone_Belongs_e.pdf.

Simpson, Leanne. "Aboriginal Peoples and Knowledge: Decolonizing Our Processes." *Canadian Journal of Native Studies* 21, no. 1 (2001): 137–48.

———. *Dancing on Our Turtle's Back: Stories of Nishnaabeg Re-Creation, Resurgence, and a New Emergence*. Winnipeg: Arbeiter Ring, 2011.

———. "Dancing the World into Being: A Conversation with Idle No More's Leanne Simpson." By Naomi Klein. *Yes! Magazine*, March 5, 2013. http://www.yesmagazine.org/peace-justice/dancing-the-world-into-being-a-conversation-with-idle-no-more-leanne-simpson.

———. "Oshkimaadiziig, the New People." In *Lighting the Eighth Fire: The Liberation, Resurgence, and Protection of Indigenous Nations*, edited by Leanne Simpson, 13–21. Winnipeg: Arbeiter Ring, 2008.

Sinclair, Raven. "Identity Lost and Found: Lessons from the Sixties Scoop." *First Peoples Child and Family Review* 3, no. 1 (2007): 65–82. http://journals.sfu.ca/fpcfr/index.php/FPCFR/article/view/25/63.

Smith, Andrea. "Beyond the Politics of Inclusion: Violence against Women of Color and Human Rights." *Meridians* 4, no. 2 (2004): 120–24.

———. *Conquest: Sexual Violence and American Indian Genocide*. Cambridge, MA: South End Press, 2005.

———. "Unsettling the Privilege of Self-Reflexivity." In *Geographies of Privilege*, edited by France Winddance Twine and Bradley Gardener, 263–79. New York: Routledge, 2013.

Smith, Andrea, and J. Kēhaulani Kauanui. "Native Feminisms Engage American Studies." *American Quarterly* 60, no. 2 (2008): 241–49. doi:10.1353/aq.0.0001.

Smith, Ariel. "Indigenous Cinema and the Horrific Reality of Colonial Violence." *Decolonization: Indigeneity, Education, and Society*, February 13, 2015. https://decolonization.wordpress.com/2015/02/13/indigenous-cinema-and-the-horrific-reality-of-colonial-violence/.

Smith, Laurel. "*Morningstar: A Warrior's Spirit*." *Quill and Quire* 72, no. 2 (2006): 60.

Smith, Linda Tuhiwai. *Decolonizing Methodologies: Research and Indigenous Peoples*. London: Zed Books, 2012.

Smith, Sidonie. "Narrating the Right to Sexual Well-Being and the Global Management of Misery: Maria Rosa Henson's *Comfort Woman* and Charlene Smith's *Proud of Me*." *Literature and Medicine* 24, no. 2 (2005): 153–80. doi:10.1353/lm.2006.0013.

Smith, Sidonie, and Julia Watson. "Introduction: Situating Subjectivity in Women's Autobiographical Practices." In *Women, Autobiography, Theory:*

A Reader, edited by Sidonie Smith and Julia Watson, 3–52. Madison: University of Wisconsin Press, 1998.

Sommer, Doris. "Sacred Secrets: A Strategy for Survival." In *Women, Autobiography, Theory: A Reader*, edited by Sidonie Smith and Julia Watson, 197–207. Madison: University of Wisconsin Press, 1998.

Spivak, Gayatri. "Righting Wrongs." In *Human Rights, Human Wrongs: The Oxford Amnesty Lectures, 2001*, edited by Nicholas Owen, 168–227. Oxford: Oxford University Press, 2003.

Srivastava, Sarita. "'You're Calling Me a Racist?' The Moral and Emotional Regulation of Antiracism and Feminism." *Signs*, 31, no. 1 (2005): 29–62. doi:10.1086/432738.

Srivastava, Sarita, and Margot Francis. "The Problem of 'Authentic Experience': Storytelling in Anti-Racist and Anti-Homophobic Education." *Critical Sociology* 32, no. 2/3 (2006): 275–307. doi:10.1163/156916306777835330.

———. "Troubles with Anti-Racist Multiculturalism: The Challenges of Anti-Racist and Feminist Activism." In *Race and Racism in 21st Century Canada: Continuity, Complexity and Change*, edited by Sean Hier and Singh Bolaria, 291–311. Peterborough, ON: Broadview, 2007.

St. Denis, Verna. "Feminism Is for Everybody: Aboriginal Women, Feminism and Diversity." In *Making Space for Indigenous Feminism*, edited by Joyce Green, 33–52. Winnipeg: Fernwood, 2007.

Stenning, Philip, and Carol LaPrairie. "'Politics by Other Means': The Role of Commissions of Inquiry in Establishing the 'Truth' about 'Aboriginal Justice' in Canada." In *Crime, Truth and Justice: Official Inquiry, Discourse, Knowledge*, edited by George Gilligan and John Pratt, 138–60. Portland, OR: Willan, 2004.

Stevenson, Winona. "Colonialism and First Nations Women in Canada." In *Scratching the Surface: Canadian Anti-Racist Feminist Thought*, edited by Enakshi Dua and Angela Robertson, 49–80. Toronto: Women's Press, 1999.

Stone, Anne, and Amber Dean. "Representations of Murdered and Missing Women: Introduction." *West Coast Line 53*, 41, no. 1 (2007): 8–13.

Stone-Mediatore, Shari. *Reading across Borders: Storytelling and Knowledges of Resistance*. New York: Palgrave Macmillian, 2003.

"Study Commission Added to Missing Women Inquiry." *BC Gov News,* March

28, 2011. https://news.gov.bc.ca/stories/study-commission-added-to-missing-women-inquiry.

Suthers, Laura. "Film Illustrates Hope and Strength." *Windspeaker* 25, no. 2 (2007): 18.

Suzack, Cheryl. "Law, Literature, Location: Contemporary Aboriginal/Indigenous Women's Writing and the Politics of Identity." PhD diss., University of Alberta, 2004. http://search.proquest.com.ezproxy.library.ubc.ca/docview/305097267?pq-origsite=summon.

———. "Law Stories as Life Stories: Jeanette Lavell, Yvonne Bédard, and *Halfbreed*." In *Tracing the Autobiographical*, edited by Marlene Kadar, Linda Warley, Jeanne Perreault, and Susanna Egan, 117–41. Waterloo, ON: Wilfrid Laurier University Press, 2005.

Tator, Carol, Frances Henry, and Winston Mattis. *Challenging Racism in the Arts: Case Studies of Controversy and Conflict*. Toronto: University of Toronto Press, 1998.

Thomas, Robina Anne. "Honouring the Oral Traditions of My Ancestors through Storytelling." In *Research as Resistance*, edited by Leslie Brown and Susan Strega, 237–54. Toronto: Canadian Scholars' Press, 2005.

Tingley, Ken. "Strong Voice Emerges from the Dark." Review of *Morningstar: A Warrior's Spirit*. *Edmonton Journal*, October 29, 2006.

Truth and Reconciliation Commission of Canada. *They Came for the Children: Canada, Aboriginal Peoples, and Residential Schools*. Winnipeg: Truth and Reconciliation Commission of Canada, 2012.

Tuck, Eve, and K. Wayne Yang. "Decolonization Is Not a Metaphor." *Decolonization: Indigeneity, Education, and Society* 1, no. 1 (2012): 1–40.

Tuharsky, Anita. "Play Promotes Racism, Sexism and Oppression." *Windspeaker*, March 12, 1991, 5.

Valaskakis, Gail Guthrie. *Indian Country: Essays on Contemporary Native Culture*. Waterloo, ON: Wilfrid Laurier University Press, 2005.

———. "Parallel Voices: Indians and Others—Narratives of Cultural Struggle." *Canadian Journal of Communication* 18, no. 3 (1999): 283–94.

Van Kirk, Sylvia. *Many Tender Ties: Women in Fur Trade Society, 1670–1870*. Norman: University of Oklahoma Press, 1980.

Verstraten, Katelyn. "For Indigenous Women, Radical Art as a Last Resort." *The Tyee*, June 22, 2013. https://thetyee.ca/ArtsAndCulture/2013/06/22/Radical-Art/.

Vizenor, Gerald. "Aesthetics of Survivance: Literary Theory and Practice." In *Survivance: Narratives of Native Presence*, edited by Gerald Vizenor, 1–23. Lincoln: University of Nebraska Press, 2008.

Wade Rose, Barbara. "Race and Feminism Trouble at Nellie's." *Globe and Mail*, May 9, 1992.

Wakeham, Pauline. "The Cunning of Reconciliation: Reinventing White Civility in Canada's Culture of Redress." In *Shifting the Ground of Canadian Literary Studies: Nation-State, Indigeneity, Culture*, edited by Smaro Kamboureli and Robert Zacharias, 209–33. Waterloo, ON: Wilfrid Laurier University Press, 2012.

———. "Settler Colonialism, Slow Violence, and the Time of Idle No More." Presentation at the Annual Conference of the Native American and Indigenous Studies Association. University of Saskatoon, Saskatoon, SK. June 15, 2013.

Walia, Harsha. "Decolonizing Together: Moving Beyond a Politics of Solidarity Toward a Practice of Decolonization." In *The Winter We Danced: Voices from the Past, the Future, and the Idle No More Movement*, edited by the Kino-nda-niimi Collective, 44–50. Winnipeg: Arbeiter Ring, 2014.

Whonnock, Karen. Presentation at the Kitsumkalum Community Forum, Terrace. September 13, 2011. http://www.missingwomeninquiry.ca/forums/.

Wine, Jeri Dawn, and Janice L. Ristock. "Introduction." In *Women and Social Change: Feminist Activism in Canada*, edited by Jeri Dawn Wine and Janice L. Ristock, 1–18. Toronto: James Lorimer, 1991.

Withey, Elizabeth. "Discovery of '23rd Woman's' DNA at Pickton Farm Inspires Film." *Edmonton Journal*, March 6, 2007.

Witt, Shirley Hill. "The Brave-Hearted Women." *Akwesasne Notes* 8, no. 2 (1976): 16–17.

Womack, Craig. *Art as Performance, Story as Criticism: Reflections on Native Literary Aesthetics*. Norman: University of Oklahoma Press, 2009.

———. "Theorizing American Indian Experience." In *Reasoning Together: The Native Critics Collective*, edited by Craig S. Womack, Daniel Heath Justice, and Christopher B. Teuton, 353–410. Norman: University of Oklahoma Press, 2008.

Young, Alison. *The Scene of Violence: Cinema, Crime, Affect*. New York: Routledge, 2009.

Young, Robert. "Introduction to Gayatri Spivak." In *Human Rights, Human Wrongs: The Oxford Amnesty Lectures, 2001*, edited by Nicholas Owen, 164–67. Oxford: Oxford University Press, 2003.

Younging, Gregory. "Inherited History, International Law, and the UN Declaration." In *Response, Responsibility, and Renewal: Canada's Truth and Reconciliation Journey*, edited by Gregory Younging, Jonathan Dewar, and Mike DeGagné, 323–36. Ottawa: Aboriginal Healing Foundation, 2009.

Younging, Gregory, Jonathan Dewar, and Mike DeGagné. "Conclusion." In *Response, Responsibility, and Renewal: Canada's Truth and Reconciliation Journey*, edited by Gregory Younging, Jonathan Dewar, and Mike DeGagné, 339–44. Ottawa: Aboriginal Healing Foundation, 2009.

INDEX

"Aboriginal," as term, 5
Aboriginal Justice Inquiry of Manitoba (1988), 22, 76, 77, 85, 89, 138, 234n94
Aboriginal organizations, Canadian, 208n2
Aboriginal Women's Action Network, 57
Absolon, Kathleen, 52
Acoose, Janice, 21, 51
adaptive inclusions, 4
addiction, 13
Alfred, Taiaiake, 16
Allen, Paula Gunn, 132
American Indian Movement (AIM), 135; sexism in, 152–53, 157; suspected of Aquash's murder, 237n143
Amnesty International, 5, 24, 66, 72–84, 103. See also *Stolen Sisters* report
anger: of Indigenous women, 131; as response to Indigenous literature, 128; as response to violence, 181
Annie Mae's Movement (Nolan), 26, 151–63, 235n117

anti-oppression training, storytelling in, 118–23
anti-racist multiculturalism, 219n26
anti-violence activism, 22, 159, 161, 166; feminist, 104; and legitimate victims, 139; opposite effect of, 23; as tool of activism, 84
apologies, public, 25, 26, 101–2, 114, 121–22, 128, 140–46
Archibald, Jo-ann, 59
Arlo Looking Cloud, 230n18
Armstrong, Jeannette, 25, 130
Arvin, Maile, 9, 191n41
assimilation, cultural, 2, 166; as factor in Osborne's murder, 78; and Indian Act, 10; and kinship relations, 36; and residential school system, 11, 77; and violence against Indigenous women, 35
Atleo, Shawn, 41
autobiography, 104, 122, 123–32. *See also* life stories; stories/storytelling
awareness-raising initiatives, 14, 20, 26, 166; and narrative accounts of violence, 103; in storytelling, 104

Bannerji, Himani, 112
Barker, Donna, and Carolann Wright, 111, 222n64
Barker, Joanne, 10
Barthes, Roland, 94–95
Beads, Tina, 34, 80, 211n94
Belmore, Rebecca, 158, 159, 237–38n144
Benjamin, Akua, Judy Rebick, and Amy Go, 116, 224n102
Berton, Pierre, 115
Blackstock, Cindy, 13
Blackstone, Madison, 146
Blaney, Fay, 51
"blood memory," 130–31
Bosse, Daleen, 51
Bourgeois, Robyn, 3, 14, 168
Braker, Hugh, 42
Brant, Beth, 97–98
Brown, Wendy, 82, 98, 119, 222n68
Butler, Judith, 134, 137

Callwood, June, 110–17, 223n86
Cameron, Stevie, 127, 228–29n182
campaigns, anti-violence, 14; as converging with dominant paradigms, 98; emblematic figures of victimry in, 134; limitations of, 20; storytelling in, 103, 133
Campbell, Kim, 151–52
Campbell, Maria, 20, 129–30, 159
Canadian government: apology for residential school system, 101, 128, 144; indifference to Indigenous women, 32, 34, 35, 77, 103, 136, 137
Canadian public, indifference of, 3, 18, 35, 95, 134, 136, 138
Cannon, Margaret, 111
Cardinal, Richard, 88
child welfare system, 13, 88, 89
Coalition of Women of Color Working in Women's and Community Services, 110–11, 114, 118, 222n60
Collins, Shannon M., 236n129
colonial gaze, Indigenous stories seen through, 124–26
colonialism, and Indigenous women: academic studies of, 14; and apologies, 144; in *Finding Dawn*, 59; in "Helen Betty Osborne," 87–88; and "obliteration of memory," 64; persistence in the present, 145; and public visibility of violence, 16; role of literature, 1
colonial violence, gendered: narrative disclosures of, 102; as "past," 144, 149, 163, 166; seen through literature, 163; and *Stolen Sisters* report findings, 79; structural facets leading to, 23, 34–35; as systemic vs. interpersonal, 177. *See also* violence against Indigenous women
commemoration, 155–56, 185; and "grievability," 134; and poetry, 24, 71, 84–100; as premised upon injustice, 141; public, 25–26
commissions, types of, 43–44
Community Resource Guide (NWAC), 70

confessional text, 227n172
Coulthard, Glen, 16, 39, 81, 181
Crawford, John, 91, 214n158
Cree poetic discourse, 86
Crey, Dawn, 29, 51, 52, 56–61
Crey, Ernie, 40, 59, 64
critical race theory, 106
Culhane, Dara, 56
Culleton, Beatrice, 159
Cultural Memory Group, 143

Dean, Amber, 165
decolonized approaches to anti-violence, 18
Decolonizing Methodologies: Research and Indigenous Peoples (Smith), 6
Deer, Sarah, 82
Deerchild, Rosanna, 180
Department of Indian Affairs and Northern Development, 10, 78
depoliticization, 112, 119, 123, 165, 222n68
Developing an Antiracism Action Plan, 107
Dewar, Elaine, 115, 224n102
dispossession, 2, 36, 39, 64; Canada premised on, 80; colonialism as structured, 87; government-mandated, 75–76; in "Helen Betty Osborne," 87
Doré, Gustave, 127
Downtown Eastside (Vancouver), 2, 29, 30, 33, 40, 127; described in *Finding Dawn*, 56–57; vs. Highway of Tears victims, 198n13

Dumont, Marilyn, 24–25, 66, 71, 84–100, 167, 216n177

elegy, 85–86, 92
empathy, 19, 111, 130, 145, 147, 148, 150, 195n92
Episkenew, Jo-Ann, 6, 9, 19, 21, 122, 137, 215–16n177

families, of missing and murdered women, 56, 61, 68; in "Helen Betty Osborne," 86–87; qualitative research involving, 68–69
Families of Sisters in Spirit, 168–69
FBI, 135, 157, 237n143
Fellows, Mary Louise, and Sherene Razack, 106, 112
feminist anti-violence agencies, 103–17; anti-racist challenges in, 113; and Indigenous women, 105–6; multicultural diversity in, 8, 25; Nellie's, 109–17; positions of innocence in, 112–13, 116; and storytelling, 118–23
Finding Dawn (Welsh), 24, 29–64, 127, 167, 197n9; and Indigenous feminism, 36; and non-Indigenous viewers, 54–55; pedagogical value, 54
First Nations University, 51
Flowers, Rachel, 3, 4, 87, 99, 131, 172, 174, 181, 183
Fontaine, Phil, 102, 132
Foucault, Michel, 98
Fox, Stacey Edzerza, 42–43, 202n57

gendered disenfranchisement, 20–21

General Social Survey, 68
genocide, cultural, 123, 124, 132, 148
George, Pamela, 231–32n41
Gingell, Susan, 15
Goeman, Mishuana, 19
Gray, Lynda, 178
Green, Shirley, 90, 91
Greyeyes, Trevor, 127, 128, 132
"grievability" (Butler), 26, 134, 137, 138, 139, 140, 141, 150, 160, 163

Halfbreed (Campbell), 20–21, 129
"handouts," for Indigenous people, 178
Haraway, Donna, 126
Harper, Stephen, 145, 177
"Helen Betty Osborne" (poem, Dumont), 24–25, 84–100
Helen Betty Osborne Memorial Foundation, 146
Henderson, James (Sákéj) Youngblood, 121
Henderson, Jennifer, 179
Henderson, Jennifer, and Pauline Wakeham, 101, 144
Highway, Tomson, 22
Highway of Tears, 14, 32, 33; vs. Downtown Eastside victims, 198n13; and Northern Community Forums, 44–50
Highway of Tears Symposium Report, 44, 203n64
Hill Wit, Shirley, 154–55
Hudson's Bay Company, 90
Huhndorf, Shari M., and Cheryl Suzack, 10

human rights activism: and Indigenous practices of resistance, 83; as "moral-political project," 82
human rights discourse, 5; life narratives refracted through, 24, 73, 74; paternalism and Eurocentrism in, 211–12n97; in *Stolen Sisters* report, 75, 80, 210n62; and storytelling, 92
human rights reporting, 85, 166, 215n167
Hum-Ishu-Ma, 20
Hunt, Sarah, 4, 23, 88, 172, 174, 184

identification, 19, 111
imagining, 50, 55, 130; and literature, 19–20, 22, 84, 130, 147, 159; resistance, 95
inclusionary politics, 9
incommensurability, ethic of, 4
"Indian," as term, 5
Indian Act, 10–11, 75, 191n51; amended in 1985, 11; gendered provisions of, 10–11
Indian Agents, 12
Indian status, 10, 11
"Indigenous," as term, 5
Indigenous and Northern Affairs, 10
Indigenous feminism, 32, 35–36, 53, 66, 106, 171, 181
Indigenous peoples; initiatives led by, 169; as needing rescue, 60; as "Other," 16; popular representations of, 21; reliance on colonial structures, 17; state's authority over, 3

Indigenous women: in activist politics, 152–53, 159; in *Annie Mae's Movement*, 158–59, 162; as counting less, 134; in fur trade, 90–91; homicide rates, 2, 32, 188n7; and Indian status, 11; insights overlooked, 26; and life writing, 122–23, 129; and mainstream feminism, 105–6; as mutually supportive, 182; pathologized, 26, 57; stereotypes of, 15, 57, 89–91, 139, 174, 179–80; voices co-opted, 3, 4; voices under-represented, 7. *See also* violence against Indigenous women

Indigenous women's literature, 5, 105, 226n147; anti-violent theory/praxis in, 159; activist implications of, 9; anger as response to, 128; and "implicating the audience," 216–17n177; and male writers, 21–22; politically interventionist potential of, 4, 7; as refusing closure, 132; as site of knowledge and resistance, 18–20; as sustaining Indigenous communities, 19. *See also* literature

inquiries, public, 48; as asserting state authority over Indigenous people, 3, 38, 39; government influence on, 43; limitations of, 168–69. *See also* individual inquiries

institutions, as embedded in colonial relations of power, 9. *See also* justice system; nation-state

interpretation, of life stories, 70, 71, 95, 121

interviews, 69

Invisible Empire: Racism in Canada, The (Cannon), 111

Jacobs, Beverley, 72, 101–2, 121–22, 129

Jacobs, Beverley, and Andrea J. Williams, 10

Jerrold, Blanchard, 127

Johnson, E. Pauline, 20, 181, 184

Johnson, Joan, 111–15, 118, 120, 126, 128, 129

Jordan, Gilbert Paul, 91, 214n158

Justice, Daniel Heath, 5, 21

justice system: and apologies, 144; denial of racism in, 89; failure of, 78, 88, 146; as favouring dominant group, 88; and human rights, 80; Indigenous peoples' overrepresentation in, 198–99n18; Indigenous rights articulated within, 81; as instrumental in violence, 8, 35; racism in, 96; in *A Red Girl's Reasoning*, 171, 172; in *Stolen Sisters* report, 82. *See also* nation-state

Kaandossiwin: How We Come to Know (Absolon), 52

Kauanui, J. Kēhaulani, 102

Keeshig-Tobias, Lenore, 25

Kelly, Doug, 41

Kill Bill (Tarantino), 172, 173

King, Jennifer, 68, 71, 96

kinship relations, disruption in, 11, 36
Kohli, Rita, 107
Kovach, Margaret, 5–6, 7, 69, 74
Kuokkanen, Rauna, 80, 175

La Flamme, Michelle, 84
LaRocque, Emma, 15, 89, 148
Lawrence, Bonita, 191n51, 197n7
"let's talk" approach to reform, 119, 122
liberalism, 150; and anti-oppression movements, 103; as assimilating Indigenous stories, 128; and colonial power, 102–3; and contrition, 140, 145, 161; and discourse of equality, 107; and framework for redress, 99; and Osborne's death, 161; post-colonial, 81, 127; and recognition, 140; state-centred measures of reform, 80; and "telling," 98
Life of Helen Betty Osborne, The (Robertson), 26, 139, 140, 146–51, 163, 168
life stories, 66, 71, 74, 85. *See also* autobiography; storytelling
listening/listeners: as active participation, 71, 121, 125, 126; implicating, in "Helen Betty Osborne," 95; and looking, 125, 126; passive, 93; relational, 49; and witnessing genocide, 132
literature: analyzing, 5; contribution to policy analysis and debate, 23; as discursive site, 166; dominant tradition of, 21; and empathy, 19, 195n92; as instructive, 1, 5; as site of knowledge and resistance, 18–19; as term, 5. *See also* Indigenous women's literature
London (Ontario), memorial march in, 8
London: A Pilgrimage, 127
looking, 94–95, 125

Mackintosh, Gord, 142, 143, 146
Manitoba, apology to Osborne family, 26, 140–46, 151. *See also* Aboriginal Justice Inquiry of Manitoba
Manuel, Arthur, 178
Maracle, Lee, 120, 152
Marshall, Donald, 88
McCall, Sophie, 116–17
McClung, Nellie, 109, 221n48
McIvor, Sharon D., and Teressa Nahanee, 14
McLeod, Neal, 37, 86
media coverage, as discursive form of violence, 134
memoir, 104; in *Morningstar*, 123–32. *See also* autobiography; life stories; stories/storytelling
Memorial Foundation Act (2000), 26, 141–42, 144
memory/memorialization, 64, 130–31; in *Annie Mae's Movement*, 155, 160. *See also* remembering
Mercredi, Morningstar, 25, 104, 123–32, 168
Mihesuah, Devon Abbott, 152–54
Million, Dian, 4, 82, 120, 184
Missing Women Commission of

Inquiry (2010), 2, 22, 29–64, 198n13; boycott of, 38; limitations/criticisms of, 24, 38, 56, 202n55; terms of reference, 23, 37, 41–42, 48, 201n47; treatment of testimony, 37

Missing Women Investigation Review, 57

Monture-Angus, Patricia, 9, 113, 198n18

Morningstar: A Warrior's Spirit (Mercredi), 25, 104, 123–32; ambiguity as resistive text, 132; as story of ongoing gendered violence, 129

Moses, Daniel David, 153

multiculturalism: adaptive inclusions, 4; vs. anti-racism, 106, 219n26; and education, 119; and feminist agencies, 8, 25; and recognition, 81, 122; state-mandated, 103; and tolerance, 128

Multicultural Women Writers of Canada, 117

narrative. *See* stories/storytelling method

Nason, Dory, 182

National Action Committee on the Status of Women, 108

National Inquiry into Missing and Murdered Indigenous Women and Girls: potential for further harm, 169; terms of reference, 3, 65

nation-state: failure to protect Indigenous women, 75; and Indigenous lands, 1–2; as responsible for protecting rights, 73, 75, 80; violence endemic to, 17, 82, 184. *See also* justice system

Native Women's Association of Canada (NWAC), 14, 24, 32, 66, 101; and Amnesty International, 72–73; background, 67; Community Resource Guide, 70. *See also* Sisters in Spirit campaign

Native Youth Sexual Health Network, 168–69

Nellie's shelter, 25, 107–18, 128, 220n34, 222n60

Nolan, Yvette, 26, 151–63

No More Silence, 168–69

"No More Stolen Sisters" campaign, 72

non-racism, 223n85

Northern Community Forums, 31, 44–50; weaknesses of, 46–48

Oppal, Wally, 40, 42, 201n50

oral histories, 37

Osborne, Helen Betty, 135, 140–51; as illustrative victim, 137; as "legitimate"/"grievable" victim, 138–39, 150, 161

Osborne, Helen Betty, death of, 22, 84–100, 135; commemorative representations of, 26; compared with Pictou-Aquash's death, 133–40, 161; failure of non-Indigenous community to bring evidence, 78; in Highway's work, 22; in *Stolen Sisters* report, 76–79; as unique, 142–43

Pemmican Eaters, The (Dumont), 85
PEN Congress, 117–18
Percival, Millie, 46
petal flower metaphor, 52–53
Philip, M. Nourbese, 117–18
photography, 94–95
Pickton, Robert, 23, 33–34, 40, 57
Pickton File, The (Cameron), 127, 228–29n182
Pictou-Aquash, Anna Mae, 26, 88, 135, 151–63; as agential, 154, 161, 162; compared with Osborne, 133–40, 161; as illustrative victim, 137; killers of, 230n18; as martyr, 154–55, 160, 161
poetry, commemorative, 24; "Helen Betty Osborne," 84–100
police: adversarial relationship with Indigenous communities, 34–35; collusion of, 3; sensitivity training for, 79–80, 211n94; treatment of missing women cases, 34, 41, 48, 78, 197n7
policy documents, 22
Portage and Main Press, 233n76
poverty, 13
Povinelli, Elizabeth, 81, 101, 127, 128
public commemoration. *See* commemoration
public inquiries. *See* commissions; inquiries
Public Inquiries Act, 23, 37
publishing industry: challenged by Indigenous writers, 108; institutional racism and white privilege in, 25, 117–18

Racial Minority Writers Committee (RMWC), 108
racism: and depoliticization, 119–20; in feminist service agencies, 105–18; as foundational to Aboriginal public policy, 42; institutional, 25; as intentional act, 89; in justice system, 89, 96; and liberalism, 119, 219n26; and multicultural education, 119; and violence against Indigenous women, 30, 35, 78, 106
Razack, Sherene, 35, 88, 89, 92, 132, 232n41
RCMP. *See* police
readers: "implicating," 216–17n177; of memoirs, 125
Really Good Brown Girl, A (Dumont), 84
recognition: liberal politics of, 16–17, 181; and models of liberal pluralism, 3; multicultural, 81; storytelling as tool of, 103, 122; of "worthy" victims, 137–39, 142–43, 152, 161
reconciliation, 19, 101, 102, 128, 131, 149–50; and Manitoba's public apology, 143–46; and residential schools, 233n60
"Red Girl's Reasoning, A" (Johnson), 181, 184
Red Girl's Reasoning, A (Tailfeathers), 169–85
Red Power movement, 152, 157
remembering/remembrance/re-membering, 31; in *Annie Mae's*

Movement, 160; and anti-violence critique, 84; and commemoration, 134, 140, 141; in *Finding Dawn*, 36–37, 53, 59; in "Helen Betty Osborne," 86–87; as research process, 62–64; and Women's Memorial March, 165–66. *See also* memory

"Report on Anna Mae's Remains" (Moses), 153

representation: and anti-violence critique, 84; and photography, 94–95; political stakes of, 7; politics of, 22, 155; responsible, 97; and violence, 6

re-search, 51

research approaches, 5, 7, 37, 42; extractive, 32, 37, 48, 49; in *Finding Dawn*, 52, 55; petal flower metaphor, 52–53; relationship-based, 69; in Sisters in Spirit campaign, 68–69

research for change, 69

reserve system, 10

residential school system, 11–12, 75, 77, 192n56; Canadian government's apology for, 101, 128; genocidal intent of, 12; in *Morningstar*, 123–32; redress movement, 179, 233n60, 233n64

resistance, 70, 132, 134, 207n141; in *Annie Mae's Movement*, 156; vs. human rights activism, 83; imagining, 22–23, 95; Indigenous-led practices of, 169; and literature, 166; and telling of secrets, 97

revenge narrative, 170, 171
Rezai-Rashti, Goli, 119, 219n26
Robertson, David, 26, 139, 140, 146–51, 163, 168
Rollo, Toby, 178
Rosenberg, Sharon, 165, 166, 183
Royal Commission on Aboriginal Peoples (1991), 39, 178
Rugaru, 157, 236–37n141
Rupert's Land, 90–91

Schabus, Nicole, 43
Schaffer, Kay, and Sidonie Smith, 73, 74
Scott, Duncan Campbell, 12
searches, community-coordinated, 61, 207n138
Sellars, Bev, 176
sexual assault: and public incredulity, 174; tribunals, 179
Simon, Roger, 83
Simpson, George, 90–92
Simpson, Leanne, 1, 50, 60–61, 63, 64, 81, 207n141
Sinclair, Niigonwedom James, 7
Sinclair, Raven, 13
Sisters in Spirit campaign, 14, 24, 66; and Amnesty International, 72–73; background, 67; database, 67–68; federal funding for, 208n6; as promoting awareness, 167; reporting of traumatic experiences, 96
"Sixties Scoop," 13
Smith, Andrea, 54, 102
Smith, Ariel, 182

Smith, Laurel, 127–28
Smith, Linda Tuhiwai, 6, 17, 47, 49, 55, 62
Smith, Sidonie, 80, 124
social transformation, as creative process, 50
speechlessness, 97–98
Srivastava, Sarita, 107, 113, 119, 223n85
Srivastava, Sarita, and Margot Francis, 93, 219n26
St. Denis, Verna, 105
Statistics Canada, 68
Status of Women Canada, 67
Stevenson, Winona, 11, 74
Stolen Sisters: Discrimination and Violence against Women in Canada (2004), 24, 66, 72–84, 85, 88, 103, 136; compared with "Helen Betty Osborne," 94; limitations, 80, 98, 100; as promoting awareness, 167; recommendations, 79–80, 96. *See also* Amnesty International
Stó:lô Nation, 58–60
Stone, Anne, and Amber Dean, 196n3
Stone-Mediatore, Shari, 73–74
stories/storytelling method, 24, 25, 49, 50, 66, 103; as amenable to colonial strategies of power, 129; anger as response to, 128; in anti-oppression training, 118–23; and co-optation, 132; as direct action, 184; in feminist organizations, 104; in *Finding Dawn*, 37; in "Helen Betty Osborne," 84–100; and imagining, 130; interpreting, 71; locating oneself in, 58, 59, 60; prominence of, 92–93; and raising awareness, 98; risks of, 70–71, 132; in Sisters in Spirit campaign, 68–71; as site of critique and transformation, 159; in *Stolen Sisters* report, 72–84. *See also* Indigenous women's literature; life stories
survival schools, 236n138
survivance, 55–56, 60; vs. victimry, 59, 83
Suzack, Cheryl, 4, 21

Tailfeathers, Elle-Máijá, 169–85
Take Back the Highway demonstrations, 61
Tarantino, Quentin, 172
"Telling" (Brant), 97–98
The Pas (Manitoba), 77
Thomas, Robina Anne, 69, 71
Tingley, Ken, 126–27
Trail of Broken Treaties, The, 135
Truth and Reconciliation Commission of Canada, 192n56
truth-telling, 17
Tuck, Eve, and K. Wayne Yang, 4, 19, 173
Two Shoes, Minnie, 159

United Nations, 5; Commission on Human Rights, 145; Declaration on the Rights of Indigenous Peoples, 145; Development Program, 210n62; Permanent Forum on Indigenous Issues, 178

Valaskakis, Gail Guthrie, 95, 108
Vancouver. *See* Downtown Eastside
Vancouver Police Department, 57
Van Kirk, Sylvia, 90
victim(s): blaming, 57; "grievability" (Butler) of, 134, 137, 139, 160; hierarchization of, 160; invisibility of, 159; "legitimate" (Ehrlich), 138–39; in *A Red Girl's Reasoning*, 174
Vigil (Belmore), 158, 159
violence against Indigenous women: archetypal victims of, 134; colonial origins of, 8, 9, 23, 34–35, 59–60, 105; in family/community settings, 13; lack of representation in public/critical discourse, 15; local instances of, 33; media coverage of, 134; by non-Indigenous men, 13, 68; number of victims, 2, 32, 188n7; and pattern of state-sponsored violence, 33, 75–76, 81–82; public visibility of, 18; and role of literature, 6, 163; in *A Red Girl's Reasoning*, 171; as state-sponsored, 35; as tool of patriarchal control, 8; white male violence as root cause, 23, 88, 91–92, 96, 174
Vision 21, 117
Vizenor, Gerald, 55–56
voice appropriation, in literature, 108, 117–18
voyeurism, in reading Indigenous stories, 125, 126, 127

Wakeham, Pauline, 121
Walia, Harsha, 116, 166
Walk4Justice, 14
walking, as political expression, 61–63
Warrior, Robert, and Paul Chaat Smith, 152
Welsh, Christine, 24, 29–64, 127, 167, 206n122
white privilege: and narrative disclosures, 102; in Nellie's controversy, 116; Osborne's death as enlightenment for, 151; and responsibility, 131; and storytelling approach to reform, 118–20
"whitestream feminism," 191n41
Whonnock, Karen, 47
Wilson, Matilda, 62–64
Wilson, Ramona, 51, 62–64
Womack, Craig, 5, 58, 121, 181, 225n133
Women of Colour Caucus (Nellie's), 107, 109, 110, 114–18
Women's Memorial March (Vancouver), 8, 61, 165, 174
Women's Press, 117
Worme, Donald, 42
Wounded Knee, 135
Wright, Carolann, 116
Writers Union of Canada, 108
Writing Thru Race Conference (1994), 108, 117

Younging, Greg, 130–31

BOOKS IN THE INDIGENOUS STUDIES SERIES PUBLISHED BY WILFRID LAURIER UNIVERSITY PRESS

Blockades and Resistance: Studies in Actions of Peace and the Temagami Blockades of 1988–89 / Bruce W. Hodgins, Ute Lischke, and David T. McNab, editors / 2003 / xi + 276 pp. / illus. / ISBN 0-88920-381-4

Indian Country: Essays on Contemporary Native Culture / Gail Guthrie Valaskakis / 2005 / x + 293 pp. / illus. / ISBN 0-88920-479-9

Walking a Tightrope: Aboriginal People and Their Representations / Ute Lischke and David T. McNab, editors / 2005 / xix + 377 pp. / illus. / ISBN 978-0-88920-484-3

The Long Journey of a Forgotten People: Métis Identities and Family Histories / Ute Lischke and David T. McNab, editors / 2007 / viii + 386 pp. / illus. / ISBN 978-0-88920-523-9

Words of the Huron / John L. Steckley / 2007 / xvii + 259 pp. / ISBN 978-0-88920-516-1

Essential Song: Three Decades of Northern Cree Music / Lynn Whidden / 2007 / xvi + 176 pp. / illus., musical examples, audio CD / ISBN 978-0-88920-459-1

From the Iron House: Imprisonment in First Nations Writing / Deena Rymhs / 2008 / ix + 147 pp. / ISBN 978-1-55458-021-7

Lines Drawn upon the Water: First Nations and the Great Lakes Borders and Borderlands / Karl S. Hele, editor / 2008 / xxiii + 351 pp. / illus. / ISBN 978-1-55458-004-0

Troubling Tricksters: Revisioning Critical Conversations / Linda M. Morra and Deanna Reder, editors / 2009 / xii+ 336 pp. / illus. / ISBN 978-1-55458-181-8

Aboriginal Peoples in Canadian Cities: Transformations and Continuities / Heather A. Howard and Craig Proulx, editors / 2011 / viii + 256 pp. / illus. / ISBN 978-1-055458-260-0

Bridging Two Peoples: Chief Peter E. Jones, 1843–1909 / Allan Sherwin / 2012 / xxiv + 246 pp. / illus. / ISBN 978-1-55458-633-2

The Nature of Empires and the Empires of Nature: Indigenous Peoples and the Great Lakes Environment / Karl S. Hele, editor / 2013 / xxii + 350 / illus. / ISBN 978-1-55458-328-7

The Eighteenth-Century Wyandot: A Clan-Based Study / John L. Steckley / 2014 / x + 306 pp. / ISBN 978-1-55458-956-2

Indigenous Poetics in Canada / Neal McLeod, editor / 2014 / xii + 404 pp. / ISBN 978-1-55458-982-1

Literary Land Claims: The "Indian Land Question" from Pontiac's War to Attawapiskat / Margery Fee / 2015 / x + 318 pp. / illus. / ISBN 978-1-77112-119-4

Arts of Engagement: Taking Aesthetic Action in and beyond Canada's Truth and Reconciliation Commission / Dylan Robinson and Keavy Martin, editors / 2016 / viii + 376 pp. / illus. / ISBN 978-1-77112-169-9

Learn, Teach, Challenge: Approaching Indigenous Literature / Deanna Reder and Linda M. Morra, editors / 2016 / xii + 580 pp. / ISBN 978-1-77112-185-9

Read, Listen, Tell: Indigenous Stories from Turtle Island / Sophie McCall, Deanna Reder, David Gaertner, and Gabrielle L'Hirondelle Hill, editors / 2017 / xviii + 392 pp. / ISBN 978-1-77112-300-6

Violence against Indigenous Women: Literature, Activism, Resistance / Allison Hargreaves / 2017 / xvi + 284 pp. / ISBN 978-1-77112-239-9